THE LIVING WORD OF THE LIVING GOD

A BEGINNER'S GUIDE TO READING
AND UNDERSTANDING THE BIBLE

REV. TOM FURRER

The Living Word of the Living God:
A Beginner's Guide to Reading and Understanding the Bible
Copyright © 2011 Thomas Furrer

Published by Barnabas Books
An imprint of Winged Lion Press
Hamden, CT

Scripture quotations are from the Revised Standard Version of the Bible, copyright 1952 [2nd edition, 1971] by the Division of Christian Education of the National Council of the Churches of Christ in the United States of America. Used by permission. All rights reserved.

All rights reserved. Except in the case of quotations embodied in critical articles or reviews, no part of this book may be reproduced or transmitted in any form or by any means, electronic or mechanical, including photocopying, recording, or by any information storage or retrieval system, without written permission of the publisher.
For information, contact Winged Lion Press www.WingedLionPress.com

Winged Lion Press titles may be purchased for business or promotional use or special sales.

10-9-8-7-6-5-4-3-2-1

ISBN-13 978-1-936294-08-4

DEDICATION

To my parents, George and Katherine,
who taught me, by word and example,
the most important things in life.

ACKNOWLEDGMENTS

I wish to thank everyone who has helped me to fall in love with the Word of God and to write this book.

First and foremost, I thank my wife, Maryjane, for her encouragement of my active life of faith and discernment of a vocation and in my theological studies and ordained ministry over the past thirty years.

I want to thank the people of Grace Church in Old Saybrook, Connecticut in whose company, fellowship and prayer I dedicated my life to Jesus Christ as a young man. I want to thank all of my teachers at Wesleyan University and Yale Divinity School for opening me to the great height and breadth of the Scriptures and the normative interpretive tradition of Judaism and Christianity.

I am also deeply grateful for the work and ministry of St. George's College in Jerusalem through whom I learned to appreciate the relevance of "the fifth gospel (i.e. the Holy Land) in the work of reading and understanding the Bible in its cultural and social context.

I am grateful to the hundreds of children, teens and adults of St. Paul's Church in Huntington and Trinity Church in Tariffville who have been the recipients of my various Bible studies, sermons, confirmation classes, retreats and other learning events over the past twenty five years. Through their many questions and "I don't understand you" gestures, they have taught me (I hope) to be a better communicator and teacher of the Word of God.

I wish to thank my publisher, Robert Trexler, and his team of proof-readers (Fr. Jonah, Fr. Shane, and Lawrence) who provided helpful editorial comments in the completion of the manuscript. I am particularly grateful in this regard to The Rev. Christopher Webber who was very generous with his time and with many helpful comments and suggestions.

Finally, I am grateful to the people of Trinity Church in Tariffville who granted me a three-month sabbatical from my pastoral duties to be able to devote my attention to completing this book. Without this luxury of uninterrupted focus, I would never have been able to do so.

TABLE OF CONTENTS

	Foreword	iv
Chapter 1	What Is The Bible And How Do I Interpret It?	1
Chapter 2	Creation: "Behold It Is Very Good"	14
Chapter 3	Adam and Eve: "Paradise Lost"	26
Chapter 4	Abraham: "You Will Be a Blessing To All Nations"	34
Chapter 5	Exodus: "Let My People Go"	45
Chapter 6	Promised Land: Judges, Kings, Priests and Prophets	57
Chapter 7	Psalms and Wisdom Literature: "Sing to the Lord a New Song"	76
Chapter 8	Exile and the Great Homecoming: "Comfort, Comfort My People"	91
Chapter 9	"When the Time Had Fully Come, God Sent His Son": What's "New" in The New Testament?	105
Chapter 10	Jesus' Resurrection: What Happened and Why It Matters	115
Chapter 11	Matthew: The Messiah-King	136
Chapter 12	Mark: Triumph of The Suffering Servant	150

Chapter 13	Luke: The Man of Compassion	160
Chapter 14	John: The Eternal Word Of God	170
Chapter 15	Acts: Gospel of the Holy Spirit	184
Chapter 16	Paul's Great Epistles: "I Am Not Ashamed of the Gospel"	193
Chapter 17	The Later Epistles: "Now You Are God's People"	209
Chapter 18	Revelation: "A New Heaven and A New Earth"	226

Appendices:

Timeline of the Old Testament	236
Timeline of the New Testament	240
When the New Testament Books Were Written	243
Old Testament Prefiguration/ New Testament Recapitulation	244
Other Resources For Reading and Understanding the Bible	246

LIVING WORD OF THE LIVING GOD

A Beginner's Guide to Reading and Understanding the Bible

> *"The Word of God is living and active, sharper that any two-edged sword, piercing to the division of soul and spirit, of joints and marrow, and discerning the thoughts and intentions of the heart. And before him no creature is hidden, but all are open and laid bare to the eyes of him with whom we have to do."*
>
> Hebrews 4:12-13

The title of this book is inspired by the Bible passage quoted above. It speaks of the awe-inspiring, bone-chilling, soul-stirring, gut-wrenching and priority-changing personal encounter with the living God. It reminds us of Moses and the Burning Bush, Isaiah in the Temple, Peter, James and John at Jesus' Transfiguration and Paul on the Damascus Road. It asserts that the Living Word of the Living God is a powerful, life-changing and world-changing force which we need to take very seriously.

We need to do business with the Living God. God's self-revelation is, in the first instance, a direct personal encounter with human beings. The God of the Bible is not one of the many anthropomorphic deities of "polytheism", not the Great Absentee Landlord of "deism", and not the impersonal Life Force of "pantheism." The God of the Bible is a living God who speaks and acts and loves with an overarching purpose for people and for all creation. The Bible is, first of all, a written record of many of these direct encounters with the living God. Secondarily, it is an extended history and commentary on living out the implications of these encounters over time.

This little book is written with the conviction that God is not finished with the human race, that people may still expect to encounter the Living Word which is sharper than any two-edged sword and which cuts to the innermost intentions of the heart. My hope is that this little book will help people to read the Big Book with increased understanding and expectation of an encounter with the Living God.

My subtitle is inspired by a second biblical text:

> *"But as for you, continue in what you have learned and have firmly believed, knowing from whom you learned it and how from childhood you have been acquainted with the sacred writings which are able to instruct you for salvation through faith in Christ Jesus. All scripture is*

Foreword

inspired by God and profitable for teaching, for reproof, for correction, and for training in righteousness, that the man of God may be complete, equipped for every good work."

2 Timothy 3:14-16

This passage is less dramatic but no less important. It reminds us that knowing, loving and following God is a life-long process of discovery and growth, beginning with childhood and continuing to old age. The passage calls us to devote our lives to studying, being instructed, corrected, trained and equipped, by the sacred writings which are "inspired by God" (literally translated "God-breathed").

I have written this book after twenty two years in parish ministry, teaching small children, adolescents and adults. My observation is that most of the people (in every age group) who attend worship and participate in various educational opportunities have a good knowledge of favorite Bible stories, such as: Adam and Eve; Noah's Ark; Moses and the Ten Commandments; David and Goliath; The Prodigal Son; The Lost Sheep; The Good Samaritan; The Beatitudes; Jesus' miracles; The Last Supper; The Crucifixion; The Resurrection; Pentecost. My further observation is that most people (in every age group) do not have a very good sense of how their favorite biblical stories fit into The Big Story of the Bible. This lack of understanding is not because people are not interested but because many parts of the Bible are, frankly, difficult for a modern reader to understand.

The purpose of this book is to help the reader understand the Bible as one coherent narrative. My intention here is to provide a summary of some of the main themes and to encourage everyone to dig deeper into the passages that are unfamiliar to them. This is intended to be an introduction – not "the last word." Because this is a summary, there are many passages, and characters and themes that will not be discussed. My hope is that this book will help the reader place his or her favorite stories into the context of the Bible's big story and that it will stimulate further study, deeper reflection.

In each chapter, I have included questions which I hope will help the reader connect the biblical passage with contemporary issues and questions. I have tried to include questions which relate to "big picture" contemporary issues and also personal spiritual development and ethical decisions. In one appendix, I have also listed some other books which may be helpful for further study.

I have also included a memory verse at the conclusion of each chapter which summarizes at least one of the themes discussed in the chapter. I believe that there is a great value in memorizing key passages of the Bible. Memorizing helps one to solidify important spiritual and moral truths in the heart, mind and soul. There are many good translations of the Bible available, but this is a mixed blessing at best. Reading more than one translation can help clarify a difficult passage, but it will never help to solidify a passage in one's memory. For this reason, my advice to readers is to choose one good translation and stick with it. Only then can one consistently memorize key passages. This book will usually quote the Revised Standard Version because it is the translation that I have read and memorized over many years.

It is my hope that reading this book will give everyone a greater hunger to read, understand and respond to The Living Word of The Living God. It is my hope and prayer that God's Word will take root and bear fruit in the lives of all who read, hear and respond.

> "Seek the Lord while he may be found; call upon him while he is near ....

> For as the rain and the snow come down from heaven; and return not again but water the earth, making it bring forth and sprout, giving seed to the sower and bread to the eater, so shall my word be that goes forth from my mouth; it shall not return to me empty, but it shall accomplish that which I purpose, and prosper in the thing for which I sent it."

Isaiah 55:6-1

Chapter 1
WHAT IS THE BIBLE AND HOW DO I INTERPRET IT?

I. What Is The Bible?

1) Most importantly, The Bible is a witness to the God who speaks.[1]

In the beginning, God *said* "Let there be light." God *said* to Abram "Go from your country …to the land I will show you." God *said* to Moses "I have seen the affliction of my people…and I have come to deliver them." God *said* to Isaiah "Go and say to this people…" God *said* to Jeremiah "I appointed you as a prophet…whatever I command you, you shall speak." God *said* "This is my beloved Son. Listen to him."

We humans learn to speak long before we learn to write. We write about things we deem to be important. The Bible is a living witness to the God who speaks to his people and who has acted in history. The various books of the Bible were written, edited, collated and copied by nameless authors because they were convinced that God had spoken and that their efforts would make God's word available to future generations. The various books of the Bible have been received, judged to be authentic, and recognized as "inspired" by Jewish and Christian faith communities over thousands of years because these communities have experienced the presence and power of God in reading and responding to them in faith. Moreover, the final codification of the biblical "canon" was affirmed by official councils of Jewish teachers and of the early Church. The Bible continues to be the most widely published, translated and read book in the world because growing numbers of people in every culture have found in it the voice of God giving inspiration, meaning,

[1] I borrowed this insight and much of the information in this section from Jaraslov Pelikan in *Whose Bible Is It?: A History of the Scriptures Through The Ages* Penguin Publishing (New York 2005)

direction, purpose and hope to their lives. There is one Author in whose hand the countless human scribes are writing instruments; one Voice which speaks through many and various human voices.

2) The Bible is a collection of books

The English word "Bible" is derived from the Greek work "*biblion*" which means "book" or "scroll." The Bible is a collection of books which were written, edited and collated over a period of more than 1,000 years. As such, these books reflect many different historical eras, social circumstances and "lifestyles" of the respective human authors and subjects: primitive hunters and farmers, nomadic shepherds, brutish tribal warriors; sophisticated and educated city dwellers, military and political elites, kings and queens; slaves, slave owners and slave liberators; empire builders, empire bureaucrats and empire destroyers; poets, priests, prophets and prostitutes; magicians, miracle workers and mad men; saints, sinners and scoundrels. If modern readers of the Bible feel as if they have entered an alien world, they have ! We are entering a world and a world-view very different from our own, but the alien world of the Bible has a take-home message for our world.

The Bible also contains many different types of writing. Within this collection of books, we find heroic military sagas, detailed lists of ancestors and descendants, legal codes and case law, royal histories, love poems, personal and national laments, poetry, worship hymns and liturgies, biographies and personal letters, just to name a few. The Bible often speaks in symbols, images and metaphors which are not familiar to modern readers. If the modern reader thinks the Bible "talks funny", it does ! Like reading Shakespeare or Dante or Moby Dick, listening to Bach or Beethoven or rap music, the Bible requires effort to interpret, translate, understand and apply to ones life.

The various books of the one Bible are arranged in roughly chronological order and divided into two main parts, the Old Testament and the New Testament.

The Old Testament (or "Hebrew Scriptures" or "Tanakh")

The first and largest section of the Bible (comprising nearly 75% of the whole) is called by Christians "The Old Testament." Many Jewish scholars (and some Christians) object to this terminology because it is often taken to mean that the Old has been superceded by the New, and therefore not as important. For this reason, some prefer the term: "Hebrew Scriptures" and still others prefer a much older name: *"Tanakh."* This is an acronym comprised of the three Hebrew names for each section: **Torah** (The First Five Books),

What is the Bible?

Nevi'im (The Prophets) and ***Kethuvim*** (The Writings). The Tanakh tells the story of the people of God (variously called Hebrews, the people of Israel, Judeans and Jews in the Bible) before the time of Jesus Christ. It is a time in which God set aside a "chosen people" to bear witness to the One God in a polytheistic (belief in many gods) world. During that long period of time, God prepared his chosen people to expect, prepare for, and receive the Messiah. Christians believe that the long awaited Messiah has come in the person of Jesus Christ. Hence the need for a "New Testament" to tell the whole story. This book will use the term "Old Testament" because it remains the normative usage the overwhelming majority of Christians in the world today.

The Old Testament contains 39 books according to the Christian count. (The Jewish count totals 24 because some books are consolidated.)

The Apocrypha

The Apocrypha is an additional part of the Old Testament which covers the period of time immediately before Jesus was born. Its status is not settled among various Christian groups. (Roman Catholics and Eastern Orthodox Christians accept it as part of the Bible. Most Protestants do not accept it. Anglicans accept it as a source of inspiration but not of doctrine.)

The Apocrypha contains 18 books.

The New Testament

The New Testament is arranged in three parts: The Four Gospels tell the story of the birth, life, death and resurrection of Jesus Christ. **The Acts of the Apostles** tells the early history of the followers of Jesus as they went out to make disciples of the whole world. **The Epistles** are letters written by early church leaders to help followers of Jesus understand how to live faithfully in the world. Christians believe that Jesus Christ is the fulfillment and culmination of God's saving work and that through him, God extends the scope of salvation to all humanity. In the New Testament, God extends the status of "chosen people" to all people and the "Promised Land" to all creation.

The New Testament contains 27 books.

3) The Bible is One Book – One Big Story

In all of the variety and complexity of the Bible, it is sometimes easy to lose sight of the essential unity of the narrative. **In sum, the Bible is a love story: God's love for the human race from the beginning of time until the end of time. History has a divine purpose from start to finish.**

As noted above, the Bible was written, edited, compiled, received and ratified over a period of 900 years (from 500 B.C. to 400 A.D.). It is the record of God's dealing with specific groups of people over many centuries. It recounts God's self-revelation and the growing understanding of God's nature, will and purpose for humanity. As such, we can see an evolution of perception in the Bible which reflects a growing and deepening understanding of God over time. For example, in the early sections of the Bible, we find a polytheistic world-view (a belief in many gods of which Yahweh is only one). By the end of the Bible, we find a very clear understanding of one (and only one) true God. In the early Bible, God's primary concern is Israel's success in warfare against other tribes. By the end of the Bible, we find that "God is love" and concerned for the redemption of all humanity. In the early Bible, we find a God who commands sacrifice of animals as part of worship. By the end, we find that God takes no delight in such sacrifices but desires "steadfast love" instead. In the early Bible, we find God demanding (and then condemning) human sacrifice. By the end, we find God sending his own Son as an "atoning sacrifice" for the sins of humanity. In the early Bible, we find no expectation of life after death. By the end, we find that the Resurrection is the culmination of God's redeeming work in the world.

Does this mean that God had a "mid-life crisis" and decided to give himself a complete makeover? No. It reflects the deliberate timing of God self-revelation and perhaps the slowness of human beings to grasp the full nature, character and purpose of God. When reading the Bible, especially the some of the sections which seem to modern eyes to be so brutal or primitive, we need to keep the big picture in mind. We need to read these passages within the context of the culture in which they were revealed and of the whole story of the self-revelation of God.

4) The Bible is the authoritative book for the Church of Jesus Christ.

The Bible is "the Church's Book." In other words, it is read, understood, interpreted and its implications lived out in the ongoing community of faith. While there are many different interpretations within the various Christian communities about how to interpret the Bible, all authentic Christian communities live under its authority. It is the primary means through which God teaches, reproves, corrects, trains and equips God's people for "every good work" in the world. The story of the Bible is not over. God continues the love relationship with his people which is recorded in the Bible.

What is the Bible?

II. How Did The Bible Take Shape In History?

Many people have the (often unspoken and perhaps not even fully conscious) idea that God dropped the Bible from heaven directly. In fact, God chose a more scenic route through the twists and turns of human history. Christians believe that, this process of inspiration, oral transmission, written transmission, reception and canonization is guided by the Holy Spirit every step of the way. Here is a brief summary:

- **Direct revelation**

God speaks, inspires and acts in history.
Example: Moses, Burning Bush, Exodus, Ten Commandments, Manna, Promised Land

- **Oral transmission**

People tell other people what God has done.
Example: Jesus tells his disciples to tell the whole world about his death, resurrection and to make disciples of all nations. (Matthew 28)

- **Written transmission**

Write it down for future generations.
Example: Luke 1:1-4 "I am writing…that you may know the truth…John 20:31 "These   are written that you may believe."

- **Faith Community Reception**

Local faith communities accept writings as truly inspired writings.
Example: Local Jewish groups accept individual prophets as authentic. Local Churches accept one of the Gospels as authentic.

- **Canonization** (definitively recognized and codified by Jewish and Christian authoritative councils).

Individual books are grouped together by larger faith communities.
Torah (First Five Books) canonized by Jewish authorities 500 B.C.
Prophets (Isaiah, Jeremiah, Amos etc.) canonized by   200 B.C.
Writings (Psalms, Job etc.) canonized by 100 B.C.
Four Gospels and Paul's Epistles canonized by the whole
Church 200 A.D.
Other Epistles and Revelation canonized by 400 AD

5) Criteria for Canonical books of New Testament

There were many early Christian writings which were not included in the New Testament, even though some of them were judged to be theologically sound and spiritually edifying. Here are four of the criteria for choosing some and rejecting others:

a) Apostolic Origin: written by the apostles (Matthew, Mark, Luke John, Peter, James) or one of their close associates (Paul).

b) Importance of the early Christian community to whom the writing is addressed (Rome, Corinth, Ephesus, Galatia)

c) Conformity to the rule of faith: some early Christian writings about Jesus were radically at odds with the theology of the authentic apostolic gospels and were rejected as forgeries (for example "The Gospel of Peter").

d) Widespread liturgical usage in local Christian communities.

6) Universal Acceptance and Official Codification by Universal Church
(Synod of Rome - 382, Council of Hippo - 393, Council of Carthage - 397)

After nearly 400 years of prayerful consideration of the books which were chosen (and not chosen) to be included in the "canon" of the New Testament, several councils of regional gatherings of Bishops affirmed and officially recognized what was a near universal consensus.

As may be seen from the above timetable, the process of "canonization" was a long, prayerful and deliberative process. Each of the books of the Bible has stood the test of time in communities of faith, guided by the Holy Spirit, before it could even be considered "inspired."

In recent years, the process of canonization has come under criticism from some Bible scholars. Some scholars claim that these books were included and other books excluded by a very small group of people who were primarily concerned with maintaining their own institutional power and enforcing "orthodoxy" on others. Other scholars claim that canonization was largely a "from the bottom up" process in which Jewish and Church authorities ratified a near universal consensus from local communities. Solving this historical problem is beyond the scope of this little book, but we can say that whatever the original context of canonization was, the process has continued to this day. If there was ever a time when a small group of people could enforce biblical "orthodoxy" on others, that time is long past. Since the time of final canonization in the fourth century AD, several billion Jews and Christians have read the Bible and through their own experience found it to be the inspired word of God. Taken as a whole, this is the work of the Holy Spirit confirming and ratifying and "canonizing" the Bible even to this day.

III. How Do We Interpret The Bible?

The Bible, as noted above, is an ancient book with many different types of writing. To understand its meaning, we need to interpret it. We do the work of interpretation in other areas of our lives as well, sometimes without even realizing it. For example, think about the kinds of programming one might see on T.V. in a few minutes of "channel surfing": a news report, a comedy news show, a documentary, a "talk show," a situation comedy, a cops and bad guys drama, a "reality" show, a cartoon, a home shopping channel, a sports program, a rock concert, C-SPAN and so on. At first glance, many of these programs might look alike. The cops and bad guys drama might look like the local news report of the latest car chase. The comedy news show might look like a serious news show, or *vice versa*. The baseball game might look like the sports section of the evening news. A "reality" show might look like a documentary. A commercial may look like a situation comedy. When flipping through channels, we make interpretations. Sometimes these interpretations are instant. Sometimes they take a while to figure out. We decide what kind of program we are watching. We decide whether or not we want to watch it. We decide how to interpret the message of the program. And we decide what, if anything, we are going to do to respond to the message we have heard. If we see a news report of a tornado heading for our neighborhood, we may decide to take immediate action. If we see a commercial for a product we need or want, we may decide to buy it. If we see a political debate, we may decide to vote for a certain candidate. If we see a comedy, we may just relax and enjoy it and tell someone about it later. And so on. Every day, in a hundred different ways, we make decisions about how to interpret things we see, hear and read. We then decide how we will respond or react to our interpretations.

Three Questions to ask when interpreting a Bible passage:

1) What kind of message is this? What kind of truth is being told in the original context of the passage?

2) What is the enduring message? How do I translate this message from the Bible context to our present day context?

3) How is God leading me to respond to this message? How is God calling me to respond to God's Word contained in this passage?

THE LIVING WORD OF THE LIVING GOD

1) What kind of message is this? What kind of truth is being told in the original context of the passage?

What kind of language? One important aspect of interpreting a Bible passage is to consider what kind of language. In everyday conversation, we often use symbolic language. For example: "I have a million things to do today." "My car is a lemon." "Her boyfriend is a hunk" "She has stars in her eyes." "My baseball team crashed and burned last night." "My supervisor at work is a pain in the posterior." We all know that these expressions are not to be understood literally. Similarly, we use different speech forms to communicate. A television news report, a poetry reading, a Shakespeare play, rap music, a fortune cookie message, a text message between two 13 year girls, and a stock market report may each be written in English language and yet each will contain its own unique code words, shorthand and speech patterns. To understand the communication, you need to understand the differences. This is also true of different Bible passages.

When Isaiah says *"You shall go out in joy, and be led forth in peace; the mountains and the hills before you shall break forth in singing and the trees shall clap their hands"* (Isaiah 55:12) he does not mean that mountains will miraculously grow mouths and trees develop hands. He means "you will be so happy that it will seem as if the whole creation is celebrating with you."

When Jesus says: *"I Am the Bread of Life"*, (John 6) he does not mean he will turn into a piece of whole wheat toast. He is placing his own life and ministry in the context of God's care and provision for the people of Israel dating back to the Exodus.

When Genesis tells us that Adam and Eve were hiding in the Garden and God had to ask *"Where are you?"* (Genesis 3:9) it doesn't mean that God is near-sighted. It brings home the point that God sought them out.

More often than not, the Bible speaks of great relational, moral and spiritual truths in highly symbolic language. Here are some examples.

God is: The Shepherd of Israel…the Fear of Jacob…a Consuming Fire…the Ancient of Days…The Father

Jesus is: The Vine…the Lamb of God…the True Door…the Lion of Judah…the Son of Man…the Living Water…the Alpha and the Omega…Bright Morning Star

The Kingdom of God is like: a mustard seed…a pearl of great price…a wedding banquet…a fishing expedition…a field of wheat and weeds…a city with streets paved with gold.

What is the Bible?

God's willingness to forgive is like: A father welcoming his errant son home…an employer paying equal wages to workers who didn't work as long as others…a landlord who sends his son to reconcile wayward tenants…a shepherd who leaves ninety-nine sheep to seek out one that is lost.

What kind of truth? In a court of law, each witness promises "to tell the truth, the whole truth and nothing but the truth." But every good lawyer knows that there are many different ways to tell the truth. Some versions will land their client in jail; others, hopefully, will not. When reading the Bible, we need to keep in mind that there are many different kinds of truth statements. We need to try to determine what kind of truth is being presented in each biblical text. For example, when Jesus says: "Man shall not live by bread alone", he is not giving dietary advice. Instead, he is telling us that we are spiritual as well as material creatures; and that we need to feed our souls as well as our bodies.

Historical/factual Truth

Historical/factual truth can be measured and verified against other historical records. The Bible gives us a history of the Hebrew people and of the early Christian movement. It gives us detailed genealogies (lists of ancestors and descendants). It identifies events with the dates of certain kings and Roman emperors. Some of these historical records have been verified by historians and archeologists, and some not. But the Bible is much more than a "history book" in the modern sense of the word. It is history with a divine purpose. The historical accounts are always presented in service to this divine purpose – God's plan of redemption. The historical accounts always point to a deeper, relational truth.

Relational Truth - the meaning behind the facts

Relational truth is not the kind that can be measured by historical review or scientific inquiry. For example: "John Smith got married to Mary Wilson in Oshkosh, Wisconsin on October 1, 1988." This is a statement that can be verified by checking marriage license records. But everyone who knows John and Mary very well will tell you that while this historical fact is true, it does not even begin to come close to telling "the whole truth." Here is the larger truth: "John and Mary love each other more than any couple we know. Their love is a shining light to everyone they know. They are role models for what a good marriage should be." This is the deeper truth behind the mere historical truth that can be verified at the court house. You can verify it only through close observation and personal friendship with John and Mary.

The Bible is a book which is primarily concerned with Relational Truth: the relationship between God and the people of Israel; the relationship between Jesus and God; the relationship between Jesus and his disciples; the relationship between Jesus and all who believe in him throughout history. The Relational Truth of the Bible begins with Creation, continues through the Covenant with Abraham and Moses and reaches its fulfillment in Jesus Christ. "God so loved the world that he gave his only begotten Son that whoever believes in him may not perish but have eternal life." That is the "story behind the story" of the Bible. It happened in history, but it goes deeper than historical study can verify. As with John and Mary, the only way one can know its truth is to get to know Jesus in a personal and prayerful relationship of love.

Moral Truth

The Bible contains many moral truth statements. In a few instances, these are stated in simple and straightforward commands or exhortations, such as the Ten Commandments (Exodus 20) or the Sermon on the Mount (Matthew 5) and many instances in the Epistles. More often, however, the moral truths are embedded in parables or stories. The heart of the biblical moral vision is what Jesus calls "the first and great commandment": To love the Lord your God with your whole heart, soul, mind and strength." And the Second: "To love your neighbor as yourself." These two bedrock commandments are the basis for the entire biblical moral vision.

Spiritual Truth

The Bible tells us about the ultimate meaning of human life; the relationship with God that begins on this earth and extends to eternity; the relationship and responsibility we have to honor the image and likeness of God in other people; the spiritual character of relationships with other Christians in the Body of Christ. All of these can be classified as spiritual truths which lie at the heart of, and give direction and purpose to, our material existence.

What kind of message?

Reading the Bible also involves interpreting what kind of message we are receiving and what we are going to do with what we have read. Just as there are different kinds of television programs that look alike at first glance, so there are different kinds of writing in the Bible which contain different messages and call for a different response. To interpret and apply these passages, we need to first try to understand the message. Sometimes, the message is short and blunt and easy to understand and apply, for example: "You shall not steal" (Exodus 20:15). In other cases, the message is contained in a short story which requires a bit of interpretation and translation into our present day context. For example the parable of the Good Samaritan (Luke 10:25-37) ends with the exhortation: "You go and do likewise." In this case, the reader needs to translate this exhortation into the daily circumstances of life on an ongoing basis. In other cases, the message is contained in the form of beautiful poetry. For example, Psalm 104 does not exhort us to "do" anything. It invites us to contemplate the majesty and power of God in Creation and therefore to see the world with a new set of eyes. In other cases, the Bible invites us to relive an ancient epic story and to see our lives as a continuation of the story. One example is the Wilderness saga (told in the book of Exodus and commented upon throughout the rest of the Bible). This story of heroic effort by the people of Israel, and of miraculous provision and protection by God, is an invitation to view our own life as a pilgrimage of faith through the wilderness of an uncertain world, trusting in the protection and provision of God. The Resurrection passages of the New Testament invite us to interpret every aspect of our life (and death) in light of God's redeeming love. At every step of the way, the Bible invites us into the big love story between God and the human race. It is not primarily a "to do" list. Rather, it is an invitation to see our lives in light of God's awesome power and love and to live accordingly.

2) "What is the enduring message? How do I translate this message from the Bible context to my context?"

Once one has determined the meaning of a biblical passage in its original context, then we need to try to translate the message to our own context. One helpful analogy is to compare the text to an ear of corn. One needs to peel back the contextual "husk" to get to the "eternal kernel" of truth for our lives today. Sometimes this is relatively easy and straightforward and sometimes it is quite difficult. For example, the exhortations of the Ten Commandments or the Sermon on the Mount are quite easily transferable to life today. Others are much more difficult. For example, the ancient Israelite legal system and ritual sacrifices; the relations between kings and subjects, masters and slaves, men and women, church and state are all vastly different from the norms and practices of our own cultural context. It takes considerable reflection to translate what, if any, application those texts may have for us. (We will explore this topic at the end of each chapter of this book.)

3) "How is God leading me to respond to this message? How is God calling me to respond to God's Word contained in this passage?"

Remember, "all Scripture is inspired by God (God-breathed) and profitable for teaching, reproof, correction and training in righteousness, that the person of God might be complete, equipped for every good work."

God speaks to us through the Bible and calls us to live our lives in response to his Word. If we want to learn to know God more, to grow in our relationship with God, to formed and taught and reproved and corrected and equipped by God, then we need to be attentive to our response. To grow into a mature relationship with God, to be useful for the work of the Kingdom of God, to help other people to grow in their own relationship with God, we need to go beyond merely reading the Bible as an interesting religious book. We need to carefully, prayerfully and consistently ask ourselves: "How is God speaking to me through his word today? How does what I have read today affect my actions and decisions and priorities today? How will my attitudes toward other people, myself and God be shaped by what I have read and heard and learned this day?

4) Reading the Bible "with the Church."

Remember the point made earlier in this chapter: the Bible is the Church's book. When we read the Bible, we can learn a lot from the collective wisdom of others who have read it before us. As one progresses in reading and interpreting the Bible, it is helpful to consult a commentary which reflects the normative interpretation, scholarship and wisdom of the Church over time. There are many good biblical commentaries which reflect the various interpretive norms of different Christian traditions (i.e Roman Catholic, Eastern Orthodox, Anglican, Classical Protestant, Evangelical etc). For a beginner, the best place to start is to ask for a recommendation from the pastor of one's own faith community.

Because reading and interpreting the Bible can be difficult, many people find it helpful to join a group Bible study. When discussing how God is speaking through the Bible, the Holy Spirit often works through the group to bring out a greater wisdom than is available to individuals. Also, when discerning major life decisions, it is always helpful and advisable to pray and discuss these matters with fellow Christians. Jesus promised to send the Holy Spirit to lead his followers "into all truth" and we can expect the Holy Spirit to show up when we ask. And he promised to be personally present in our communal prayer and discernment: "When two or three of you are gathered in my name, I am in the midst of you."

QUESTIONS FOR REFLECTION AND DISCUSSION

Read the following Bible passages one at a time.

Psalm 104

Exodus 20:1-18

Matthew 1:1-17

Matthew 5:1-16

Matthew 25:31-46

Luke 10:25-27

Revelation 21:1-8

Choose one or two of these biblical passages and discuss the following questions:

1) What kind of truth statements are being made here? Should the passage be interpreted as historical/factual truth, as relational truth, as moral truth, as spiritual truth, or as a combination of two or more?

2) How would the truth statements in each of these passages be translated to our historical context. What is the "eternal kernel" of truth from God to us? How might God be speaking to us through these passages?

3) How is God speaking to me through these passages? What are the "take home" messages for my life, my priorities, my attitudes, my relationships with other people?

Chapter 2

CREATION: "BEHOLD, IT IS VERY GOOD"

Main focus of this chapter: Who is in charge of the world and what is the meaning and purpose of human life?
(Before reading this chapter, please read Genesis, chapters 1 and 2)

There are two creation stories in Genesis. The first one gives us "the big picture" of the whole world; the second give us a "close up" of the first human beings.

I. The First Creation Story (Genesis 1:1 to 2:3)

This first creation story of Genesis is a powerful statement of **relational truth** about God, the universe, the earth and all living creatures, including human beings. To understand the full impact of this account of creation, we need to first discuss the context in which it was written. Genesis 1 is a **powerful rebuke** directed against the prevailing religions, cultures and worldview of the ancient Middle East. To appreciate the full impact of Genesis 1, we need to first understand the polytheistic world-view against which it argues.

1) The Polytheistic ("Pagan") World-View

Polytheism (a belief in many "gods") was the dominant world-view of the ancient world. (This world-view has often been called "paganism", but that pejorative term now has many modern connotations which are not relevant or helpful for our discussion here. So we will use the more descriptive term "polytheistic.") Israel's near neighbors, the Babylonians (modern day Iraq) believed that the world was created in a battle between two opposing gods. In the Babylonian creation story (called the *"Enuma Elish"*), Marduk (the patron god of Babylon) defeated Tiamat (the dragon of watery chaos) in an epic battle. Maduk won the battle, established order and life as we know it began to flourish. Marduk was the leader of all the lesser "gods", which included the sun, moon and stars, wind and other natural forces. All of these lesser "gods" were to be respected, worshiped and feared in proportion to their influence over the natural forces which affect humans for good or ill.

Other polytheistic cultures in the ancient world had other names for the greater and lesser "gods", but the basic pattern was the same. In polytheism, the "gods" are rival powers which are in charge of various necessary aspects of the world around us: sun, rain, wind, the sea, crop yields, animal fertility, human love and fertility, revenge, war and so on. In this world-view, none of the "gods" was ever in complete control. Some were favorable toward humans; others not. The main point of polytheistic religion is to persuade the "gods" to work in your favor and, when necessary, to work against your enemies. For this reason, humans were constantly devising sacrifices to persuade certain "gods" to act kindly - and curses to persuade them to act unkindly to your enemies. Human beings were seen as slaves (or at best pawns) of the "gods." Human beings had no dignified or predictable place in this world-view and no real choices about their destiny. They were subject to the whims of capricious powers in a chaotic universe.

It is critically important to understand this polytheistic world-view to fully appreciate the alternative world-view presented by Genesis. Genesis is a stunning rebuke to polytheism and all of its implications.

2) The Genesis World-View: One God Plans Creation

In the beginning God created the heavens and the earth. The earth was without form and void, and the darkness was on the face of the deep; and the spirit of God was moving across the face of the waters. And God said, "Let there be light"; and there was light. And God saw that the light was good and God separated the light from the darkness. God called the light Day and the darkness Night. And there was evening and there was morning, one day.
Genesis 1:1-5

And God said "Let there be lights in the firmament of heaven to separate the day from the night; and let them be for signs and for seasons and for days and for years and let them be lights in the firmament of the heavens to give light."
Genesis 1:14-15

As opposed to the polytheistic view, creation was not the result of a primordial battle between "gods" of order and chaos. It has a beginning, originating in the mind and will of the one God, who alone brings order out of chaos. In polytheistic religion, the sun and lesser lights were "gods" to be worshiped. In Genesis, one God creates, and orders and directs "the Light" which is the motive force of the sun and all other stars.

One God Gives Life to All

> *And God said, "Let the earth put forth vegetation, plants yielding seed and fruit trees bearing fruit in which is their seed, each according to its kind upon the earth. And it was so. The earth brought forth vegetation, plants yielding seed according to their own kinds, and trees bearing fruit which is their seed, each according to its kind....*
>
> Genesis 1:11-12

> *And God said "Let the waters bring forth swarms of living creatures, and let the birds fly above the earth across the firmament of heaven." So God created the great sea monster and every living creature that moves, with which the waters swarm, according to their kinds, and every winged bird according to its kind....*
>
> Genesis 1:20-22

> *And God made the beasts of the earth according to their kind and cattle according to their kind, and everything that creeps upon the ground according to their kind.*
>
> Genesis 1:25

In the Genesis account, God is the author of all life and every aspect of life, from "creeping things" to "birds" to "sea monsters." God's creative purpose is at work in the minutest processes of plant propagation ("each producing fruit which is their seed") and species differentiation ("each according to its kind"). The teeming energy, vitality and diversity of the natural world of plants and animals are an expression of the creative power and purpose of the One God who creates and governs all living things.

Humans Created in God's Image and Likeness

> *Then God said, "Let us make man in our image, after our likeness; and let them have dominion over the fish of the sea, and over the birds of the air, and over the cattle, and over all the earth, and over every creeping thing that creeps upon the earth."*

Creation: "Behold it is Very Good"

> *So God created man in his own image and likeness, in the image of God he created him; male and female he created them. And God blessed them and said to them "Be fruitful and multiply, and fill the earth and subdue it; and have dominion over the fish of the sea and over the birds of the air and over every living thing that moves upon the earth. And God said "Behold, I have given you every plant yielding seed which is upon the face of all the earth, and every tree with seed in its fruit; you shall have them for food."*
>
> Genesis 1:26-29

Here the difference between Genesis and the polytheistic world-view reaches its climax. In the polytheistic religions, human beings are slaves and playthings of capricious and malicious "gods." By contrast, in Genesis human beings are the "crown of creation" - created in "the image and likeness" of the one God who gives life and order and purpose to all creation. Human beings are created with the capacity to have knowledge of, and friendship with, the one God. Human beings are given the role of having "dominion" over all other living things and the natural world – God's "junior partners", so to speak, in managing the created world.

> *And God saw everything that he had made, and behold, it was very good.*
>
> Genesis 1:31

After each of the first five days of creation, God pronounces it "good." But on this last day, it is pronounced "very good." In contrast to the polytheistic view, the world is not a chaotic, disorderly and hostile place. It is fundamentally "very good" because it reflects the will and purpose of a God whose purpose is good. The beauty of Creation reflects the beauty of its Creator. It is orderly, rational, predictable and beneficent.

The Sanctification of Time

> *And on the seventh day God finished his work which he had done, and he rested on the seventh day from all his work which he had done. So God blessed the seventh day and hallowed it, because God rested from all of his work which he had done in creation.*
>
> Genesis 2:2-3

God "hallows" (makes "holy") the seventh day when the work of creation is completed. Does this mean that the Master of the Universe was physically exhausted and needed a break? No, the Sabbath is "holy" – that is set apart for a special purpose. It is a day for humans to stop work, contemplate and give thanks for the great gift of life that the one God has given us. The Sabbath is a day to reflect on the gift of Creation and of our role as stewards of creation.

Summary of the difference between polytheistic and Genesis world-views:

Polytheistic world-view

- Many competing "gods", many of them unfriendly.
- World is disorderly, chaotic and capricious.
- Humans are slaves and playthings of the "gods."
- The main objective of religion is to persuade or bribe the "gods" to act favorably to you in their respective fields of influence.

Genesis world-view

- One God plans and orders creation.
- The created order is orderly, predictable and rational reflecting the mind and purpose of God.
- Human beings are the "crown of creation" and partners with God in caring for the created world.
- The main objective of religion is obedience to God's purpose in ordering the created world (stewardship) to thank God for the gift of creation (Sabbath).

II. The Second Creation Story (Genesis 2:4-25)

In the first creation story, we have the "big picture" of God's relationship to the whole created order. In this second account, we get a much different perspective. This "close up" picture tells us about the relationship between God and the first man and woman. Their names are highly symbolic and make them representatives for all human beings. Adam is a Hebrew word meaning "man" and is a word play on another Hebrew word *adama*, meaning "earth." Eve is similar to a Hebrew word meaning "life" and can be translated as "mother of all living." In other words, the story of Adam and Eve is the story of humanity in relationship to God. As we shall see in the next chapter, and in the New Testament, Adam and Eve play a central role in our understanding of God's will and purpose for all humanity.

Creation: "Behold it is Very Good"

1) The Man

These are the generations of the heavens and the earth when they were created. In the day that the Lord God made the earth and the heavens, when no plant of the field was yet in the earth and no herb of the field had yet sprung up – for the Lord God had not yet caused it to rain upon the earth, and there was no man to till the ground; but a mist went up from the earth and watered the whole face of the ground- then the Lord God formed the man of dust from the ground, and breathed into his nostrils the breath of life; and the man became a living being.
Genesis 2:4-7

Man (*adam*) is created from the earth (*adama*) and infused with the breath (spirit) of God. Humans are both material and spiritual beings, created with the capacity to relate to God thus reiterating, with different terminology, the "image and likeness" of God message in the first creation story.

2) The Woman

Then the Lord God said "It is not good that the man should be alone; I will make a helper fit for him"...So the Lord God caused a deep sleep to fall upon the man, and while he slept took one of his ribs and closed up the place in his flesh; and the rib which the Lord God had taken from the man he made into a woman and brought her to the man. Then the man said "This at last is bone of my bone and flesh of my flesh; she shall be called woman for she was taken out of man. Therefore a man leaves his father and mother and cleaves to his wife, and they become one flesh. And the man and his wife were both naked and they were not ashamed.
Genesis 2:18, 21-25

God creates many other creatures to keep the man company in the garden. But none are a fit helper for him. God says the man needs a companion, and the man apparently agrees. God takes the substance of the man ("rib" and "life" are very similar words) to create the woman. The moment he sees her, he cries out in joy: "This at last is bone of my bone and flesh of my flesh." There is an equal and mutual partnership. This echoes back to the first creation story: "in the image of God he created him. Male and female he created them." Then the man and woman are joined together in the "one flesh" union of marriage and sexual intercourse. This passage is the foundation for the Judeo-Christian understanding of marriage and sexual ethics. We are informed "they were naked and they were not ashamed." In other words, they were in a state of moral innocence with regard to their sexual attraction to each other and in relation to God.

3) The Garden and the Tree

> *And the Lord God planted a garden in Eden, in the east; and there he put the man whom he had formed. And out of the ground the Lord God made to grow every tree that is pleasant to the sight and good for food, the tree of life also in the midst of the garden, and the tree of the knowledge of good and evil.... And the Lord God commanded the man saying, "You may eat freely of every tree of the garden; but of the tree of the knowledge of good and evil you shall not eat, for in the day you eat of it, you shall die."*
>
> Genesis 2:8-9 and 16-17

God intentionally places Man in a harmonious place with "the tree of life" at the center–symbolizing everything he needs for a good life in a harmonious balance between Man and nature. But there is trouble on the horizon. There is another, more problematic tree in the garden. There are limits to Man's enjoyment of the harmonious life. To eat of the fruit of this one tree will bring the harmony to an end.

Summary of the Relational Truth in the Second Creation Story

➢ Man is created by God as both material (earth) and spiritual (breath of God).
➢ Woman is created as an equal and mutual partner with Man.
➢ This mutual partnership is consummated in the "one flesh" bond of marriage.
➢ Man and Woman are "naked but not ashamed", in a state of moral innocence.
➢ Man and Woman are placed in a beautiful Garden in which they enjoy a harmonious relationship with God, nature and with each other.
➢ The harmonious relationship with each other, with nature and with God is conditional. They must not eat of the fruit of the tree of the knowledge of Good and Evil.

Creation: "Behold it is Very Good"

III. How To Interpret The Genesis Creation Narratives

1) Is Modern Science at War with Genesis?

The answer, according to many news reports, is a resounding **YES!!!** And if one interprets Genesis as a science textbook, then there is indeed a problem. We learn in science class that the universe was born several billion years ago, that it took a few billion years for the earth to cool down before life on it was possible, and that plants and animals developed for many millions of years before humans arrived on the scene. A literal interpretation of Genesis tells us that it all happened in six days, that humans arrived one day after (Genesis 1), or just before (Genesis 2), the other living creatures. We learn in science class that plants, animals and humans developed and adapted to different environments over millions of years. But a literal interpretation of Genesis gives the impression that every creature instantly appeared in its present-day form. So, for those who read Genesis as a science textbook, there appear to be some major contradictions. This conflict is often distilled to its essence under the heading of "Evolutionism vs. Creationism." And there are occasional battles between parent groups and local school boards regarding the content of science courses. News media people love to report on these conflicts because it gets people riled up and therefore sells news and advertising. On the other hand, news media outlets almost never report an alternative (boring and therefore not "newsworthy") set of facts: that a fairly high percentage (40 -50%) of academic scientists identify themselves as believing in God, that an even higher percentage (about 70%) of practicing Protestant and Catholic Christians do not believe that Genesis and the insights of science are incompatible, and that *The Catechism of the Catholic Church* teaches (what many devout Christians probably believe, either implicitly or explicitly):

> "The question about the origin of the world and of man has been the object of many scientific studies which have splendidly enriched our knowledge of the age and dimensions of the cosmos, the development of life-forms and the appearance of man. These discoveries invite us to an even greater admiration for the Creator, prompting us to give him thanks for all his works and for the understanding he gives to scholars and researchers."
> (Section 2, Article 1, Paragraph 4 Catechesis on Creation # 283)

2) A Hymn of Praise to the one Creator God, Not A Science Textbook

Many believing Jews and Christians (both scholars and everyday believers) think that Genesis should be interpreted as a "Hymn of Praise" to the One Creator God. Its message – as opposed to the dominant polytheistic world-view it refuted – is this: *The One God has given us this awesome, majestic and beautiful world. It is teeming with life and has everything needed to sustain life. And he has given us the privilege and responsibility to take care of, and bring order to, this beautiful world. And, unlike the other creatures, he has given us the capacity to relate to him in reflection and worship and praise. We can trust and obey and even love this God who has created us in his own image and likeness. Praise the Creator God.*

Genesis chapter 1 is very similar in tone and message to another beautiful hymn of praise to the Creator God, Psalm 104: *"O Lord, how manifold are your works! In wisdom you have made them all; the earth is full of your creatures, … May the glory of the Lord endure forever,; may the Lord rejoice in all his works. …I will sing to the Lord as long as I live; I will praise my God while I have my being."*

Going back to our discussion in the introduction, Genesis is presenting relational truth in symbolic language. It tells us about the relationship between God, the created order and human beings. It tells us that there is one God who plans, creates and sustains the beautiful world we live in. It tells us that we are created in this one God's image and likeness and that we have a God-given responsibility to care for the gift of creation that we have inherited. If we interpret Genesis in this way, then there is no inherent conflict with modern science. Each is telling the truth in a different language. Genesis tells us **that** God created the world and all creatures. Science investigates **how** the creative process has happened over time how the various life-forms relate to each other in this marvelously intricate universe. Genesis tells us **why** we are here and how we are to live in relationship to God, to our fellow human beings and to the other creatures on the planet. Genesis tells us that we have a responsibility to use scientific knowledge to protect and conserve the world God has given us. Science can tell us how to understand and manipulate our environment to fulfill that God-given duty.

CREATION: "BEHOLD IT IS VERY GOOD"

QUESTIONS FOR REFLECTION AND DISCUSSION

1) Our responsibility for caring for Creation.

In Genesis 1, God tells humans to "be fruitful and multiply, and fill the earth and subdue it; and have dominion over the fish of the sea and the birds of the air and over every living thing that moves upon the earth." In the past, this passage has been interpreted to give us a license to use, develop and manipulate "nature" for human advantage, prosperity and happiness. Everything we enjoy in "modern" life (electricity and all of the labor-saving devices that electricity makes possible, world-wide communication, life-saving medicine, good housing, easy transportation, longer life expectancy, greater agricultural output per person, cell phones, internet and so on) is the direct result of the human "dominion" of nature.

More recently this interpretation has come under intense criticism. Some people say that this notion of "dominion" is the cause of our current environmental crisis. We have become too successful at manipulating our environment and we are killing ourselves and every other living thing because of overpopulation, massive starvation, species extinction, air and water pollution and global warming.

Evaluate and discuss these two points of view. Are they true? Can you believe that both are true? Does accepting one mean that we must reject the other? Given our current state of environmental affairs, what is the best way to honor the Creator and the rest of Creation? How is love for God and our neighbor expressed in our use of resources? How does our use of electricity, cars, cell phones, modern medicine and airplanes relate to a desire to "save" the environment?

2) Human population.

In Genesis 1, God commands humans to "be fruitful and multiply." In the thousands of years since that was written, we have been pretty successful at doing so. In 2011, the human population crossed the 7 billion threshold. In light of the environmental crisis noted in question 1, how should we view God's command? Is there a contradiction between human population growth and care for the rest of Creation?

Evaluate the following strategies for slowing human population growth from a Biblical point of view: 1) government – enforced sterilization and abortion; 2) government sponsored education about family planning, responsible fertility and the impact of population growth. What is the essential difference between these two strategies?

Is it ever morally permissible for one person or one group of people to decide that the life of another person or group of people is expendable?

What do you think God thinks about the following human activities:
- Raising animals for human food and clothing.
- Hunting animals for "trophies", or harvesting fur for luxury coats.
- Experimenting on animals to develop medicine to cure human diseases.
- Experimenting on animals to develop better perfumes and beauty products.

The Bible tells us that God created human beings in God's "image and likeness." Do you think that cloning human beings is something that we should do if we are able? How about cloning certain human body parts (heart, liver, kidney) for transplants to save peoples' lives? Are these activities like "playing God" and therefore a bad thing to do? Or are they a legitimate application of God's gift of reason to humans?

3) Compare Psalms 8, 104 and 139 to Genesis 1 and 2.

How are these different "Hymns of Praise" to the Creator the same? What are the different emphases in each one?

4) Sabbath Rest

Rabbi Abraham Heschel, in his book *Sabbath Time*, says this: *"There is a realm of time where the goal is not to have but to be, not to own but to give, not to control but to share, not to subdue but to be in accord."* How does this statement compare with the way most people in our society behave on the weekend? How does this compare with your own personal view of the meaning of Sunday as a day of worship, rest, reflection and prayer.

PERSONAL REFLECTION AND PRAYER

Blaise Pascal (17th century French philosopher and mathematician) said this:
> *"There are only three kinds of people: those who have sought God and found Him- these are reasonable and happy; those who have sought God and not yet found Him – these are reasonable but unhappy; and those that neither seek God nor find Him – and*

CREATION: "BEHOLD IT IS VERY GOOD"

these are both unhappy and unreasonable."

Do you think this is a reasonable (and true and useful) observation about human beings? Does this statement have any relevance for your own spiritual life and search for God?

Are there times in your life when you felt empty of meaning and purpose? How has faith, trust and love of God and of other people affected your view of your own happiness?

Someone (anonymous) once said, "If God seems far away, who moved?"

Read Psalm 139 quietly and slowly.. It speaks of God's intimate knowledge of every aspect of our life? Is this a comforting or a frightening thought? Think about the times in your life when God seemed far away from you – when you felt lost, ashamed, depressed and without purpose. How does this psalm speak to your feelings at those times? Think about a thought pattern or behavior pattern of which you are ashamed. How does this psalm speak to your shame? Is there any sin or shame that God does not already know about? Is there anything God is not willing or able to forgive when we acknowledge it and ask for help?

BIBLE MEMORY VERSE

And God saw everything that he had made, and behold, it was very good. Thus the heavens and the earth were finished, and all the host of them. And on the seventh day God finished his work which he had done, and he rested on the seventh day from all his work which he had done. So God blessed the seventh day and hallowed it, because God rested from all of his work which he had done in creation.

Genesis 1:31-2:3

Chapter 3

ADAM AND EVE: "PARADISE LOST"

Main focus of this chapter:
Who is responsible for evil in the world?
(Read Genesis chapter 3 before continuing)

I.   Adam and Eve Rebel Against God

Some of the oldest and most enduring religious questions are these: Why is there evil in the world? Where did it come from? Who is responsible for it? Why do people hurt and hate each other? Why do nations go to war? Why does God allow these things to happen?

Polytheistic religions of the ancient world had answers to these questions. Evil gods cause bad things to happen. Human beings are under the influence of evil powers and/or fate. The gods are responsible for evil.

As we have seen, Genesis presents a radical alternative to the prevailing polytheistic worldview. This account of Adam and Eve's temptation and fall is the Bible's foundational statement of "relational truth" about "the human condition." It tells us about the origin of sin, who is responsible, the consequences and God's response.

As we saw in the last chapter, Man and Woman are living in the Garden of Eden. To remain in this wonderful garden, Adam and Eve had to follow one rule: they could not eat of the fruit of the knowledge of good and evil. They couldn't resist for long.

> *"Now the serpent was more subtle than any other wild creature that the Lord God had made. He said to the woman, 'Did God say 'You shall not eat of any tree in the garden'? And the woman said to the serpent. 'We may eat of the fruit of the trees in the garden; but God said, 'You shall not eat of the fruit of the tree which is in the midst of the garden, neither shall you touch it, lest you die'. But the serpent said to the woman, 'You shall not die. For God knows that when you eat of it your eyes will be opened, and you will be like God, knowing good and evil.' So*

when the woman saw that the tree was good for food, and that it was a delight to the eyes, and that the tree was desired to make one wise, she took of its fruit and ate; and she also gave some to her husband, and he ate. Then the eyes of both were opened, and they know that they were naked; and they sewed fig leaves together and made themselves aprons.

"And they heard the sound of the Lord God walking in the garden in the cool of the day, and the man and his wife hid themselves from the presence of the Lord God among the trees of the garden. But the Lord God called to the man, and said to him, 'Where are you?' And he said, 'I heard the sound of thee in the garden, and I was afraid, because I was naked; and I hid myself.' He said, 'Who told you that you were naked? Have you eaten of the tree of which I commanded you not to eat? The man said, 'The woman whom thou gavest to me to be with me, she gave me the fruit of the tree and I ate.' Then God said to the woman, 'What is this that you have done?' The woman said, 'The serpent beguiled me, and I ate.'

Genesis 3:1-13

To understand the meaning of this passage, we need to translate some of the symbolic language.

The Garden of Eden: a state of peace, happiness and harmony between God, human beings and nature.

Naked, but not ashamed: a state of child-like moral innocence.

The Tree of the Knowledge of Good and Evil: the possibility of being "like God" in knowledge and power.

The Serpent: a tempter, the source of temptation but not the one responsible for disobedience. In later Christian reflection, the serpent is identified as Satan, but not in this passage.

Eating the Fruit: an act of disobedience and rebellion against God. The author does not spell out the exact nature of the disobedience, but clearly pride and envy are major factors. The act indicates the ability to make moral judgments and the freedom to choose between right and wrong.

What happened?

Man and Woman give in to the Serpent's temptation, eat the forbidden fruit, rebel against God, and try to evade their moral responsibility by blaming the Serpent and each other.

What's the relational truth?

Man and Woman are morally responsible for rebellion against God. Through their own choice they have forfeited their harmonious relationship with God, nature and with each other. They have lost their innocence. Evil has entered the world through the misuse of human freedom. We call this misuse of freedom "sin."

II. Adam and Eve Expelled From the Garden

> *"The Lord God said to the serpent, 'Because you have done this, cursed are you above all cattle and above all wild animals; upon your belly you shall go, and dust you shall eat all of the days of your life. I will put enmity between you and the woman, and between your seed and her seed; he shall bruise your head, and you shall bruise his heel.'*
>
> *"And to the woman he said, 'I will greatly multiply your pain in childbearing; in pain shall you bring forth children, yet your desire shall be for your husband, and he shall rule over you.'*
>
> *"And to Adam he said, 'Because you have listened to the voice of your wife, and have eaten of the tree of which I commanded you,' You shall not eat of it.', cursed is the ground because of you; in toil shall you eat of it all the days of your life; thorns and thistles it shall bring forth to you; and you shall eat the plants of the field. In the sweat of your face you shall eat bread till you return to the ground, for out of it you were taken; you are dust and to dust you shall return.' "* Genesis 3:14-19

As a consequence of their act of rebellion, Adam and Eve are ejected from the Garden of Eden. On the way out the door, so to speak, God issues a three-fold "curse": first to the serpent, then to Eve and finally, to Adam.

The serpent is destined to crawl on the ground and to be in perpetual battle with the offspring of Eve.

Eve is destined to suffer pain in childbirth and to be ruled over by her husband. The mutual relationship she enjoyed with her mate is gone.

Adam is destined to a life of hard labor eking out a living from the "cursed" ground and is destined to return to the earth from which he was formed. The harmony he enjoyed with nature is gone.

What is the relational truth?

The threefold "curse" is a statement of the consequence of sin. Adam and Eve have exercised their God-given freedom. As a result of sinful choices they have brought themselves a hardness of heart and a harshness of life. Furthermore, they have passed this condition on to their descendants. We all inherit a web of sinful behavior that precedes and distorts our own moral choices.

However, (and this is a very important "however") even though God has kicked Adam and Eve (representatives of all humanity) out of the Garden, he has not given up on them (us). Even though the blissful state of moral innocence is lost forever, there still exists a moral sense. Even though the peaceful coexistence with God and all other creatures is ended, there is still a distant memory and a desire for a return. Even though the "image and likeness of God" is distorted, it is not destroyed. Even in the act of ejecting them from the Garden, God acknowledges a kinship with, and protection of, his creatures.

> *"And the Lord God made for Adam and for his wife garments of skins and he clothed them. Then the Lord God said, 'Behold, the man has become like one of us, knowing good and evil; and now, lest he put forth his hand and take also the tree of life, and eat, and live forever' – therefore the Lord God sent him forth from the garden of Eden...and at the east of the garden of Eden, he placed the cherubim, and a flaming sword which turned every way, to guard the way to the tree of life."*
>
> Genesis 3:21-25

The way back to the tree of life is not closed forever. We encounter it again in the very last book of the Bible, when God's work of redeeming his lost creation is complete. And there, we are told, "the leaves of the tree of life were for the healing of the nations."

III. The Web of Sin Grows

After Adam and Eve (and with them, all humanity) are ejected from the garden, Genesis continues to spell out the consequences of sin. Several stories follow which demonstrate the ever growing web of sin in which the human race is entangled:

> ➤ **Chapter 4: Cain kills Abel:** the first murder, brother is alienated from brother.

- **Chapters 6 & 7: The Great Flood** God brings judgment upon sinful people, but saves a few righteous people in the Ark and leaves a sign of hope (the rainbow).
- **Chapter 11: Tower of Babel** God punishes pride through confusion of tongues which results in separation of races and ethnic groups which leads to further alienation and war.
- **Chapter 19: Sodom and Gomorrah** God punishes hostility and sexual immorality.

It is important to note in all of these cases, God punishes to teach a lesson – never simply for vengeance. God always saves a few righteous persons to bear witness to His saving purpose.

IV. Consequences of "The Fall"

The first three chapters of Genesis are the basis for our understanding of what it means to be human. As such they are foundational for understanding the entire Bible and the Christian faith.

Adam ("Man") and Eve ("Mother of All Living") are a representative image of all humanity. Their story is our story. Their experience with God and with moral choices is our story. Their experiences with the consequences of sin are the prototype for our experiences with sin. We are in the same mess as they are.

During many centuries of study and reflection on the relational truth contained in the Adam and Eve story, Christians came to refer to it as **"The Fall."** Because of sin, Adam and Eve "fell" from their honored place in the garden: from their state of harmony with God and each other. Also, because the story of Adam and Eve is a prototype for our own experience with sin and alienation from God and each other, we call their act **"Original Sin."**

God's Response to "Original Sin"

The doctrine of "Original Sin" is the Church's teaching about the consequences of Adam and Eve's "fall." The doctrine teaches that we all inherit from Adam And Eve a "fallen" humanity. Because of their sin, all other humans have been born into a web of sinful relationships, sinful behaviors, sinful institutions, and sinful individuals.

And inevitably, we are all caught up in this web of sin and suffer the same consequences. We too are alienated from God, from nature and from one another. Because of original sin, we need to be redeemed. We need to be reconciled to God and to one another. We need a savior who will restore what has been lost through sin. The Bible tells us the story of God's answer to our need - God's response to the human condition. In the Old Testament God calls a group of "Chosen People" to bear witness to God's saving purpose. In the New Testament, God completes the saving purpose by sending His only begotten Son.

The story of the Bible – the story of God's response to the mess we are in – may be summarized in the following verse, which Martin Luther called "the Gospel in miniature."

> *"For God so loved the world that he gave his only begotten Son, that whoever believes in Him shall not perish but have eternal life. For God sent his Son into the world, not to condemn the world, but that the world might be saved through Him.*
>
> John 3:16-17

QUESTIONS FOR DISCUSSION AND REFLECTION

1) The book and film "Lord of the Flies" is about a group of fourteen year-old boys who get stranded on an island after their plane goes down at sea. As time passes, all of the boys except one turn to savages. The point of the story is that people are basically evil. When removed from the cultural peer pressure and legal restraints of civilized society, our natural "badness" comes out. In this view, the way to "fix" human evil is to have clear cultural standards, strict laws and swift punishment for bad behavior. This picture of "human nature" is often identified as a "conservative" view.

The book "Catcher in the Rye" gives us an opposite perspective. In this book, a young man starts out good, but learns to do bad things through the bad example of the adults around him. The point of this story is that people are basically good, but we are corrupted by a bad society. In this view, the way to "fix" human evil is to reform society, and then individuals will respond positively to their improved surroundings. This picture of "human nature" is often identified as a "liberal" view.

Based on your own life experiences, which of these two views is the most accurate? Are people "basically bad" and in need of restraint? Or are we "basically good" and in need of better cultural climate? Try to give some real life examples to support your answers.

Are these "mutually exclusive" points of view? (In other words, if one is true does that mean the other is necessarily false?) Or do they each point to one aspect of the whole truth?

Which of these points of view is closest to the book of Genesis point of view? Give some specific biblical examples to support your opinion.

2) Genesis points out that each new generation is caught up in a growing web of sin. Over many centuries of reflection, Christians have called this inherited entanglement of bad choices by the name "original sin." On the day we are born, we first breathe air that has been polluted by others. Similarly, we enter a world in which previous human choices have created a moral context within which we make choices. We in turn will make choices which affect the choices to be made by people not yet born.

Discuss how the following realities are affected by individual and societal choices. How can different choices made now affect positively or negatively on choices that will be made 50 years into the future?

➢ air pollution from cars, power plants and economic development

➢ pornographic magazines, web sites and magazines

- sexual promiscuity, sexually transmitted diseases, children born not knowing who their parents are
- violence of one ethnic group against another
- alcoholism and drug addiction
- music, movies, games which portray violence as a good thing

3) Adam and Eve do not want to admit that they have sinned. Each tries to blame it on someone else. Why do you think it is so hard for us to admit our own rebellion against God? Is it possible to have an honest relationship with God without admitting our sins?

PRAYER EXERCISE

Read slowly Psalm 51. Reflect on the ways that you are personally entangled in the "web of sin" and ways that you contribute to it. Make a list and ask God for forgiveness and amendment of life.

BIBLE MEMORY VERSE

But the serpent said to the woman, 'You shall not die. For God knows that when you eat of it your eyes will be opened, and you will be like God, knowing good and evil.' So when the woman saw that the tree was good for food, and that it was a delight to the eyes, and that the tree was desired to make one wise, she took of its fruit and ate; and she also gave some to her husband, and he ate. Then the eyes of both were opened, and they know that they were naked; and they sewed fig leaves together and made themselves aprons.

Genesis 3:4-7

Chapter 4

ABRAHAM
"YOU WILL BE A BLESSING TO ALL NATIONS"

Main Focus of This Chapter: How God began the work of redeeming the human race by making a "covenant" with his "Chosen People."

I. God's Plan of Salvation

In the last two chapters, we have focused on the first 11 chapters of Genesis: the Creation, "the Fall" of Adam and Eve, and the consequences of their "original sin." We have seen that God created the world and everything in it and declared it "very good." Human beings were created in the "image and likeness of God" and therefore have the ability to make moral choices and to live in spiritual communion with God. Adam and Eve chose to disobey and rebel against God and because they did, the harmonious relationship with God was ended. The "image and likeness of God" was distorted and an ever-expanding web of sinful behavior spread throughout all humanity.

These early chapters of Genesis "set the stage" for the rest of the Bible. God was not (and is not) content to have us alienated from God and from each other because of sin. God wants to restore us to the harmonious state which Adam and Eve enjoyed before their disobedience. God wants to fix what is broken. We call this "God's plan of salvation." The rest of the Bible tells us about all that God has done to restore the harmonious relationship that was broken by sin. The Bible is, from beginning to end the story of God's redeeming love.

1) How Did God Set Out to Fix what was Broken?

God might have revoked our free will and not allowed us the capacity to sin. But redemption by force is alien to a relationship of love. God chose not to revoke our moral freedom because to do so would have wiped away "the image and likeness of God" in which we are created. We are created for fellowship and even friendship with God and true friendship can never be forced. For love to be genuine, it is necessary for the lover to allow the freedom of the beloved.

And true freedom necessarily means that the beloved can choose to reject the love offered. Instead of forcing us to love and obey, God chose to win our love and obedience by persuasion. To do this, God established a relationship with a particular group of people: the people of Israel; God's "chosen" people. God chose the people of Israel for a specific purpose: to know and tell the world about God's plan of salvation.

2) Chosen People:
God's Instrument for the Salvation of All People

Why a "chosen people"? Why not everybody? In our modern culture, imbued as it is with democratic sensibilities and concern for "inclusivity" of marginalized people, it often seems unfair that God would be "exclusive"- that God would choose a particular group of people for this special relationship. Why were all other ethnic groups excluded from this special relationship with God?

At the most basic level, we must simply acknowledge that God does not operate according to our expectations. And in other cases, we simply don't know the mind of God. The following is one possibility.

Those who study people's working habits have a saying: "Everybody's job is nobody's job." This means that we human beings need to be motivated by a clear sense of mission and purpose, and a clear sense of who is responsible for carrying out the mission. If no one is designated as the responsible person, the job usually does not get done. God may well have had this human tendency in mind when deciding to establish a special relationship with the people of Israel. God set apart a special group of people for a special mission – to know, love and serve the living God and to tell others about God's saving purpose for all humanity.

God chose to begin with a small group of people, but the scope of God's saving purpose extends to every human being who has ever lived. In other words, God's exclusive relationship with a particular group was a temporary measure which was necessary to fulfill the larger mission of redeeming all humanity. In the Old Testament period, we have many indications of the universal scope of salvation. For example, the books of Ruth and Jonah both focus on non-Jews being included within the scope of God's saving purpose. And the book of Isaiah has many references to the universal mission of Israel to be a "light to the nations" and to the temple in Jerusalem as "a house of prayer for all people." However, it is in the New Testament that the universal scope of salvation comes to full and explicit expression. To cite two (out of many) examples, Jesus commands his followers to "make disciples of all nations" (Matthew 28:19) and Paul tells us: "God desires all people to be saved and come to acknowledge of the truth." (1 Timothy 2:4)

II. The Calling of Abram (later renamed "Abraham")

In Genesis, chapters 1 through 11, we are reading "pre-history." They are accounts which, as we have seen, are primarily meant to convey "relational" truth and are told with very symbolic language. With chapter 12, we begin the historical portion of the Bible. From this point forward, we are dealing with people who are clearly fixed in time and place in the recorded history of the world. Bible scholars have different opinions on when to date the life of Abram, but most agree to sometime around 1,750 B.C.

An important note on sources: Before we begin the accounts of Abram, it is helpful to know that the episodes recorded in Genesis, as well as many other sections of the Old and New Testaments were compiled from several different sources. For that reason, we have several different accounts of Abram's life which tell different aspects of the story. These different accounts sometimes seem to be overly repetitive, and sometimes contradictory. But each account gives a different perspective on Abram's relationship with God. In the following discussion, we are combining several different accounts of God's covenant with Abram to get the full picture.

1) The Call from God

Abram came from the city of Ur, which was located in the area called Mesopotamia (the modern state of Iraq). Ur was an important cultural and commercial center. Archeologists have found ample evidence in Egypt that there were itinerant families of metal workers and traders who traveled extensively throughout the area we now call the "Middle East." These archeological discoveries confirm many of the details recounted in the story of Abram and his wife. It is possible that he and his family may even have been itinerant metal workers and traders.

Besides its commercial status, Ur was an important polytheistic religious center. The patron deity of the city was the moon god Nanna. Nanna was considered to be the father of the Sun god, the guardian of mankind and the master of destinies. Recalling our discussion of polytheistic religions in chapter 2, each god was thought to have power over some aspect of the universe, but no god was in charge of everything. Hence the quest to propitiate the relevant god for favors in specific areas of life. Abram was raised in this culture, but he was called by God to leave the city and its moon god.

> *Now the Lord said to Abram, "Go from your country and your kindred and you father's house to the land that I will show you. And I will make you a great nation, and I will bless you, and*

Abraham: "You Will be a Blessing to All Nations"

make your name great, so that you will be a blessing. ...and by you all the families of the earth will bless themselves." So Abram went as the Lord had told him.
Genesis 12:1-4

Abram is called out by God. He is told to leave his home and family and go to a "land that I will show you." God promises that he will be a great nation" and that he will be a blessing to "all families of the earth." Here in God's earliest contact with Abram is the promise of God's universal plan of salvation. At this stage, however, it is still very unclear what exactly God has in mind for Abram and his descendants. As the narrative goes on, it becomes clearer.

2) God's Promises to Abram (Abraham)

The Promise Land

Abram dwelt in the land of Canaan, ...The Lord said to Abram, ... "Lift up your eyes, and look from the place where you are, northward and southward, eastward and westward; for all the land which you see I will give to you and your descendants forever."

The Promise of Many Descendants

"I will make your descendants as the dust of the earth; so that if one can count the dust of the earth, your descendants also can be counted. Arise, walk through the length and breadth of the land, for I will give it to you."
Genesis 13:12,14-17

God promises Abram and his descendants the land of Canaan. (This corresponds roughly with the modern state of Israel.) Here again, the modern reader might wonder why God chose that particular piece of ground as "the promised land" and not some other place. Again, we might speculate that God wanted the chosen people with a mission to have a specific focal point for carrying out the mission. (Teachers need school buildings to educate students; farmers need fields to grow and store crops; the sheriff needs a jail to lock up the bad guys; the people of Israel needed a land of their own to shape their unique identity as the chosen people of God.)

The Promise of Blessing to All People of the Earth

"I will indeed bless you, and I will multiply your descendants as the stars of the heavens...and by your descendants shall all nations of the earth bless themselves."

Genesis 22:17-19

Here, we see specifically, God's universal saving purpose. He called this particular people of Israel for a universal mission. He blessed this particular group of people with a land and a special relationship with God to equip this small group to extend God's blessing to all people. Later in this book (chapter 16) we shall see this theme developed in the writings of Paul.

The Promise of a "Shield" of Protection

"After these things the word of the Lord came to Abram in a vision, 'Fear not, Abram, I am your shield; your reward shall be very great. But Abram said, 'O Lord God, what wilt thou give me, for I continue childless. ...And he brought him outside and said, 'Look toward heaven, and number the stars, if you are able to number them.' Then he said to him, 'So shall your descendants be.' And (Abram) believed the Lord and he reckoned it to him as righteousness."

Genesis 15:1-2;5-6

Some time has elapsed since God's initial promise to Abram, yet he still had not been able to conceive a child with his wife. As time went on, Abram began to doubt the validity of God's promise. But after this reassurance, Abram believed (trusted deeply) God's promise, and God accepted his act of faith and trust. This passage will have crucial importance when we come to the New Testament and especially to the writings of St. Paul.

2) The Covenant

"Covenant" means "agreement." In this covenant, God promises four things:

    1) many descendants – a great nation and a blessing to all families of the earth.

    2) a promise land

    3) People of Israel would be a blessing to all nations

    4) God will be Abram's "shield."

In return, Abram must do two things:

1) follow God's call
2) believe and trust God's promise

As we shall see in the next chapter, God gives Moses an important clarification of this covenant – the Law (Torah). The Torah includes the Ten Commandments plus dietary, ritual and ceremonial laws. It specifies what exactly it means to "believe, trust and follow" God's will and purpose.

3) Signs of the Covenant

Throughout the Bible, God reveals His purpose in "outward and visible signs." The covenant with Abram is marked by three signs. The meaning behind these signs is that God was beginning the long process of preparing and setting apart a people for himself – people with a distinct identity rooted in a common trust in God.

Animal Sacrifice:

> "And (God) said to (Abram) 'I am the Lord who brought you from Ur of the Chaldeans, to give you this land to possess.' But he said, 'Oh Lord God, how am I to know that I shall possess it?' He said to him, 'Bring me a heifer three years old, a ram three years old, a turtle dove, and a young pigeon.' And he brought him all these, cut them in two, and laid each half over against the other; but he did not cut the birds in two. ...When the sun had gone down and it was dark, behold, a smoking fire pot and a flaming torch passed between these pieces. On that day the Lord made a covenant with Abram, saying, 'To your descendants I will give this land'."
>
> Genesis 15:7-11;17-18

For modern readers, the idea of the animal sacrifice is probably one of the most difficult biblical practices to understand. However, as we shall see in chapter 6, sacrifice is an ever-present reality in both the Old and New Testaments. To understand the Bible, we need to learn the meaning behind the various sacrificial rites. In this case, the idea seems to be that Abram shows his trust in God by offering valuable livestock in sacrifice. God's presence and promise are symbolized by the smoking fire pot and flaming torch passing through the center of the sacrifice. Abram gives something of value – God gives his Word.

A new name: Abraham

> *"God said to Abram, 'Behold, my covenant is with you, and you shall be the father of a multitude of nations, No longer shall your name be Abram, but your name shall be Abraham."*

IV. The (Non) Sacrifice of Isaac

Abraham and his wife Sarah had great difficulty in conceiving a child. After many years without success, Sarah agreed to allow her slave woman (Hagar) to bear a child with Abraham. Hagar conceived a child whose name was Ishmael.

This was a common practice at a time when producing children was an absolute necessity for one's survival in old age. In effect, it was the "Social Security" system. In an age of very high infant and child mortality, it was necessary to produce many children in hopes that a few would survive to care for the parents in old age. Archeological evidence of ancient marriage contracts tells us that wives were obligated to produce children. If wives were infertile, they were required to provide substitute wives for childbearing. To modern people, this may sound cruel, but it reflects the realities of survival in a harsh environment.

After many years, Sarah finally conceived and bore a son whose name was Isaac. At last, God began to fulfill the promise made so long ago to Abraham – the promise of descendants "as many as the stars in the sky".

Imagine how happy Abraham and Sarah were at the birth of their son after many years of waiting. But after a few years of happiness, Abraham was asked to make the ultimate sacrifice:

> *"God tested Abraham and said to him, 'Abraham!' And he said, 'Here I am.' (God) said 'Take your son, your only son, whom you love, and go to the land of Moriah, and offer him there as a burnt offering upon one of the mountains which I shall tell you."*
>
> Genesis 22:1-2

Again the modern reader will be horrified and ask, "Why did God tell Abraham to do such a cruel deed?" To interpret this passage rightly, you need to know that human sacrifice was widely practiced in the polytheistic religions of Israel's near neighbors. Archeologists have discovered in the land of Canaan many skeletons of children buried under the doorposts of houses and at city gates. Apparently, pagans did this to bribe spirits to stay away or to buy protection from friendly gods. In Abraham's time child sacrifice was a common act of religious devotion.

Once we understand this cultural and religious context, then we begin to see that God was not telling Abraham to sacrifice his son. Instead, God was about to teach Abraham that human sacrifice was not in God's will. God was leading Abraham into a new way of thinking about God. Abraham led his son up on a mountain to offer the sacrifice.

> *"And when they came to the place of which God had told him, Abraham built an altar there, and laid the wood in order, and bound Isaac his son, and laid him on the altar, upon the wood. Then Abraham put forth his hand, and took the knife to slay his son. But the angel of the Lord called to him from heaven, and said 'Abraham, Abraham!' And he said 'Here am I.' He said, 'Do not lay your hand on the lad or do anything to him; for now I know that you fear God, seeing you have not withheld your son, your only son from me.' And Abraham looked up, and behold, behind him was a ram, caught in the thicket by his horns; and Abraham went and took the ram, and offered it up instead of his son. So Abraham called the name of that place, 'The Lord will provide'."*   Genesis 22:9-14

This passage is very important because it is a further development in God forming the religious consciousness of the people of Israel. The two main points are these:

1) God abolishes human sacrifice.

2) This is one of the many ways that God calls his people to be different from their polytheistic neighbors.

The "non-sacrifice" of Isaac is a prefiguration of Jesus Christ. God does not require Abraham to sacrifice his only son to God, but God will offer up His only son as a perfect sacrifice for the whole world. God provides Abraham with the ram to sacrifice. God will later provide the "Lamb of God, who takes away the sin of the world" on the ultimate sacrifice of Calvary.

V. Jacob (Israel) – "One Who Wrestles With God"

Isaac grew up and married Rebecca. They had twin sons Jacob and Esau. Esau was honest, honorable and gullible. Jacob was a dishonest and dishonorable swindler. "Scoundrel" might be too strong a word for Jacob, but not far from the truth! Nevertheless, God passed on the promises of the Covenant with Abraham first to Isaac and then to his son Jacob. (Genesis 28:1-17)

In one appearance, God gives Jacob a new name: "Israel". This name means "one who wrestles with God". (Genesis 32:28 and 35:10)

The Patriarchs and Twelve Tribes

Abraham, Isaac and Jacob are often referred to as "The Patriarchs" of the people of Israel. Often throughout the rest of the Bible, God is identified as "The God of our fathers, the God of Abraham, Isaac and Jacob". Later on, the descendants of Abraham, Isaac and Jacob were referred to as "the children of Israel" or simply, "Israel".

Jacob had twelve sons. Each of these sons became the namesake of one of the twelve tribes of Israel. Their names are: Reuben, Simeon, Levi, Judah, Zebulon, Issachar, Dan, Asher, Naphtali, Gad, Benjamin and Joseph. (Genesis 49:1-27) These tribal designations were still in use two thousand years later. Jesus was a member of the tribe of Judah and Paul was a member of the tribe of Benjamin. (Matthew 1:1-17 and Philippians 3:5)

VI. Joseph

The following is brief synopsis of Genesis Chapters 37 though 50. These chapters are some of the most dramatic, suspenseful and readable chapters in the entire Bible. At least one Hollywood movie has recreated this drama – "but the book is better than the movie".

Joseph was Jacob's youngest and favorite son. Joseph's brothers were jealous of his favored status with their father. They plotted against him and sold him into slavery in Egypt. They lied to their father, telling him that Joseph had been killed by a wild animal. Joseph became a slave in an Egyptian household, but because he had a gift for interpreting dreams, he quickly rose in social status. He became a special advisor to the ruler (called Pharaoh) of Egypt. Joseph predicted seven good crop years and seven years of famine. He advised Pharaoh to store up food in the good years to prevent disaster in the bad years. Pharaoh was impressed with Joseph's wisdom and put him in charge of all food production and storage in Egypt. After seven years of good crops, the predicted seven-year famine struck the land. Because of the precautions suggested by Joseph, Egypt was able to survive the drought and was even able to sell extra food to foreigners.

Joseph's brothers came to Egypt to buy food because they too were stricken with drought in the land of Canaan. They did not know who Joseph was, but he recognized them. After several dramatic and suspenseful encounters with his long-lost brothers, Joseph finally told them who he was. They apologized for selling him into slavery. He forgave them, invited them all (including their aging father Jacob) to come live in Egypt, and they all lived happily ever after.

Abraham: "You Will be a Blessing to All Nations"

The descendants of Jacob (Israel) lived in Egypt for the next four hundred years. The Bible is silent on what happened during most of those years. However, it does tell us that the good relations that Joseph had with Pharaoh were forgotten in later generations. A new Pharaoh "who did not know Joseph" came to power and enslaved the people of Israel. This sets the stage for the most dramatic events in the history of Israel, which will be discussed in the next chapter.

QUESTIONS FOR DISCUSSION AND REFLECTION

1) God calls Abraham to leave his own city and culture behind and to enter a new relationship with the living God. This was in the days before telephones, television, air travel, mail or e-mail. To obey God probably meant that he would never again see any of his family and friends. Have you ever had to move to a new town? New school? New job? Meet new friends and make new contacts? Describe how it felt. Did it help you to trust God more –or less? To trust yourself more – or less? How do you think Abraham's trust of God and of himself changed as a result of "leaving everything" to follow God's call on his life?

2) Have you ever been "called" by God to do something? How would you know if it was God's call and not your own wishes? Do you think God often calls people to do things? Do you think that God's call is the same as, or radically different from, your own "game plan" for life?

3) God promised Abraham many descendants. But God took a long time to fulfill that promise. In the mean time Abraham got discouraged and had doubts about God's intentions toward him. Are there times in your own life when God seems to have forgotten you? Are there times when you even doubt God's existence? Are there times when you want to give up following God because it's too difficult? If so, how should we respond to doubt and despair? Should we: deny it and hope it goes away? give up? seek out a faithful believer for prayer and counsel? pray for greater faith? Do you think God gives up on us when we give up on God?

4) Jacob was not a great example of moral integrity. In fact, he was a very dishonest person. And yet God called him "Israel" – "one who wrestles with God". The name stuck and Jacob's descendants became known as "the people of Israel". Why do you think God chose Jacob as the namesake and role model for his people? Why name your favorite group of people after a crook? What does this teach us about God's character in this instance? What does it teach us about our own shortcomings and sins? Do they make it difficult for us to follow and serve God faithfully?

PRAYER EXERCISE

Read Psalm 139: 1-17 slowly and out loud. Then take several minutes to write down all of the times in your life that God has searched out and known you, has rescued you from doubt and despair, has lifted you up when you were down. Then read the Psalm again slowly, thanking God for those times.

BIBLE MEMORY VERSE:

"Now the Lord sad to Abram, 'Go from your country and your kindred and you father's house to the land that I will show you. And I will make you a great nation, and I will bless you, and make your name great, so that you will be a blessing. ...and by you all the families of the earth will bless themselves.' So Abram went as the Lord had told him."

Genesis 12:1-4

Chapter 5

EXODUS: "LET MY PEOPLE GO"

Main focus of this chapter: Has God forgotten his promise to Abraham? Have the people of Israel forgotten their God?

I. Slavery in Egypt

As we read in the last chapter, Jacob inherited the promise originally given to Abraham - many descendants and a promised land. Jacob's youngest son Joseph was sold by his brothers into slavery in Egypt, but rose through the ranks of Egyptians society to be a close advisor to the Pharaoh. Because of a severe drought and a shortage of food in the land of Canaan, Joseph invited his father Jacob and his entire family to Egypt for food and a better life. They accepted the invitation, but in so doing, they abandoned the "promised land." But the promise of God is still valid. Thus ends the book of Genesis.

The book of Exodus begins 400 years later. The good relations which Joseph enjoyed with Pharaoh have long since been forgotten. The descendants of Joseph and his brothers have been made slaves by the rulers of Egypt. Furthermore, they have greatly increased in number, thus fulfilling God's promise of many descendants to Abraham. They have been so prolific that they are now perceived as a threat to the rulers of Egypt who fear a slave revolt.

> *"Behold, the people of Israel are too many and too mighty for us. Come, let us deal shrewdly with them, lest they multiply, and if war befall us, they join our enemies and fight against us and escape from the land. Therefore they set taskmasters over them to afflict them with heavy burdens, ...But the more they were oppressed the more they multiplied and the more they spread abroad. And the Egyptians were in dread of the people of Israel. So they made the people of Israel serve with rigor, and made their lives bitter with hard service, in mortar and brick, and in all kinds of work in the field; in all their work they made them serve with rigor."*
>
> Exodus 1:9-14

Later, Pharaoh went even further in his oppression of the people of Israel. He ordered that all male babies be killed by the midwives who delivered them at birth. When the midwives refused to kill the male babies at birth, Pharaoh ordered that all male children be thrown into the Nile (the main river in Egypt.)

II. The Early Life of Moses

Moses is the central character in the book of Exodus. Moses was born to an Israelite mother and was hidden in a waterproof basket in the river to protect him from being harmed by the Egyptians. Pharaoh's daughter came to the river to bathe. While there, she discovered Moses in the basket and recognized him as an Israelite child. For some reason, she decided not to have the child destroyed according to her father's edict. Instead, she decided to adopt the child as her own. She raised Moses in the royal household. There is no biblical record of Moses life in Pharaoh's house, but we may surmise that he enjoyed a very privileged life and that he was educated in the ways of Egyptian high society and power politics.

One day Moses observed an Egyptian slave master beating an Israelite slave. He had compassion on the slave and killed the abusive overseer. After this, Moses was forced to flee the country for fear of punishment from Pharaoh for killing an Egyptian. *"When Pharaoh heard of it, he sought to kill Moses. But Moses fled from Pharaoh to the land of Midian"* (Exodus 2:15)

III. God calls Moses

Moses made a new life for himself in Midian. He married a local woman (Zipporah) and began a family. He evidently had no intentions of returning to Egypt. He was not busy starting a chapter of the "Anti-slavery League" or the "Israeli-Liberation Organization." He was apparently quite content in his quiet life as a husband, father and shepherd. But God had other plans for Moses.

> "In the course of many days the king of Egypt died. And the people of Israel groaned under their bondage and cried out for help, and their cry under bondage came up to God. And God heard their groaning, and God remembered his covenant with Abraham, with Isaac and with Jacob. And God saw the people of Israel and knew their conditions.
>
> Exodus 2:23-25

Exodus: "Let My People Go"

One day, Moses was herding his father-in-law's sheep near a mountain. While there, he saw a strange sight.

> *"An angel of the Lord appeared to him in a flame of fire out of the midst of a bush; and he looked, and lo, the bush was burning but it was not consumed. And Moses said, 'I will turn aside and see this great sight, why the bush is not burnt.' When the Lord saw that he had turned aside to see God called to him out of the bush, 'Moses, Moses!' And he said, 'Here am I'. Then he said, 'Do not come near; put off your shoes from your feet, for the place on which you are standing is holy ground.' And he said, 'I am the God of your father, the God of Abraham, the God of Isaac, and the God of Jacob.' And Moses hid his face for he was afraid to look at God."*
>
> Exodus 3:2-6

After doing something dramatic to get Moses' attention, God identifies himself as the God of Abraham, Isaac and Jacob. This recalls the promises of God to those ancestors – descendants, land and God's protection. Then God tells Moses that he has not forgotten that promise and that Moses has a special role in the fulfillment of the promise.

> *"I have seen the affliction of my people who are in Egypt, and I have heard their cry because of their taskmasters; I know their sufferings, and I have come down to deliver them out of the hand of the Egyptians, and to bring them up out of that land to a good and broad land, a land flowing with milk and honey... Come, I will send you to Pharaoh that you may bring forth my people, the sons of Israel, out of Egypt."*
>
> Exodus 3:7-10

Moses is reluctant to accept the job and tries several times to make excuses why he couldn't do it, but God won't take "No" for an answer. Instead, God gives Moses several kinds of help to accomplish this mission.

First of all, God gives Moses God's name: *"God said to Moses, 'I AM WHO I AM'. And he said, 'Say this to the people of Israel, 'I AM' sent me to you.'"* (Exodus 3:14)

Remember, in ancient times, the name was a sign of power and intimacy. In a polytheistic world inhabited by every manner of spiritual power – both good and evil, to possess the name of God was to be on God's "good side", so to speak. This name is, in the original language of Hebrew spelled out like this: **YHWH**. In English, it has been variously translated as: "Jehovah", "Yahweh", or "The Lord."

Secondly, God gives Moses a staff with miraculous powers. Among other things, it is able to turn into a snake and back to wood again. Moses needs some audiovisual aids to get the attention of both the Israelite slaves and the Egyptian slave holders.

Finally, God gives Moses a spokesperson named Aaron. Moses did not have good public speaking ability; Aaron did.

IV. Moses Demands Freedom – Ten Plagues Are His Bargaining Chips

Moses' unusual early life was a preparation for what was about to happen. He was uniquely qualified for the job that God had given him. Moses knew his way around the Egyptian court. He knew how to speak the language of the upper classes. He went directly to the court of Pharaoh and demanded that Israel be allowed to go out in the wilderness to worship God. But Pharaoh refused and retaliated by ordering an increased work load for the slaves. Because he refused God set into motion a series of nine plagues which were commanded by Moses and put in motion by his miraculous staff.

The First Nine Plagues   (listed in Exodus chapters 7-10)
1. the Nile is changed to blood
2. frogs cover the whole land
3. gnats swarm over the whole land
4. flies swarm over the whole land
5. cattle get sick and die
6. skin boils cover people and livestock
7. hail storm kills trees and crops
8. locusts eat every plant in sight
9. darkness covers the whole land.

After each of these plagues, Pharaoh was given a chance to let the people go. Each time, he agreed to let them go and then changed his mind and refused. Each refusal was followed by a new plague.

To the modern reader, these plagues (and especially the last one) may seem a cruel punishment to visit on every family in Egypt for the hardheartedness of one man. It's important to keep in mind that this is an account of Gods judgment upon a nation's collective guilt. The nation of Egypt as a whole took the lives of all Israelite male babies. This is seen a just retribution.

Exodus: "Let My People Go"

The Tenth Plague – Death of All First Born Egyptians

Finally, God sent the tenth and most terrible plague. The first-born child in every household in Egypt died, including Pharaoh's own son. The Bible does not say exactly how they died, but gives the strong impression that it was some form of disease. However, God gave the people of Israel a way to escape this plague of death. We call that escape, and a series of related events, "Passover."

V. Passover

1) The Passover Meal

God gave Moses advanced warning of the last plague and told him how the people of Israel were to save themselves from this calamity.

> *"Tell all the congregation of Israel that on the tenth day of this month they shall take every man a lamb according to their father's houses, a lamb for the household; and if the household is too small for a lamb, then a man and his neighbor next to this house shall take according to the number of persons; according to what you can eat you shall make your count for the lamb... Then they shall take some of the blood (of the lamb) and put it on the two doorposts and the lintel of the house in which they eat them...The blood shall be a sign for you, upon the houses where you are; and when I see the blood, I will pass over you, and no plague shall fall upon you to destroy you when I smite the land of Egypt."*
>
> Exodus 12:3-13

In the last chapter, we mentioned the sacrifice offered by Abraham to seal the covenant. This Passover meal also has a sacrificial aspect. The lamb's life is sacrificed as a substitution for the lives of the people of Israel. The lamb died and its blood was used to ward off the plague of death that struck the land of Egypt. In this case, it is a sacrificial meal to initiate a new covenantal relationship with the people of God. God is about to liberate the people from slavery and lead them into freedom, and eventually, the promised land.

God also commanded the people of Israel to celebrate this sacrificial meal every year to remember what God had done for them. Thus the Passover meal anticipated something God is about to do and, in later generations, celebrates something God has already done. We will see this theme of substitutionary sacrifice and sacrificial meals many more times in the Bible. This is a key element in understanding both the Old and New Testaments.

2) Passing Through The Red Sea

After the last plague, Pharaoh finally agreed to let the people of Israel go free. But shortly after they left, he changed his mind again and sent his army after them. When the people of Israel came to a large body of water known as the Red Sea, they noticed that they were being pursued by Pharaoh's army. And they were sure they were about to be recaptured or killed.

> *"And all the people of Israel cried out to the Lord; and they said to Moses, 'Is it because there are no graves in Egypt that you have taken us away to die in the wilderness? What have you done to us bringing us out of Egypt?' ...And Moses said to the people, 'Fear not, stand firm, and see the salvation of the Lord, which he will work for you today; for the Egyptians whom you see today, you shall never see again. The Lord will fight for you, and you have only to be still.'"*
>
> Exodus 14:10-14

Then the Lord did something which will be forever etched into the memory of the people of Israel, and which will reverberate throughout the Old and New Testaments.

> *"The Lord said to Moses, 'Lift up your rod and stretch out your hand over the sea and divide it, that the people of Israel may go on dry ground through the sea.' ...And the Lord drove the sea back by a strong east wind all night and made the sea dry land, and the waters were divided. And the people of Israel went into the midst of the sea on dry ground, the waters being a wall to them on their right hand and their left."*
>
> Exodus 14:15-22

After the people of Israel were safely across, the Egyptian army attempted to pursue them with horses and chariots, which soon got stuck in the mud. Then the Lord instructed Moses to pray for one more miracle.

> *"So Moses stretched forth his hand over the sea, and the sea returned to its wonted flow when the morning appeared and the Egyptians fled into it, and the Lord routed the Egyptians in the midst of the sea. The waters returned and covered the chariots and the horsemen and all the host of Pharaoh that had followed them into the sea; not so much as one of them remained."*
>
> Exodus 14:27-28

Exodus: "Let My People Go"

The "Passover" as it is remembered in the Bible (and in later Jewish and Christian reflection) is the whole series of events that led to this moment of deliverance from slavery: the ten plagues, the Passover meal, the sacrificial lamb and the saving power of its blood, the escape through the Red Sea. In this series of events, God had acted, decisively, dramatically and repeatedly to deliver his "chosen people" out of slavery and into freedom, God's act of salvation in the Passover sets the stage for all that God does in the rest of the Bible.

VI. The Ten Commandments

1) Law Given on Mt. Sinai

After the miraculous escape at the Red Sea, God led Israel into the wilderness and eventually to the foot of Mt. Sinai. There he called Moses up on the mountain for instruction. We call these instructions "The Ten Commandments." They are listed in Exodus 20:1-17 and again in Deuteronomy 5:1-21. Here is a brief summary:

2) Our Duties to God

1) You shall worship only YHWH (The Lord) and have no other gods.

2) You shall not worship idols or have graven images of God.

3) You shall not take the name of the Lord in vain.

4) You shall keep the Sabbath day holy.

3) Our Duties to our Fellow Human Beings

5) You shall honor your father and mother.

6) You shall not kill.

7) You shall not commit adultery.

8) You shall not steal.

9) You shall not bear false witness against your neighbor.

10) You shall not covet your neighbor's wife or property.

These Ten Commandments form the foundation for the entire Old

Testament Law. The law is the code of legal, moral, ceremonial and sacrificial customs practiced by the people of Israel. The Ten Commandments also have continuing use and validity in the New Testament and for Christians.

3) God's Covenant with Moses

Recalling our previous discussion of Abraham, we said that a covenant is a solemn agreement between two parties. We might compare it to a marriage. Marriage is more than a legal contract. It's a solemn promise of life-long commitment between two people. The Ten Commandments (and the rest of the Old Testament Law) are the basis for the covenant between God and the people of Israel. This covenant between God and Moses is a clarification of God's covenant with Abraham. It still includes the promise of land, descendants, protection and blessing, but requires more of the human participants. Abraham had to follow and trust, but now God gives moral laws which more clearly define what it means to trust and follow God

Summary of Covenant with Moses

God (YHWH)	People of Israel
1) Deliver Israel from Slavery	1) Worship YHWH only
2) Give Law	2) Obey the Law, be holy people
3) Give Promised Land	3) Inhabit Land; keep it for God only
4) Protect Israel from enemies	4) Tell world God's saving deeds

Historians say that the Constitution of the United States is a defining document in the American government. We keep going back to it, arguing about it and reinterpreting it in each new generation. This Covenant with Moses is the same for Israel. As we shall see, this Covenant will be tested continuously throughout Israel's history.

VII. Forty Years in the Wilderness

God did not immediately bring the people of Israel into the Promised Land. Instead, he tested them for forty long years in the wilderness. Why did God do that? To teach the people of Israel to rely on God, and God alone, for their survival as a people. During their time in the wilderness, God provided food in the form of "Manna" – a bread-like substance that appeared miraculously for forty years and ceased when they entered the Promised Land.

At the end of their wilderness trek, Moses addressed the people of Israel with these words – a challenge which is repeatedly echoed by the prophets in later history:

Exodus: "Let My People Go"

> *"You shall remember all the way that the Lord your God has led you these forty years in the wilderness that he might humble you, testing you to know what was in your heart, whether you would keep his commandments or not. And he humbled you and let you hunger and fed you with manna, which you did not know nor did your fathers know; that He might make you know that man does not live by bread alone, but that man lives by ever word that proceeds from the mouth of the Lord... Take heed lest you forget the Lord your God by not keeping his commandments... and you forget the Lord your God who brought you out of Egypt, out of the house of bondage, who led you through this terrible wilderness... Beware lest you say in your heart 'My power and the might of my hand have gotten me this wealth.'"*
>
> Deuteronomy 8:2-17

VIII. Prefiguration

Now that we have discussed several important Old Testament events and people, it is time to mention an important aspect of Biblical interpretation: **"Prefiguration."**

Prefiguration is a literary device which is found in many kinds of literature – not just the Bible. The Bible often uses prefiguration to interpret God's will and to provide continuity to the ongoing story of God's dealings with the human race. It is a key element in explaining the relationship between the Old Testament and the New Testament and to understand the inner logic of the Bible.

1) Prefiguration means that:

a) Certain events contain within themselves the promise of future events;

b) Certain people whom God calls are examples and models of later people whom God will call and through whom God will work;

c) God's actions in one time contain the promise of future actions which will be even greater than the first.

2) The logic supporting the idea of Prefiguration.

a) God's will and purpose are always the same – Salvation.

b) God is working His purpose out in history. Time is moving from a beginning to an end. The "end" is the final consummation of God's perfect will – the "Kingdom of God."

c) Therefore, we may look back to God's previous dealings with the human race as an indication of God's future dealings with us. We may see in past events the promise (or warning) of future events in God's plan of salvation.

3) Some examples of Prefiguration from the Bible.

a) Adam is a prefiguration of Christ – the "second Adam" who reverses the damage done by the first. (Romans 5:6-17 and I Corinthians 15:20-28)

b) Abraham's faith is a prefiguration of Christian faith. (Romans 4:1-25 and Galatians 3:6-29)

c) The Passover lamb is a prefigurations of Jesus "our paschal lamb" who was sacrificed for us. (I Corinthians 5:7)

d) The people of Israel traveling in the wilderness toward the promised land are a prefiguration of the Christian people traveling through a world of temptation towards the promised land of heaven. (I Corinthians 10:1-13)

e) The sacrifices of the Old Testament are a prefiguration of the sacrifice of Christ. (Hebrews 9:1-24)

These are few (out of many) examples of prefiguration in the Bible. We will see many more instances when we read the New Testament. Jesus is the "Promised One" in all the major events of Scripture. The salvation that God began with Abraham, Isaac, Jacob, Joseph, Moses and the people of Israel was completed in Jesus Christ.

EXODUS: "LET MY PEOPLE GO"

QUESTIONS FOR DISCUSSION AND REFLECTION

1) In this chapter, we have discussed how God acted to free the Israelites from slavery. We have also discussed the concept of "prefiguration", which is based on the conviction that God's will remains consistent throughout history. God called Moses to tell Pharaoh (the mightiest King in the world at that time) to "Let my people go !"

What do you think God thinks about the following situations in the world today? Does God care about these people? Does God approve of the conditions under which many people are forced to live? Does God want us to do something to change these situations? Does God still call people to do what Moses did?

– Persecution against Christians in Sudan (north east Africa) including mass murder, forced starvation, slavery and forced marriages.

– Extreme poverty and hunger for millions of people in the underdeveloped (sometimes called "third world') nations.

– Illegal immigrants from China and South America being smuggled into the United States and forced to work without pay for years to "pay back" those who smuggled them in.

– Children working long hours in "sweat shop" factories in poor countries to produce inexpensive designer clothing and sneakers for sale in rich countries.

Does it seem 1) probable, 2) possible, 3) highly improbable, or 4) absolutely impossible that you personally could do anything meaningful to change the injustices mentioned above?

If you believed that God might be calling you, like God called Moses, to do something to change these terrible realities, what would it be? Would you be reluctant to do something? Would you feel overwhelmed as Moses did? Would you be reluctant to trust God as Moses was? How would you overcome your fears and lack of trust?

2) Read Exodus chapter 16. Why were the people of Israel complaining? Why did they forget the benefits of being freed from slavery so quickly? How did God respond to their complaints? Why do you think God made them wander around for forty years before going into the promised land?

Do you see any parallels between their behavior and your own life? Are there times when we trust God because there are no other options except to do so? Times when we forget all that God has done for us and complain? Times when God tests us and teaches us to trust him more? Times when we are ready to give up on God altogether? Times when life is going so well that we forget about God or act as if God doesn't matter to us?

PRAYER EXERCISE

Read Palm 136 slowly and out loud. Reflect on the way the people of Israel must have felt when they were liberated from slavery and when they entered the promise land. Now read the Psalm again. This time, think about the times in your own life hen God has done "great wonders" for you, when God has had mercy on you, when God has remembered you in your low estate. Now read the Psalm again, this time use it as a prayer of thanksgiving to God for all the help and mercy and underserved good gifts you have been given in your life.

BIBLE MEMORY VERSE

"I have seen the affliction of my people who are in Egypt, and I have heard their cry because of their taskmasters; I know their sufferings, and I have come down to deliver them out of the hand of the Egyptians, and to bring them up out of that land to a good and broad land, a land flowing with milk and honey... Come, I will send you to Pharaoh that you may bring forth my people, the sons of Israel, out of Egypt."

CHAPTER 6

PROMISED LAND
JUDGES, KINGS, PRIESTS AND PROPHETS

Main focus of this chapter: How will the liberated slaves use their new freedom in the promised land?

In this chapter, we will cover the six hundred years (from 1,200 B.C. to 600 B.C.) during which the people of Israel lived in the Promised Land after Moses led them out of slavery in Egypt. The period we are summarizing here is recorded in the following historical books of the Bible: **Joshua, Judges, Ruth, 1 and 2 Samuel, 1 and 2 Kings, 1 and 2 Chronicles.** It is also the period of time during which many of the "major prophets"

(**Amos, Micah, Jeremiah and Isaiah**) lived and whose words are recorded in the books bearing their names. It is also the time in which many of the **Psalms** and **"Wisdom" literature** (to be discussed in chapter 7) were written. In this chapter, we will summarize this historical period and discuss several influential groups within the people of Israel: Kings, Priests and Prophets.

I. Summary of History (1,200 B.C. to 600 B.C.)

1) Joshua leads the Conquest of Promised Land (1,200 B.C.)

Moses led the people of Israel for forty years in the wilderness, but was not allowed to enter the Promised Land. Just before he died, he appointed one of his assistants, Joshua (whose name means "Yahweh will save") to be the new leader of the people of Israel. Joshua led the people in battle to seize control of the land of Canaan from the previous inhabitants (who were called "Canaanites"). He conquered many cities and gained control of much of the land – but not all of it. The book of Joshua tells us: *"Joshua took the whole land, according to all that the Lord had spoken to Moses; and Joshua gave it for an inheritance to Israel according to their tribal allotments. And the land was at rest from war."* (Joshua 11: 23) But just a few chapters later, we are told that *"the Jebusites, the inhabitants of Jerusalem, the people of Judah did not drive out; so the Jebusites dwell with the people of Judah at Jerusalem to this very day.*" (Joshua 15:63) Furthermore, a reading of the other historical books and the prophets reveals many examples of many unhappy, and sometimes disastrous, interactions between the people of Israel and other inhabitants of "the promised land." This does not mean that the Bible is untrue in saying that "Joshua took the whole land." It means that the people of Israel succeeded in being the dominant governing force, but that many other groups lived under the umbrella of Israel's governance. This is a pattern which continues to this day in the modern State of Israel and in many other countries in the world in which social differentiation is determined by tribal identity. In these countries, a central government holds power and is usually dominated by one tribal group. The other tribal groups (more or less) acknowledged the authority of the government, but tensions between rival tribal groups are perennial. This seems to be the state of affairs in Israel during the historical period we are considering here.

2) Ongoing Conflict between the People of Israel and the Canaanites

The people of Israel continued to live "side by side" with their Canaanite neighbors for several centuries. (We use the term "Canaanites" as a generic term to cover many indigenous tribal groups.) The Canaanites were polytheists who worshipped many different gods. "Baal" was "the storm god" and the fertility goddess "Asherah" was his lover. People whose survival depended on successful agriculture thought it prudent to keep "the storm god" and his girlfriend "the fertility goddess" happy. Worship of Baal and Asherah involved drunken revelry, sexual promiscuity and cult prostitution. The general idea behind cult prostitution is that the "worshipers" participate in, and presumably benefit from, the sexual and procreative powers of the fertility deity. Based on what we know of male behavior in other contexts, we may surmise that many participants in cult prostitution were not entirely interested in the theological fine points of the practice.

"Molech" was another important god whose worship required the sacrifice of little children who were thrown alive into a fiery offering to the god. These gods were worshiped in "high places" i.e. hilltop shrines.

For obvious reasons, worship of these gods and worship of Israel's God were incompatible. This reality of the people of Israel living as close neighbors to the Canaanites provides the context for a thousand year battle for the soul of Israel. The people of Israel were constantly tempted to fall back into polytheism. When the men of Israel took Canaanite wives, the temptations became more severe. The Canaanite wives brought their "household gods" into the home and children were raised to worship many different gods. Throughout the Old Testament, we find evidence of people of Israel worshiping Yahweh on the Sabbath and then slipping off to a sexual orgy in the "high places" on another day; proclaiming trust in the One God for all good gifts but sacrificing to the fertility god to insure a good crop yield; trusting the One God in times of war but also sacrificing children to Molech for protection against a powerful enemy. This situation sets the stage for much of the conflict between prophets, priests and kings throughout the entire Old Testament history. The prophets continually insist that the people of Israel forsake the other gods and worship Yahweh, the Creator God who had brought them out of slavery into the Promised Land.

The book of Judges summarizes this struggle:

> *"And all that generation (of Moses and Joshua) also were gathered to their fathers (died); and there arose another generation after them who did not know the Lord or the work which he had done for Israel. And the people of Israel did what was evil in the sight of the Lord and served the Baals; and they forsook the Lord, the God of their fathers, who had brought them out of the land of Egypt."*
>
> Judges 2:10-11

For specific examples of this ongoing battle for the soul of Israel, see Leviticus 18:21 and 20:2-5; 2 Kings 23:10 and Jeremiah 32:35 (for Molech); 1 Kings 15:13, 2 Kings 21:7 and 23:4 (for Asherah) and 1 Kings 18:17-40 (for the epic battle between the prophet of Yahweh and the priests of Baal).

3) The Judges:
Macho Men and Wild Women (1,200 B.C. to 1,000 B.C.)

After Joshua died, there was no clear leader for all of the people of Israel. Instead, each tribe settled into its own allotted territory and ruled itself. However, in times of military crisis, the tribes needed to band together to fight a common enemy or invader. During these times of crisis, individuals would lead tribes in battle. These leaders were known as "Judges." When we hear the English word "judge", we think of a thoughtful, wise, middle-aged person wearing a black robe, sitting behind a mahogany desk, carefully evaluating complicated legal arguments, issuing judgments and writing opinions that most of us can't understand. This modern English meaning of "judge" is the polar opposite of the lead characters in the book of "Judges." These men and women are violent, hands-on and no-nonsense warriors who fight in the name of the Lord and for the sake of Israel. The Bible portrays them as "savior" figures raised up by God to restore the people of Israel to their rightful place. *"Whenever the Lord raised up judges for them, the Lord was with the judge and he saved them from the hand of their enemies all the days of the judge."* (Judges 2: 18) In addition to the "warrior judges", there were also those we might call "prophet-judges" and "priest-judges" who took leadership roles in times of crisis. There are 14 "judges" listed in the Bible: Othniel, Ehud, Shamgar, Deborah, Gideon, Tola, Jair, Jephthah, Ibzan, Elon, Abdon, Samson, Eli and Samuel. There are probably many more whose names are not recorded.

4) The Limits of the Judges and Tribal Confederacy System

The fairly loose tribal confederacy and the leadership of occasional judges worked for about 200 years, but there were serious drawbacks to this system of governance. In times of war, it was often difficult to get all of the tribes together to fight for common defense. And because defense was essential for national survival, many felt that a stronger central government was needed. Early attempts to establish a king were resisted. Many people believed that God would protect the tribes of Israel through "judges." To establish a king (and a central government) was a sign of not trusting God. One example of these conflicting opinions is found in Judges 8:22-23: *"The men of Israel said to Gideon, 'Rule over us, you and your son and grandson also; for you have delivered us from the hand of Midian'. Gideon said to them, 'I will not rule over you, and my son will not rule over you; the Lord will rule over you'."*

Eventually, however, the pressure for a stronger system of government and self-defense was overwhelming. This pressure came from a new tribal group, the Philistines. The Philistines lived on the coastal plain near Egypt (what is today called "the Gaza strip"). They were a highly organized military force which posed a new and deadly threat to Israel's survival. This leads us to the next phase of our history, the era of Kings.

5) The "Golden Age" of Israel's Kings (1,000 B.C. to 922 B.C.)

Saul was a successful warrior who was deemed worthy to be the first king and was anointed by the prophet Samuel as God's designated leader. Saul was a popular and successful king at first but he was emotionally unstable. He became jealous because of the growing popularity of David, a young shepherd who distinguished himself in battle by killing a giant, and well armed, Philistine warrior named Goliath with a simple slingshot. Saul began a feud with David that escalated into an armed conflict. At the same time, war raged on with another neighboring tribe, the Amelikites. Finally, in a battle with the Amelikites, Saul took his own life rather than be captured by the enemy. After a struggle between rival factions, David succeeded Saul as king.

David was the greatest of all of the kings of Israel. Under his reign, the conquest of the promised land (begun so long ago by Joshua) was completed.

David unified the country as never before. His chief accomplishment was to conquer and centralize authority in Jerusalem. (Up until David's time, Jerusalem was a Jebusite city. After David's conquest, Jebusites and Israelites lived together in peace even though the Israelis were in charge.) David's reign was one of relative peace, national unity and economic prosperity. In later centuries, when Israel fell on hard times, the people would look for a new king like David. This ideal king would often be referred to as the "anointed one" or "messiah" and was expected to bring another age of peace and prosperity as in David's "golden age."

Solomon succeeded his father David and continued many of his policies and to centralize political and religious authority in Jerusalem. Solomon's chief accomplishment was to build the Temple in Jerusalem. This Temple became central to Israel's political, religious and symbolic life in a way that can hardly be exaggerated. The site of the Temple continues to the present day to anchor Israel's identity even though the last Jewish Temple on that site was demolished nearly two-thousand years ago. However good Solomon's contribution may have been, he did not remain faithful to the God of Israel. He married many foreign women and they turned his heart to worship other gods. Thus, the supposed spiritual leader of Israel was openly breaking the first commandment of the Covenant. Solomon also levied heavy taxes and used forced labor of his own people to build the Temple and other public works projects. (This forced labor policy was considered entirely normal and appropriate for kings in the ancient world, but was frowned upon by a people whose central conviction about God was that he had freed them from slavery. Forced labor has probably never been popular with those forced to labor, but it must have seemed especially outrageous for laborers forced to construct a Temple to the Slave Liberating God.)

The judgment of God on Solomon's unfaithfulness is summarized in 1 Kings 11:9,11,12: *"And the Lord was angry with Solomon...and said 'Since this has been your mind and you have not kept my covenant and my statutes which I have commanded you I will surely tear the kingdom from you and will give it to your servant. Yet for the sake of David your father, I will not do it in your days, but I will tear it out of the hand of your son."* This prophecy sets the stage for the tragic events that unfolded immediately after Solomon's death.

6) The Kingdom Divides (922 B.C.)

Solomon's son succeeded him and intensified his father's policies of forced labor and heavy taxes. This brought massive resistance and discontentment. The ten northern tribes, under the leadership of Jereboam, staged a rebellion. As a result, the kingdom split in two: the northern kingdom was now called

"Israel" and the southern kingdom was now called "Judah." David's work of national unification was undone. Never again would the people of Israel enjoy the peace, prosperity and self-governance that they had under David. From a purely historical point of view, this was largely due to external factors arising from power struggles between Egypt, Assyria and Babylon. But the prophets continually tell us that the real reason was spiritual: the kings of Israel failed to uphold the Covenant. All other kings in the books of 1 and 2 Kings are evaluated on the basis of whether he obeyed the Lord "as David his father did" or that "his heart was not true to the Lord as was the heart of David, his father." Almost all of the kings that followed Solomon received a negative assessment and are seen as the cause for the calamities that followed.

7) The Northern Kingdom (Israel) Is Destroyed (722 B.C.)

In 722 B.C. the northern kingdom was attacked by King Sargon II of the Assyrian Empire (modern day northern Iran). Most of the leading citizens were killed or led away into exile and slavery, never to be heard from again. The Jews who were left behind intermarried with the Assyrian occupation forces. They came to be known as "Samaritans" and were despised as "false Jews" by those who did not intermarry. In the New Testament, we find many references to this ongoing animosity between Samaritans and Jews. The Samaritans continue to the present day as a distinct ethnic group in the modern State of Israel.

8) The Southern Kingdom (Judah) Is Destroyed (597 B.C.)

King Nebuchadnezzer of the Chaldeans (whose capital was in Babylon in modern day central Iraq) was the strongest military force in the Middle East at this time. Three successive kings of Judah (Jehoahaz, Jehoiakim and Jehoiachin) tried to form a rival alliance with Egypt as protection against Nebuchadnezzer, but their efforts failed. In two separate invasions, the entire city of Jerusalem (including the Temple) was destroyed; the king and all of the important citizens (elites, scholars, merchants and tradesmen) were carried off into exile in Babylon. This was a stunning blow to God's "chosen people." The Covenant that God had established with Abraham and further developed with Moses seemed to be completely null and void: the chosen people were scattered, the land was lost, the Temple destroyed, God's protection seemed to be absent. This caused many people to ask: "Why had God allowed this to happen?" The prophets had a ready answer: The people of Israel had not been faithful to the Covenant. God was allowing the people to suffer the consequences of their unfaithfulness. But, as we shall see in chapter 8, God did not forget his chosen people..

Now, having surveyed briefly the history, we will take a closer look at some of the leaders of the people of Israel during this period: Kings, Priests and Prophets. These are important and influential figures. Having a clear understanding of their respective roles is essential to understanding the main themes of the Old and New Testaments.

II. Kings

In the United States of America, we have a constitutional doctrine of "separation of Church and State." The exact meaning of this doctrine is widely and endlessly debated. But whatever it may mean in theory, in practice every President ends every important speech with the words "may God bless you all and may God bless America." In times of war and other national crises, every President prays for the nation in a very public way and encourages the nation to pray. And no one ever complains about this seeming contradiction between theory and practice. Why? Because at a very basic level, human beings need to know that there is a connection between their human leaders and the unseen power of God. This need is especially acute in times of national crisis. This is one expression of the "image and likeness of God" planted in every human heart. We want to connect with God when we feel vulnerable and we want our leaders to do so as well.

This basic human tendency was very much at work in ancient Israel. The king was not just a political leader, he was "the Lord's anointed" leader of the nation. He was supposed to be a reflection of the real King of Israel, the Lord. Several of the Psalms reflect this exalted status of Israel's kings: *"You are the fairest of the sons of men; grace is poured upon your lips; and therefore God has blessed you forever; Gird up your sword upon your thigh, O mighty one, in your glory and in your majesty... Your divine throne endures forever...therefore God, your God has anointed you with the oil of gladness above your fellows."* Psalm 45:2-7

1) Israel's Kings are Accountable to God

Even though the king is held is very high esteem as God's "anointed", he is not free to do whatever he pleases. He is accountable to God for his conduct in office. And even though David is consistently venerated as the model of the ideal king, the Bible is clear that he is not without sin and that God will punish him for his misdeeds. The prophets are God's agents for keeping the kings accountable. This is demonstrated in 2 Samuel chapters 11 and 12. David, who already has several wives at his disposal, commits adultery with Bathsheba. She is the wife of Uriah, one of David's soldiers. She becomes pregnant by David. David arranges to have her husband killed in battle to cover up the scandal (2 Samuel 11:27). *"But the thing that David* had done displeased the Lord" and the prophet Nathan is sent to call the King to account and to proclaim God's coming punishment for David's sin (2 Samuel 12: 1-14). This episode demonstrates a very important aspect of Israel's self-understanding. The King is a caretaker of Israel on God's behalf. In many biblical texts, both God and the king are referred to as a "shepherd" of Israel. If the shepherd is leading the people in the wrong direction, God sends prophets to turn the king back in the right direction. This is in sharp contrast with other kings in this time period who usually killed prophets who displeased them. This is another one of the enduring truths which continues to the present day in the Western societies and legal systems which have been shaped by the Bible. Human rulers are not absolute despots - they are accountable to the moral law of God.

2) The Promise of a Future Messiah-King

The exalted language about the King reflects the expectation that God will be working through the "anointed one" to bring about God's purpose for the nation. Furthermore, God has plans for a future "anointed one" who is from David's lineage and who will complete God's purpose for the people of Israel. During David's reign, the prophet Nathan gives voice to God's intention for David and his "house" (his descendants):

> *"When your days are fulfilled and you lie down with your fathers, I will raise up your offspring after you, who shall come forth from your body, and I will establish his kingdom. He shall build a house for my name, and I will establish the throne of his kingdom forever....I will not take my steadfast love from him."*
>
> 2 Samuel 7:12,13,15

The prophet Isaiah, speaking 500 years after David further develops these prophecies of the Messiah-King. He speaks of a universal king for all the "nations." This harkens back to God's promise to Abraham, that his descendants would be a "blessing to all nations of the earth."

> *"For to us a child is born, to us a son is given;*
> *and the government will be upon his shoulder,*
> *And his name shall be called Wonderful Counselor, Mighty God, Everlasting Father, Prince of Peace.*
> *Of the increase of his government and of peace there will be no end, upon the throne of David, and over his kingdom, to establish it and uphold it with justice and righteousness from this time forth and for ever more."*
>
> Isaiah 9:6-7

Promised Land

This promise of a future king from David's "house" became part of the Jewish expectation of God's promise his "chosen people." When the kingdom was destroyed by the Babylonians, this unrealized expectation added to their disillusionment. However, in the depths of Israel's national despair, Isaiah promises a future in which God will send his "messiah" or "anointed one" to restore the covenant and redeem Israel. In the following passage, Isaiah speaks of a " shoot from the stump of Jesse." (Jesse was David's father. The "stump" refers to the monarchy cut down to the ground by the Babylonians. The "shoot" refers to a new king arising from the apparently dead tree.) Isaiah promises a future time in which a messiah-king will preside over a peaceable kingdom in which all animosities and violence will cease.

> *"There shall come forth a shoot from the stump of Jesse,*
> *And a branch shall grow out of his roots,*
> *And the Spirit of the Lord shall rest upon him,*
> *the spirit of wisdom and understanding, the spirit of counsel and might,*
> *the spirit of the knowledge and fear of the Lord.*
> *And his delight will be in the fear of the Lord.*
> *He will not judge by what his eyes see, or decide by what his ears hear;*
> *but with righteousness shall he judge the poor,*
> *and decide with equity for the meek of the earth...*
> *The wolf shall lie down with the lamb, and the leopard shall lie down with the kid,*
> *and the calf and the lion and the fatling together, and a little child shall lead them.*
> *The cow and the bear shall feed; their young shall lie down together;*
> *the lion shall eat straw like an ox.*
> *The suckling child shall play over the hole of the asp,*
> *and the weaned child shall put his hand over the adder's den.*
> *They shall not hurt or destroy in all my holy mountain;*
> *for the earth shall be filled with the knowledge of the Lord as the waters cover the sea.*
> *In that day, the root of Jesse shall stand as an ensign to the peoples;*
> *him shall the nations seek, and his dwelling shall be glorious"*
>
> Isaiah 11:1-1

As we shall see in later chapters, the New Testament proclaims that these prophecies are fulfilled in the person of Jesus, the Messiah-King for all people in all times and beyond time.

III. Priests *(Please read Exodus chapters 28 and 29 before continuing.)*

The flamboyant dress code for priests in Exodus 28 and the ordination ritual of Exodus 29 were "over the top" by anyone's standard. The special clothing and ornate ritual were intended to convey a message: the priests were intermediaries between God and the people of Israel, and therefore very important. The God-given priestly duties are as follows.

1) Teaching the Law to the people (Deuteronomy 33:10). This was especially critical in a pre-literate society and in a context in which Israel had to constantly differentiate its beliefs from those of its neighbors, the Canaanite polytheists.

2) Proclaiming the oracles of God in times of battle or national crisis. This happened either through prayer or by casting lots, which were called the "Urim and Thummim." (See I Samuel 14:18-23 and 36-45)

3) Blessings and cursing people for obeying (or not) God's law. (See Numbers 5:12-28 for example).

4) Public health care – Priests were responsible for declaring someone "clean" or "unclean" with respect to various skin diseases (under the generic term "leprosy") which were a threat to public health. If the priest declared a person "unclean", the person was banished to live away from the general population in order to isolate a contagious disease. (See Leviticus 13 for several explicit directions.) Such persons were "outcasts" who had to rely on charity for food. We see this in practice in the New Testament when Jesus heals lepers and tells them to "go show yourself to the priest." (Matthew 8:1-4)

5) Offering Sacrifices – This was the most important and publicly visible duty of the priests. Here is a partial list of the different types of sacrifice.

The Kinds of Sacrifices

Burnt offerings (Leviticus 1)
Cereal offerings (Leviticus 2)
Peace offerings (Leviticus 3)
Sin offerings (Leviticus 4)
Guilt offerings (Leviticus 5)

6) The Meaning of Animal Sacrifices [2]

For many modern readers in the Western world, this is one of the most perplexing and even repugnant aspects of the Bible. Many modern readers cannot see why God would have commanded what seems to many of us to be a barbaric custom. Many cannot understand what possible relevance animal sacrifice could have to the human relationship with God. As we have seen previously, the Bible does not always have clear-cut answers to every question modern readers ask. Just as Genesis is not a biology textbook, so Leviticus is not a "comparative religions" textbook. The best we can do to understand the meaning of sacrifice in the Bible is to try to enter the world of the texts and understand the world-view of the people at that time. And in doing so, we need to know that every religion in the ancient world involved sacrifices of some kind. In the mind of our ancient ancestors, a religion without sacrifice was no religion at all. So, it may be that God worked within the prevailing world-view to "meet people where they are" as we say.

When we look at the whole story of the Bible, we can see these animal sacrifices as one step in a long process of God's self-revelation to the human race. This process reaches its conclusion in the New Testament conviction that God offers the ultimate sacrifice for the benefit of humanity in the person of Jesus Christ.

> **a) A gift to God** of something valuable to people. In an agricultural society, animals and crops were the measure of wealth. To offer the "first fruits" of a herd or a crop was a serious act of gratitude to the giver. (see Genesis 28:10-22)
>
> **b) A meal of communion with God and fellow believers.** In this case the animal sacrifice was the opportunity to share a celebratory meal with friends and family, and by extension with God who provided the food. In these cases, the people ate "before the Lord." The idea here is not very different from most people's working theology of American Thanksgiving. (See Deuteronomy 12:17-19)
>
> **c) Atonement for sin – personal sin** (Leviticus 5:5-10) *"When a man is guilty of any of these, he shall confess the sin he has committed, and he shall bring the guilt offering to the Lord for the sin he has committed."* Corporate sin (Leviticus 16:15-23) *"he shall make atonement for the holy place, because of the uncleanness of the people of*

---

[2] This is a summary of an extensive study by Gerhard Von Rad in *Old Testament Theology, Vol. I*, Harper and Rowe, New York 1962, pages 262-272

The Living Word of the Living God

Israel, and because of all of their transgressions and sins"

In both of these last cases, atonement for sin and personal sin, the idea seems to be that humans, both as individuals and as a society, sacrifice something valuable as a sign of sorrow for their sins and in the hope that God will accept the sign of sorrow and forgive. But the meaning goes further than this. It implies that God will somehow act through the sacrifice to bring forgiveness. In a special sacrifice on the annual "Day of Atonement":

> *"Aaron shall lay both his hands upon the head of the live goat, and confess over him all of the iniquities of the people of Israel, and all of their transgressions, all of their sins; and he shall put them upon the head of the goat, and send him away into the wilderness...The goat shall bear all their iniquities upon him in a solitary land."*
>
> Leviticus 16:21-22

A final passage to consider is the following. God is the speaker in this passage.

> *"For the life of the flesh is in the blood; and I have given it for you upon the altar to make atonement for your souls; for it is the blood that makes atonement by reason of the life."*
>
> Leviticus 17:11

The gift of life is given by God. Blood is the essential substance in the process of life and is the primary symbol of God's gift of life to us. In the atoning sacrifice, people acknowledge their sin and ask for God's forgiveness. Then, the animal blood is offered as a substitute for human blood. The blood is the sign of God giving new life through forgiveness and of God's willingness to channel the negative influences of sin into the animal and away from the humans.

To sum it up, the sacrifices were an outward sign of God's willingness to forgive and save. The priest's duty was to offer continuous sacrifices as a reminder to the people of their sins and of God's willingness to forgive.

As we shall see later in the New Testament book of "Hebrews", this priestly ministry was a preparation for Jesus, who is both the "*High Priest of the good things to come*" who offers himself "*taking not the blood of goats and bulls but his own blood, thus securing an eternal redemption*" for all humanity. (Hebrews 9: 11-12)

IV. Prophets [3]

1) Called By God and In Your Face

The prophets were holy men and women who had a special calling from God to challenge and exhort the people of Israel, beginning with the Kings and Priests. The English word "prophet" is a translation of the Hebrew word *"nabi"* which can be translated "one who is called" and /or "one who announces." Several of the prophets tell us their experience of being called by God. These are usually shocking, unexpected and frightening encounters with the living God. And when called in this way, the prophet can't help but tell others. The prophets were not calm and reasonable persuaders. They were loud, intentionally shocking and decidedly "in your face" most of the time. Their style of telling others often imitated the shocking nature of their own calling from God. The Prophet ("nabi" - "One who is called /one who announces") announces to his fellow humans in the same manner that God communicated to him.

The following is an account of Isaiah's calling from God.

> *"In the year that King Uzziah died, I saw the Lord sitting upon a throne, high and lifted up and his train filled the Temple. And above him stood the seraphim; each had six wings: with two he covered his face, and with two he covered his feet, and with two he flew. And one called to another and said: 'Holy. Holy. Holy. Is the Lord of Hosts; the whole earth is full of his glory'. And the foundations and the thresholds shook at the voice of him who called, and the house was filled with smoke. And I said: 'Woe is me for I am a man of unclean lips; for my eyes have seen the King, the Lord of Hosts!' Then flew one of the seraphim to me, having in his hand a burning coal which he had taken from the tongs of the altar. And he touched my mouth and said: 'Behold, this has touched your lips; your guilt has been taken away, and your sins forgiven'. And I heard the voice of the Lord saying, 'Whom shall I send and who will go for us?' Then I said 'Here am I send me'. And he said 'Go and say to this people.....'*

> Isaiah 6:1-9

---

[3] This section is a summary of an extensive study by Abraham Heschel, *The Prophets*, Harper and Rowe, New York,1969.

Notice that Isaiah's first reaction was like that of Moses at the burning bush. He felt utterly unworthy and unqualified for the mission to which God called him. But God, speaking through the angel, declared him forgiven and worthy. It was an offer that Isaiah could not refuse. (Other similar passages tell us of the calling of several other prophets: Jeremiah 1, Ezekiel 1-3 and Amos 7.)

2) Prophets Demand Accountability

The primary role of the prophet was to call the people of Israel to be accountable to the Covenant that God had established with them. The circumstances in which they preached changed dramatically, but the message was always the same. "If we are not keeping the Covenant, God won't either. Don't expect God's blessing and protection when you are flagrantly disobeying God's Law. God's judgment is coming and you aren't going to like it. Repent before it is too late !!!"

The prophets focused on three main areas of Covenant violation.

Personal morality. The prophet Nathan was one of David's greatest supporters. But when David committed the multiple sin of stealing another man's wife (Bathsheba) and arranging for the husband (Uriah) to die in battle, Nathan strongly rebukes the all-powerful and popular king:

> *"Why have you despised the word of the Lord, to do what is evil in his sight? You have smitten Uriah the Hittite with the sword and you have taken his wife…Now therefore, the sword shall never depart from your house because you have despised me, and taken the wife of Uriah the Hittite to be your wife.' Thus says the Lord, Behold I will raise up evil against you and your own house…' "*
>
> 2 Samuel 12:9-11

This is a rebuke against the king deemed to be the most faithful of all. The prophets had even stronger words for the kings deemed unfaithful. No one was above the law and kings were supposed to set the standard for everyone else. Therefore they came in for the strongest criticism.

Social Justice – Almost all of the prophets spoke out against unjust social conditions which resulted in mistreatment of those who were most vulnerable: orphans, widows and the poor. In the following passage, Amos is speaking against the rich landowners who cheat the poor out of a livable wage and use the extra money to build lavish houses for themselves.

> *"Therefore, because you trample upon the poor, and take from him exactions of wheat, you have built houses of hewn stone, but you shall not dwell in them; you have planted pleasant vineyards but you shall not drink their wine. For I know how many are your transgressions, and how great are your sins – you who afflict the righteous, who take a bribe and turn aside the needy in the gate. ...Seek good and not evil, that you may live; and so the Lord, the God of hosts, will be with you as you have said. Hate evil and love good, and establish justice in the gate; it may be that the Lord, the God of hosts, will be gracious to the remnant of Joseph."*
>
> Amos 5:10-15

The prophets also spoke out against religious leaders who put a strong emphasis on personal piety but turned a blind eye to the material poverty of their people.

> *"Fasting like yours this day will not make your voice heard on high...Is this not the fast I choose: to loose the bonds of wickedness, to undo the thongs of the yoke, to let the oppressed go free, and to break every yoke? Is it not to share your bread with the hungry, and bring the homeless poor into your house; when you see the naked to cover him and hide not yourself from your own flesh...Then you will call the Lord and he will answer; you shall cry and he will say 'Here I am'.*
>
> Isaiah 58:6,7 and 9

True Worship of the One God. As we have seen throughout this chapter, the constant challenge of Israel's spiritual leaders was to keep the people (beginning with the Kings and priests) faithful to the Covenant with the One God. There was the constant temptation to revert to the polytheistic practices of the Canaanites, which always involved idol worship, sexual immorality, cult prostitution and even child sacrifice. The longest, and certainly the most entertaining, confrontation in the Bible is the epic confrontation between Elijah and the 450 prophets of Baal at Mt. Carmel recorded in 1 Kings 18: 1-40. As this account makes clear, the confrontation was serious and the consequences deadly. In this particular instance Elijah prevails, the prophets of Baal are killed, but he still needs to flee for his life from a hostile king and queen. The prophet's vocation was a dangerous one and required immense courage and perseverance.

3) The Prophets Are Not Fortune Tellers

There is a common misconception about the biblical prophets. Many people assume that they are primarily "predictors of the future" in the "fortune teller" sense of the word. The prophets were primarily concerned with proclaiming the word of God to their own people in their own time. They told their own people very specifically where they had gone wrong, why God was punishing them and how they could be restored to a right relationship with God. Their main purpose was always to call, exhort, frighten, cajole, plead and even beg the people of Israel to return to their Covenant with God.

Having said that, we must go on to say that there was always a future aspect to everything the prophets said. But this is in a very different sense that the "fortune teller" image conveys. In chapter 5, we discussed "prefiguration." Many events and characters in the Bible "prefigure" other characters and events. They carry with them the promise of future events which are even greater and more significant. The foundation of these promises is the conviction that God's purposes remain the same even though history and people change. The main hope which runs throughout the Bible is that God will finish the work that God has begun. If God has begun to redeem humanity through his Covenant people, then God will complete the mission, no matter how bad things seem at the moment.

One helpful analogy in understanding this future aspect of the prophets' words is to reflect on the progress of modern medicine. In the 19th century, "germs" were discovered and medical practices (like washing hands before surgery) changed. This discovery led to greater awareness and greater discoveries that could not have been predicted at the time. In the early 20th century, penicillin and other "antibiotics" were developed to fight germs and various "vaccines" were discovered to help the immune system combat certain diseases. These discoveries gave reason to hope that even greater discoveries would lead us to more effective defenses against disease. In the late 20th century, great strides were made in understanding the human genome. This has led us to a much better understanding of genetically inherited diseases and how to protect against them. And this series of discoveries promises even greater cures in the near and distant future. Each new medical discovery carries with it the promise of more effective medicine in the future. In this way, the work 19th century scientists can be seen to have had a future aspect, the implications of which they themselves would not have understood at the time. We do not think of medical researchers as "fortune tellers" but their work always has a future aspect which is not fully understood until much later. It's the same with the words of the biblical prophets. Their words contain the promise of an even greater future because God is trustworthy and true.

Following this scientific and medical analogy, we can understand Jesus Christ to be the fulfillment of many words of the Hebrew prophets. These prophets probably did not have any consciousness of a distant future in which Jesus would be born of a virgin, would be a crucified Messiah, would be a King forever from the "house of David", would be "a great high priest" and "Passover lamb" and so on. The later biblical writers of the New Testament saw these aspects of Jesus ministry as the "fulfillment" of these earlier promises in the same sense that, for example, a 21st century cure for a disease is the "fulfillment" of a 19th century discovery.

The point here is that God's word is full of promise and potentiality for every generation. God's word moves in history and reaches ever greater fulfillment over time. According to the Bible, time is not just "one thing after another." History is moving to a Grand Conclusion: the fulfilled, completed and perfected Kingdom of God. Each generation is part of this great movement of history. The prophets proclaimed the word of God to their own generation, but the meaning of their words was not exhausted in their time. The New Testament generation discovered greater fulfillment. One example might be the words of Psalm 23: "The Lord is my Shepherd." In the Old Testament period, the people of Israel understood God to be the shepherd of their nation. In the New Testament period, this title was seen to be intensified and personalized in the person of Jesus. In every generation, believers are invited to seek and discover ever-deeper dimensions of meaning in the Living Word of the Living God. For this reason, the following words of Isaiah are as relevant today as they were when he spoke them.

> "Seek the Lord while he may be found; call upon him while he is near; ...
>
> *For my thoughts are not your thoughts, neither are my ways your ways says the Lord.*
>
> *For as the heavens are higher than the earth, so are my ways higher than your ways and my thoughts than your thoughts. For as the rain and snow come down from heaven, and return not again but water the earth, making it bring forth and sprout, giving seed to the sower and bread to the eater, so shall my word be that goes forth from my mouth,; it shall not return to me empty, but it shall accomplish that which I purpose, and prosper in that for which I sent it."*
>
> Isaiah 55:6-11

QUESTIONS FOR DISCUSSION

1) The people of Israel were given a "Promised Land" by God. And they had to struggle to maintain their spiritual identity among their Canaanite neighbors who worshiped many gods and who engaged in grossly immoral behavior. Some of the first European settlers in American (called the "pilgrims") also believed that God had sent them to a new "promised land." They also believed that they were called to be a holy people. Do you agree with this view of America. In what ways is our situation (faith in God, obstacles to faith, compromises of faith, challenges, temptations, neighbors, enemies, friends etc.) the same, and different, from theirs?

2) The Bible views the king as God's "anointed" and expects that God will work through him – and expects the king to be accountable to God. How does this translate into our democratic system of electing leaders in a society that has a constitutional "separation of church and state"? Should we view our political leaders as God's instruments? Should we hold them accountable (and if we should, then how) to God's revealed will on major moral issues?

3) In the Bible, we see a dramatic development in gender roles over time. Read Judges chapters 19 through 21. How would you describe gender roles as illustrated in this story? Now read Ephesians 5:21-33 in the New Testament. How would you describe the differences in gender roles in these two passages? How do you account for the difference between the two?

PERSONAL REFLECTION

The biblical prophets kept (or tried to keep) the people of Israel accountable to God and God's revealed will. The prophets got very specific about personal behavior, spiritual compromises, religious syncretism (blending polytheism with worship of One God) and social injustice.

What do you think the prophets would say about the following realities in our world today: 1) racial hatred, 2) widespread (in movies, internet and television) of gratuitous violence, objectification of women and promiscuous sex for entertainment sake, 3) environmental degradation to support a lavish lifestyle for the rich world 4) widespread starvation and poor health care in the poor world. Do you lend any support to these things by your active participation or silent acceptance? What does this have to do with your faith in, and relationship to, God? Is there anything you think should change as a result of these reflections?

BIBLE MEMORY VERSE

"Seek the Lord while he may be found; call upon him while he is near;...

For my thoughts are not your thoughts, neither are my ways your ways says the Lord.

For as the heavens are higher than the earth, so are my ways higher than your ways and my thoughts than your thoughts. For as rain and snow come down from heaven, and return not again buy water the earth, making it bring forth and sprout, giving seed to the sower and bread to the eater, so shall my word be that goes forth from my mouth; it shall not return to me empty, but it shall accomplish that which I purpose, and prosper in the thing for which I sent it."

Isaiah 55:6-11

Chapter 7

THE PSALMS AND "WISDOM" BOOKS: "SING TO THE LORD A NEW SONG"

Main focus of this chapter: How Israel preserved its faith, culture and folk wisdom in music and literature

In the last three chapters, we have been considering the historical narrative of the people of Israel, beginning with the call of Abraham. Now we are going to look at several books which were written in the same time period but are not concerned with "history" as such. Even though they sometimes make reference to the historical events we have been considering, they stand beside the historical texts. They have a different purpose, as we shall see.

I. The Psalms

"The Psalms" is a collection of songs which were originally sung in the worship of the Temple in Jerusalem and are intended to be sung in worship today. We might say that the book of Psalms is the "hymnal" of the Bible. The Psalms are also very helpful for personal prayer and meditation. They are also very helpful in fleshing out the meaning of other Bible passages and for a deeper understanding the teachings of Jesus in the New Testament. For these reasons, the Psalms have had a very wide influence on the public worship and theology of both the Jewish and Christian faith and on the personal prayer and devotion of ordinary believers. It is hard to overstate the importance of the Psalms.

The Psalms are often called "The Psalms of David" because he wrote many (but not all) of them. The Psalms are arranged in 5 "books" within the one book: Book 1 (Psalms 1 – 41; Book 2 (Psalms 42 –72); Book 3 (Psalm 73 – 89); Book 4 (Psalm 90 – 106) and Book 5 (Psalm 107 – 150). Some Bible scholars think that the editors arranged them in this way (the five books of David) to provide a parallel with the Torah (the five books of Moses).

Scholars have identified a long list of different types of Psalms, but for the purpose of this simple introduction, we will reduce the list to three: 1. Psalms of Prayer for the Nation and 2. Psalms of Personal Prayer. 3. Psalms of Praise to God.

Psalms and Wisdom Literature

1) Psalms of Prayer For The Nation

Scholars identify many different types of national psalms. For our purposes, the list may be reduced to two: "Help us" psalms and "Thanks for the help" psalms.

"Help us" psalms begin with a rehearsal of how God has helped Israel in times past and follow up with a plea for help now. A good example is Psalm 44.

> *"We have heard with our ears, O God, our forefathers have told us, the deeds you did in their days, in the days of old. How with your hand you drove the peoples out and planted our forefathers in the land; how you destroyed the nations and made you people flourish....*
>
> *Nevertheless you have rejected us and humbled us and do not go forth with our armies. You have made us fall back before our adversary and our enemies have plundered us....You have made us a laughing stock among the nations and a byword among the people. ... Rise up and help us, and save us, for the sake of your steadfast love.*

"Thanks for the help" psalms can be very specific, thanking God for a particular act of liberation. A good example of this type is Psalm 126 which gives thanks for the return from the Babylonian captivity (which we will discuss in chapter 8).

> *"When the Lord restored the fortunes of Zion, then were we like those who dream.*
>
> *Then was our mouth filled with laughter and our tongue with shouts of joy.*
>
> *Then they said among the nations, the Lord has done great things for them.*
>
> *The Lord has done great things for us and we are glad indeed."*

Other "thanks for the help" psalms have a more general focus on God's continual act of redemption throughout history. A good example is psalm 136. It recounts the act of creation, the Exodus liberation and the conquest of the promised land. Each verse ends with the refrain: *"His mercy endures forever."*

2) Psalms of Personal Prayer

The psalms are a great resource for personal prayer. Many of them can be easily committed to memory and can be a great source of strength in times of trial. They cover practically every human emotion and are therefore a great resource when we are experiencing these same emotions. Here is a list of some representative personal psalms.

Seeking Confession and Forgiveness

"Remember not the sins of my youth and my transgression; remember me for the sake of your love."   Ps. 25

"Create in me a clean heart, O God, and renew a right spirit in me.

Cast me not away from your presence, and take not your Holy Spirit from me"   Ps. 51

God's help in the face of fear and death

"Though I walk through the valley of the shadow of death, I shall fear no evil; for you are with e: you rod and your staff, they comfort me."   Ps. 23

God's protection from harm

"He who dwells in the shelter of the Most High, abides under the shadow of the Almighty. He shall say to the Lord, 'You are my refuge and my stronghold, my God in whom I put my trust'."
    Ps. 91

God's help in overcoming doubt

"How long O Lord? Will you forget me for ever? How long will you hide your face from me? How long shall I have perplexity in my mind and grief in my heart day after day?   Ps. 13

"Whom have I in heaven but you? And having you I desire nothing upon earth.

Though my flesh and my heart shall waste away,

God is the strength of my heart and my portion forever."
    Ps. 73

God's help in times of despair

"Why are you so full of heaviness O my soul?
And why are you so disquieted within me?
Put your trust in God; for I will yet give thanks to him who is the
help of my countenance and my God." Ps.42

Meditation on the intimate presence of God in my life

"Lord, you have searched me and known me; you know my sitting down and my rising up; you discern my thoughts from afar.... For you yourself created my inmost parts; you knit me together in my mother's womb." Ps.139

Thanksgiving for deliverance from death

"I will exalt you O God for you have lifted me up and have not let my enemies triumph over me. ...You brought me up, O Lord from the dead; You restored my life as I was going down to the grave." Ps. 30

Thanks giving for God's loving kindness

"For your loving kindness is greater than the heavens, and your faithfulness reaches to the clouds." Ps. 108

"I will give thanks to you O Lord with my whole heart." Ps.138

Peace in the presence of God

"Like a child upon its mother's breast; my soul is quieted within me." Ps. 131

3) Psalms of Praise to God

Many of the following psalms were (and continue to be) used in corporate worship, but they are also very appropriate for personal prayer.

Some psalms praise God's awesome power at work in Creation, such as Psalm 19.

"The heavens are telling the glory of God and the firmament shows his handiwork.

One day tells its tale to another, and one night imparts knowledge to another.

> *Although they have no words or language, and their voices are not heard,*
>
> *Their sound has gone out into all lands, and their message to the ends of the world.*

The longer psalm 104 sees the hand of God at work in every detail of the natural world.

> *"O Lord, how excellent is your greatness...You make the winds your messengers and flames of fire your servants....You send springs into the valleys; they flow between the mountains. All the beasts of the field drink from them, ... You water the mountains from your dwelling on high; the earth is fully satisfied by the fruit of your works. ...You send forth your Spirit and they are created and so you renew the face of the earth."*

Others focus on thanksgiving to God for all his gifts to us, such as 98.

> *"Sing to the Lord a new song, for he has done marvelous things....He remembers his mercy and faithfulness to the house of Israel, and all the ends of the earth have seen the victory of our God. Shout with joy to the Lord, all you lands; lift up your voice, rejoice and sing."*

Many psalms are uncomplicated, uninhibited and joyful expressions of praise to God. One might say the book ends with a "grand finale" of fireworks in psalms 145-150.

> *"I will exalt you, O God my King, and bless your name for ever and ever.*
> *Every day will I bless you, and praise your Name for ever and ever.*
> *Great is the Lord and greatly to be praised; there is no end to his greatness."*   (145)

> *"Hallelujah ! Praise the Lord O my soul ! I will praise the Lord as long as I live; I will sing praises to God while I have my being"...*
> *The Lord shall reign forever, your God, O Zion throughout all generations. Hallelujah !*   (146)

> *"Hallelujah! How good it is to sing praises to our God! How pleasant it is to honor him with praise !"*   (147)

Psalms and Wisdom Literature

"Hallelujah ! Praise the Lord in the heavens; praise him in the heights. Praise him, all you angels of his; praise him all his host. Praise him, sun and moon; praise him, all you shining stars."
(148)

"Hallelujah ! Sing to the Lord a new song;
sing his praise in the congregation of the faithful.
Let Israel rejoice in his maker;
and let the children of Zion be joyful in their King." (149)

"Hallelujah!
Praise God in his holy temple;
Praise him in the firmament of his power,
Praise him for his mighty acts;
Praise him for his excellent greatness.
Praise him with the blast of the ram's horn;
Praise him with lyre and harp.
Praise him with timbrel and dance;
Praise him with strings and pipe.
Praise him with resounding cymbals;
Praise him with loud clanging cymbals.
Let everything that has breath praise the Lord.
Hallelujah !"
(150)

One of the great Bible teachers of our day says this about the psalms:

"People look into mirrors to see how they look; they look into the Psalms to find out who they are. A mirror is an excellent way to learn about our appearance; the Psalms are the biblical way to discover ourselves. With a mirror we detect a new wrinkle here, an old wart there. We use a mirror to shave or to apply makeup to improve, if we can, the face we present to the world. With the psalms, we bring into our awareness an ancient sorrow, release a latent joy. We use the psalms to present ourselves to God as honestly and thoroughly as we are able. A mirror shows us the shape of nose and the curve of our chin...The Psalms show us the shape of our souls and the curve of our sin, realities deep within us, hidden and obscured, for which we need focus and names." [4]

---

4 *Psalms: Prayers of the Heart* Eugene H. Peterson, Intervarsity Press 1987 page 5

They can best be known and understood when they are prayed in the light of the circumstances of our own life experiences. The best way to do this is to make reading of the psalms part of one's daily prayer and Bible study time. In this way, one begins to discover the many ways that the psalms shine a mirror on our lives.

II. PROVERBS

"My mother always said…."

Fill in the blank. "My mother always said_____" Everyone has an answer to finish this sentence. Our answers may be different, but we all have at least one. Every child in every society learns little sayings from his or her parents which are easily memorized and which contain (at least a little bit of) wisdom about the conduct of our lives. *"The early bird catches the worm." "A penny saved is a penny earned." "An apple a day keeps the doctor away." "Early to bed, early to rise makes one healthy, wealthy and wise." "Don't count your chickens before they are hatched." "The squeaky wheel gets the grease." "God helps those who help themselves." "Don't put off until tomorrow what you can do today."* And so on.

A good deal of what is contained in the book of Proverbs falls into this category. There are at least 357 "one liners" in chapters 10 through 22 of this book. There are also several small essays on various subjects.

1) One Liners- a small sample:

"When words are many, transgression is not lacking, but he who restrains his lips is prudent."   10:19

"When pride comes, then comes disgrace; but with the humble is wisdom."   11:2

"Men of perverse mind are an abomination to the Lord, but those of a blameless way are his delight."   11:20

"Like a gold ring in a swine's snout is a beautiful woman without discretion."   11:21

"Wealth hastily gotten will dwindle, but he who gathers little by little will increase it."   13:11

"Hope deferred makes the heart sick, but a desire fulfilled is a tree of life."   13:12

> "Better is a little with the fear of the Lord than great treasure and trouble with it."   15:16

> "Better is a dinner of herbs with love in it than a fatted ox and hatred with it."   15:17

> "Good sense makes a man slow to anger, and it is his glory to overlook an offense."   19:12

2) Short Essays – A small sample:

On the pitfalls of too much wine (4:29-35) *"Who has woe? Who has sorrow? Who has strife? Who has complaining? Who has wounds without cause? Who has redness of eyes? Those who tarry long over wine...."*

On successful animal husbandry (27:23-27) *"Know well the condition of your flocks, and give attention to your herds..."*

On the importance of finding a good wife (31:10-31) *"A good wife, who can find? She is far more precious than jewels. The heart of her husband trusts her, and he will have no lack of gain...."*

On the importance of a husband being faithful to a good wife (5: 1-23) *"Drink water from your own cistern, flowing water from your own well...Let your fountain be blessed, and rejoice in the wife of your youth...Let her affection fill you at all times with delight...Why should you be infatuated with a loose woman and embrace the bosom of an adventuress?"*

On the benefits of hard work and the penalties of laziness (6: 6-11)
"Go to the ant O sluggard; consider her ways and be wise..."

The book is introduced as "The Proverbs of Solomon" but this should not be taken literally. A helpful analogy might be "the Temple of Solomon." King Solomon gave the order to have it built, but the stones were quarried and assembled by countless thousands of anonymous workers. Likewise, Solomon may have given the order for the proverbs to be collected in one book, but there are many authors, some named in the book and some not. Later, in chapter 1:20-33, we have the first of several songs in which "Wisdom" is personified as a woman inviting the simple to listen and learn:

> *"Wisdom cries aloud in the street; in the market she raises her voice;*

On top of the walls she cries out; at the entrance of the city gates she speaks:
'How long O simple ones will you love being simple?
How long will scoffers delight in their scoffing and fools hate knowledge?
Give heed to my reproof; behold I pour out my thoughts to you....
He who listens to me will dwell secure and will be at ease, without dread of evil."

Why is wisdom personified as a female figure in the male dominated culture in which the Bible was written? Probably because the mothers and grandmothers were the primary teachers of the folk wisdom contained in the proverbs.

The proverbs are not like the psalms in one respect. They are much more focused on "common sense" human wisdom and much less focused on God. God is the source of Wisdom we are told in another "Wisdom song" in 8:22-31, but this wisdom is mediated through human beings.

The proverbs are like the psalms in this respect: it is hard to categorize them. They cover a wide range of human problems and solutions. Like the psalms, we can only discover the truth they tell by reading them regularly and reflecting on how they apply to our lives and memorizing the ones that we find meaningful.

III. Job

"Why Does a Good God Allow Bad Stuff To Happen To Good People?"

About fifty years ago, a small boy was taught that God is All Knowing, All Powerful and All Loving. About the same time as he was learning about God, he was also gaining first-hand knowledge of a lush green plant called "Poison Ivy." In the middle of an agonizing bout of head-to-toe skin rash, the little boy had a question: "Why does this All Powerful, All Knowing, All Loving God allow Poison Ivy to exist? If God is All Knowing, then He knows how miserable I am. If God is All Loving, then doesn't want me to be miserable. If God is All Powerful, then he could banish Poison Ivy from the face of the earth. So, why God do you allow this to happen to me?"

The little boy grew up and is the author of this book. He has not yet found a conclusive answer to his question. When he went to seminary, he learned that an entire book of the Bible was devoted to this question and that it is probably one the oldest books in the Bible. In other words, people have been asking this question for a very long time. The book is named after its main character Job (rhymes with "globe").

Before a brief summary of the book, let's consider the context. If one believes in many gods, then "the problem of evil" is simple – blame it on one of the bad gods who are out to get you. But if you believe in the One God, then how do you explain evil? The conventional answer, found throughout much of the Old Testament, is this: If you are faithful to the covenant, God will give you wealth and happiness. If you are not faithful to the Covenant, God will punish you, either directly or indirectly. We see this in Moses' exhortation to the people of Israel found in Deuteronomy 8:11-20.

> *"Take heed lest you forget the Lord your God by not keeping his commandments and ordinances and statutes which I command you this day....You shall remember the Lord your God, for it is he who gives you power to get wealth; that he may confirm his covenant. ...And if you forget the Lord your God and go after other gods and serve them and worship them, I solemnly warn you that you shall perish...because you would not obey the voice of the Lord your God."*

Up to this point, we have straight -forward equation: "Honor God and God will help you – dishonor God and God will punish you." The Bible, from beginning to end, generally affirms this equation. However, the question then arises: What about a person who is righteous before God. If something bad happens, why did it happen? Whose fault is it?

And the conventional wisdom at the time was that God must be punishing the person for a secret sin – or the sin of his parents. We see this attitude behind the question posed to Jesus (in John 9:1) when he is about to heal a blind man. "Rabbi, who sinned, this man or his parents, that he was born blind?" This is the same question that is addressed in the book of Job. Job is a righteous man, but he has every imaginable calamity befall him. "Why did this happen? He must have secret sins because God is obviously punishing him."

1) Setting the stage: chapters 1 and 2

In this "opening act" of the Job drama, God and Satan are having a conversation. God is bragging about what a good man Job is. Satan argues that Job is good only because God has given him everything. Then, Satan challenges God: "Take all his toys away and then we'll see how good he is." So God allows Job to be tested by removing every material and personal comfort. In his extreme discomfort, Job curses the day he was born, but will not renounce his trust in God. This now sets the stage for a long argument between Job and three of his "friends" to determine why God has allowed this calamity to befall Job.

2) Job and God on Trial: Chapters 3 – 37

The next 34 chapters are a series of arguments and counter-arguments seeking to discover why Job is being punished. Job's friends say that there must be some secret sin. Job insists that he is blameless before God. Job's self-defense reaches its climax in chapter 31 in which he invokes 16 oaths attesting to his innocence.

3) God's Reply: Chapters 38 to 41

> *"Then the Lord answered Job out of the whirlwind: 'Who is this that darkens counsel by words without knowledge. Gird up your loins like a man, I will question you and you shall declare to me. Where were you when I laid the foundations of the earth? Tell me if you have understanding. Who determined its measurements – surely you know."*

The basic message of these four chapters is that God's perspective is much bigger than ours is. What looks like senseless tragedy to us somehow fits into the bigger picture that only God understands. The book of Job does not "solve" the problem of evil. It tells us that even though God loves us and has a good purpose for our lives if we are faithful to God, there are exceptions to this general theme that are impossible for us to understand.

In this sense, the book of Job can be seen as a complement for much of the Old Testament and a preparation for the New Testament. As we shall see in the next chapter, Israel had to go through a great calamity to rediscover the good purposes of God. In the New Testament, we shall see the full biblical answer to "the problem of evil" in the lives of innocent people. In the death and resurrection of Jesus we see God's good purpose being worked out through obedient and faithful suffering. In this sense, Job is a prefiguration of Jesus on the Cross: *"My God, my God, why have you abandoned me?"*

IV. Ecclesiastes

"Don't Expect Much Out of Life And You Won't Be Disappointed."

In every human society, it is generally young people who dream big dreams for the future, take risks and do irrational things like falling in love.

Psalms and Wisdom Literature

And generally it is the role of older people to remind young people of the practical limits of big dreams, the downside of taking risks and the pitfalls of doing irrational things like falling in love. (And fortunately, young people usually ignore the warnings and continue to dream dreams, take risks and fall in love.) It's not that older people want to spoil all of the fun. They just want to spare young people some of the pain and heartache that they have experienced themselves. This is the spirit in which Ecclesiastes in written. An old man, who calls himself "the preacher" is writing to tell younger people not to expect too much out of life.

> *"Vanity of vanities, all is vanity. What does man gain by all of the toil at which he toils under the sun? A generation goes, and a generation comes, but the earth remains forever.... All things are full of weariness; a man cannot utter it; the eye is not satisfied with seeing nor the ear with hearing. What has been is what will be, and what has been done is what will be done; and there is nothing new under the sun."*
>
> Eccles. 1:2-9

The main point of the book is that we shouldn't get our hopes too high about anything because all human striving is ultimately futile. It goes on to say that God has given us the capacity to relate to God, (what Genesis calls "the image and likeness of God") but even that is a delusion.

> *"he (God) has put eternity in man's mind, yet so that he cannot find out what God has done from the beginning to the end. ...I said in my heart with regard to the sons of men that God is testing them to show them that they are but beasts. For the fate of the sons of men and the fate of the beasts is the same; as one dies, so does the other. They all have one breath, and man has no advantage over the beasts; for all is vanity."*
>
> Eccles. 3:11-19

The best we can hope to do is enjoy ourselves with material pleasure:

> *"And I commend enjoyment, for man has no good thing under the sun but to eat and drink and enjoy himself, for this will go with him in his toil through the days of his life which God gives him under the sun."* (8:15)

There is no hope of life or meaning after death:

> *"For the living know that they will die, but the dead know nothing and they have no reward; but the memory of them is lost. Their love and their hate and their envy have already perished, and they have no more any share in all that is done under the sun."*
> (9:5-6)

The book goes on in this vein until the final chapter (which many Bible scholars think was written by a later editor to clean it up a bit).

> *"The end of the matter; all has been heard. Fear God, and keep his commandments; for this is the whole duty of man. For God will bring every deed into judgment with every secret thing, whether good or evil."*

Many people have asked why this book is included in the Bible, since it seems to be at odds with the main themes and narrative trajectory of both the Old and New Testament. My own view is that it offers a portrait of the hopelessness, futility and meaninglessness of life without Christ. In that sense it is a perfect mirror of our modern secular world which offers us many material pleasures but no hope and no meaning beyond what little bit we can invent for ourselves in the short span of our lives. Without Christ and without the hope of his eternal kingdom, life truly is "Vanity and a striving after wind."

QUESTIONS FOR DISCUSSION

1) Read Psalm 90 and Ecclesiastes chapter 1. What is the main message of these two passages? How are they different? How do these passages speak to our hopes, dreams and priorities in life? Do you find them depressing, encouraging, limiting, or hopeful?

2) Read Psalms 8, 16 and 27. How would you describe the portrait of the meaning and purpose of human life in these psalms? How would you compare the message of these three psalms to Psalm 90 and Ecclesiastes 1?

3) The book of Job addresses the "problem of evil": why does a good God allow bad things to happen to good people? Discuss times in your life when this has been an urgent question for you. Do you find the answer given in Job chapters 38 to 41 helpful in understanding this problem. Now read Romans 8:18-39. How are these two passages the same? How are they different?

4) Read Psalms 149 and 150. Describe times in your life when these psalms would be a good description of your experience of worship of God. Is this the only appropriate style of worship? What other psalms speak of other types of worship?

PERSONAL REFLECTIONS

Read Psalm 23 slowly and prayerfully, allowing time to picture each of the images in your mind. Now reflect on a time when you were (or are) afraid. Take some time to offer your fears to God and ask for strength and faith to believe and trust in God.

Read Psalm 137. How do you react to the last verse? Is it ever appropriate to share your anger, rage and hatred with God? Take some time to look into your own soul to discover anger, hurt, and hatred. Offer this part of your life to God, asking for healing and for the capacity to forgive others who have hurt you.

THE LIVING WORD OF THE LIVING GOD

BIBLE MEMORY VERSE

"Sing to the Lord a new song, for he has done marvelous things. His right hand and his holy arm have gotten him victory. ....He remembers his mercy and faithfulness to the house of Israel, and all the ends of the earth have seen the victory of our God. Shout with joy to the Lord, all you lands; lift up your voice, rejoice and sing. Make a joyful noise unto the Lord, all the earth' break forth into joyous song and sing praises."

Psalm 98:1-4

Chapter 8
EXILE AND THE GREAT HOMECOMING: "COMFORT, COMFORT, MY PEOPLE"

Main focus of this chapter: How God brings new life and hope out of total destruction and chaos

I. Exile

1) Historical Summary

In the chapter 6, we read that, in 722 B.C., the northern kingdom (Israel) was conquered by the Assyrian Empire, under the leadership of King Sargon II. Most of the Israeli people in the northern kingdom were either killed, hauled off into exile and never heard from again, or intermarried with the occupation army.

To understand these constant attacks, it is important to know that the land of the Jewish people was a "buffer zone" between Egypt and the other major "super-powers" of the day (Assyria, Babylon, Syria, and in later centuries Greece and Rome). For all of these nations, it was important to control Israel and Judah as an extra protection against invasion by other countries. Thus, the needs of world politics came in direct conflict with the promises of God to the people of Israel.

The southern kingdom (Judah) escaped the fate of the northern kingdom by becoming a vassal state of the Assyrians for the next 20 years. However, as time went on, the king of Judah attempted to form an alliance with Assyrian's rival, Egypt. This provoked the anger of Assyria's new king, Sennacherib. In 701 B.C., he successfully attacked Judah and laid siege to Jerusalem. However, shortly after the Assyrians laid siege to Jerusalem, their troops were struck down by "an angel of the Lord." The Bible gives the impression that this "angel" was a plague, for many Assyrian soldiers died mysteriously one night. As a result, the Assyrians abandoned the siege for fear of more deaths.

This was viewed (by the people of Israel) as divine protection of Jerusalem in honor of God's promise of an everlasting line of David's descendants as kings. It reinforced the popular idea that Jerusalem was indestructible because

God would protect it under every circumstance. But the prophets (Isaiah and Jeremiah) insisted that this was a false hope, that the people could not take God's protection for granted. Instead, these prophets said, there needed to be true repentance and reform. (To grasp the full weight and power of this idea and the public reaction against the prophets who challenged it, replace the word "Jerusalem" with "America" and imagine a similar conversation in the days after September 11, 2001.)

After this near disaster, Judah once again became a loyal vassal state of the Assyrian empire. This state of affairs continued for the next century. During that time, the Assyrian empire fell apart and a new power arose to take its place – the Babylonian Empire.

In 597 B.C. the Babylonians (whose king was Nebuchadnezzar) attacked Jerusalem and carried away many of its leading citizens into exile. Ten years later, in 587 B.C., they attacked again, this time effecting total destruction. They destroyed the Temple, all the major buildings and the walls around Jerusalem. They also destroyed most of the small cities in the "heartland" of Judah. All the leading citizens were taken into exile. The rest probably died of starvation and disease or escaped to other countries. This was a national disaster for the people of Israel. We call the period that followed this attack "The Babylonian Exile."

2) The Prophets Speak Out

The Babylonian Exile destroyed everything the people of Israel had received from God since the liberation from Egypt. The "Promised Land" was taken away, the Temple of the living God was defiled and destroyed, David's "everlasting" line of kings was ended. Every promise of God's protection of Israel was violated. And they asked themselves, "Where is our God in this mess? Why has God abandoned His 'chosen people'?"

The prophets had an answer: "God is here in this disaster – God is here to judge us for our unfaithfulness!!! We have abandoned the covenant and we are reaping the just reward for our sins."

God is sending the Babylonians (also called Chaldeans) as an instrument of God's judgment on Israel:

> *"For Lo, I am rousing the Chaldeans, that bitter and hasty nation, who march through the breadth of the earth, to seize habitations not their own. Dread and terrible are they; their justice and dignity proceed from themselves. Their horses are swifter than leopards, more fierce than the evening wolves; their horsemen press proudly on. Yea, their horsemen come from afar; they fly like an eagle swift to devour. They all come for violence;*

terror of them goes before them. They gather captives like sand. At kings they scoff, and of rulers they make sport. They laugh at every fortress, for they heap up earth to take it. Then they sweep like the wind and go on, guilty men whose own might is their god! ...O Lord, thou hast ordained them as a judgment; and thou O Rock hast established them as a chastisement."
Habakkuk 1:6-12

The people of Israel should not rely on false hopes of God's protection because they have utterly abandoned every aspect of the Covenant established with Abraham and Moses. Until they truly repent, God will allow them to suffer the consequences of their sins.

"Thus says the Lord of hosts, the God of Israel, Amend your ways and your doing, and I will let you dwell in this place. Do not trust in deceptive words: 'This is the temple of the Lord, the Temple of the Lord, the Temple of the Lord.'

For if you truly amend your ways, and your doings, if you truly execute justice with one another, if you do not oppress the alien, the fatherless and the widow, or shed innocent blood in this place, and if you do not go after other gods to your own hurt, then I will let you dwell in this place, in the land I gave to your fathers forever.

Behold, you trust in deceptive words to no avail. Will you steal, murder, commit adultery, swear falsely, burn incense to Baal, and go after other gods you have not known, and then come and stand before me in this house, which is called by my name, and say, 'We are delivered!' – only to go on doing these abominations? ...Therefore, I will do to the house which is called by my name, and in which you trust, and to the place which I gave you and to your fathers, as I did to Shiloh. I will cast you out of my sight."
Jeremiah 7:3-15

But even in the midst of judgment, God has not abandoned his people. Even in the midst of Israel's darkest hour, God offers the hope of salvation.

"Therefore I will judge you, O house of Israel, everyone according to his ways, says the Lord God. Repent and turn from all your transgressions. Lest iniquity be your ruin. Cast away from you all transgressions which you have committed against

me, and get yourselves a new heart and a new spirit! Why will you die, O house of Israel? For I have no pleasure in the death of anyone, says the Lord God; so turn and live."

Ezekiel 18:30-31

The Babylonian Exile was the greatest setback suffered by the people of Israel. It was a devastating blow to their national pride and to their (false) expectation that God would protect them no matter how unfaithful they were to God. But, despite this disaster, the time in Babylon proved to be a chance to "turn and live" – a chance to be reborn as the faith-filled "chosen" people of God.

3) Babylon – A Time of Renewal

There is very little recorded about the people of Israel during the Babylonian Exile. The Babylonian purpose of the exile was not slavery, but rather to neutralize any active resistance to Babylon's power in the "buffer zone" between Babylon and Egypt. For that reason, the people of Israel were allowed a certain amount of freedom in Babylon. They were free to engage in commerce and agriculture. And they were free to develop their own culture and community. The prophets understood this as a part of God's plan for rebuilding the people of Israel.

> *"Thus says the Lord of hosts, the God of Israel, to all the exiles whom I have sent into exile from Jerusalem to Babylon: Build houses and live in them; plant gardens and eat their produce. Take wives and have sons and daughters; take wives for your sons, and give your daughters in marriage, that they may bear sons and daughters; multiply there, and do not decrease. But seek the welfare of the city where I have sent you into exile, and pray to the Lord on its behalf, for in its welfare, you will find your welfare. ... For thus says the Lord: When seventy years are completed for you in Babylon, I will visit you. ...For I know my plans I have for you, says the Lord, plans for welfare and not for evil, to give you a future and a hope. ...I will restore your fortunes and gather you from all the nations and all the places where I have driven you, says the Lord, and I will bring you back to the place from which I sent you into exile."*

Jeremiah 29:4-14

In response to God's purpose, the people of Israel used the time in Babylon to rebuild their community and renew their faith in God. In this period, two important developments took place which would shape their future life.

First of all, the Law (first five books of the Bible) was written down and collated. Prior to this time, there were many oral traditions and several disparate written accounts. In later centuries, these writings were added to collections of historical books and prophets and were eventually collected into what we now call "The Old Testament."

Secondly, the "synagogue" movement began. The people of Israel could no longer worship God at the temple in Jerusalem, so they gathered together to study, interpret and live according to, the written word of God. (The word synagogue" means "to gather together"). Because they had an acute sense of what had been lost, there was greater devotion to rediscover the truth about God. There was much more emphasis than before on educating the people about the moral demands of the Law. It was time for Israel to rediscover and renew its Covenant relationship with God. The focus of religious devotion shifted from sacrifice to study of God's word, from priests to teachers, from Temple to synagogue. This had a profound impact on the shape of Israel's faith and worship. It was the beginning of the religious culture which we will see in the New Testament.

II. Return to the Promised Land

1) Historical Summary

The Babylonian empire (modern-day Iraq) was short-lived. Soon after the people of Israel were taken into exile, king Nebuchadnezzar died and the empire soon fell victim to the self-destructive forces of internal corruption and poor leadership. At the same time, the Persian Empire (modern-day Iran) was gaining in power and eventually took over the Babylonian empire. The Persian king (Cyrus) decided to allow the Israelis to return to their homeland in 538 B.C. But they didn't all return at once. First a small group returned and began the arduous work of rebuilding the city walls of Jerusalem. Then, in successive migrations, many of the Israelis returned home to reclaim the Promised Land. Eventually, the temple and the city of Jerusalem were rebuilt and once again became the center of Israel's worship of God.

2) The Prophets Speak Out

Once again, the prophets spoke of the purpose and will of God in this return. According to the prophets, the return was the work and plan of God. Just as the Babylonians had been God's instrument of judgment on Israel, so Cyrus was God's agent to redeem Israel. This return to the Promised Land as nothing less than a "new Exodus."

Suffering Redeemed

The broken people of God were now the rebuilt people of God. And God would honor and reward the suffering of the faithful remnant of his people. The prophet Isaiah is the author of four "servant songs" which refer to Israel as God's servant: (Isaiah 2:1-9; 49:1-7; 50:4-10 and 52:13-53:12) The last one is the most explicit and most eloquent in its portrayal of the redemptive value of Israel's suffering. It is called the "Suffering Servant Song."

> *"Surely be has borne our grief's and carried our sorrows; yet we esteemed him stricken, smitten by God and afflicted. But he was wounded for our transgressions, he was bruised for our iniquities; upon him was the chastisement that made us whole, and with his stripes we are healed. All we like sheep have gone astray; and the Lord has laid on him the iniquity of us all. ... yet it was the will of the Lord to bruise him; he has put him to grief; when he made himself an offering for sin, ...he shall see the fruit of the travail of his soul and be satisfied; by his knowledge shall the righteous one, my servant, make many to be accounted righteous; and he shall bear their iniquities. Therefore, I will divide him a portion with the great, and he shall divide his spoil with the strong; because he poured out his soul unto death, and was numbered among the transgressors; yet he bore the sin of many, and made intercession for the transgressors."*
>
> Isaiah 53:4-12

The idea behind this passage is one of **substitutionary sacrifice**. The reader should now recall all that we have been saying about "prefiguration" in the Bible. (Events and people contain within themselves the promise of future events and people to be used by God.) Now we can trace the evolution of this concept throughout the Bible.

Remember that Abraham was given a wild ram as a substitute for the life of his son Isaac; and that the Passover Lamb was seen as a substitutionary sacrifice – it's life was given in order that the life of the first born of Israel would be spared. Likewise, in the "scapegoat" on the day of Atonement and in animal sacrifices of the Temple, the animal's life was given as a sign that God forgave (and thus gave new life to) the people of Israel. Now in this passage, the idea is taken to a new level. The people of Israel were taken into exile and suffered on behalf of all the other Israelites who had violated the Covenant, but had not suffered the consequences. They suffered on behalf of others. And God honored and redeemed their suffering. **In the New Testament, we will see this idea taken to its ultimate conclusion: God gives His only begotten Son as a substitutionary sacrifice for the sins of the whole world.**

Universal Mission of Redemption

Isaiah also saw Israel's return to the Promised Land as a sign of a new mission. In this liberation from exile, God has shown his sovereignty over the pagan idols. God was triumphant over the most powerful nations of the world. Furthermore, God was restoring his people for the purpose of establishing God's universal kingdom over the whole earth. God was going to call all people to be his people.

> *"Thus says the Lord, ...'It is too light a thing that you should be my servant to raise up the tribes of Jacob and to restore the preserved of Israel; I will give you as a light to the nations, that my salvation may reach to the ends of the earth."*
> Isaiah 49:6

> *And the foreigners who join themselves to the Lord, to minister to him, to love the name of the Lord, and to be his servants, everyone who keeps the Sabbath and does not profane it, and holds fast my covenant – these I will bring to my holy mountain and make them joyful in my house of prayer; their burnt offerings and their sacrifices will be accepted on my altar; for my house shall be called a house of prayer for all peoples."*
> Isaiah 56:6-7

Many scholars have noticed three distinct time periods covered in the present book of Isaiah, spanning nearly 200years: 1) the tumultuous period before the exile, approximately 742 to 687 BC (chapters 1 through 39), 2) the time of return from the exile, approximately 539 BC (chapters 40 through 55), and 3) a time of new challenges in the Promised Land, approximately 530 to 510 BC (chapters 56 through 66). This has led many (but not all) scholars to conclude that the present book of Isaiah is the composite work of at least three different authors.

V. Rebuilding the City of Jerusalem – Nehemiah's Dream Come True

When the people of Israel returned from exile, they had an enormous job of rebuilding to do. Remember that the city of Jerusalem had been completely destroyed by the army of Nebuchadnezzar in 587 B.C. The Temple, all important buildings and the city wall had all been torn down. Remember also that, from the time of King David (500 years earlier), Jerusalem had been the center of Jewish cultural and worship life. It was then, as it is today, the symbolic geographic center of the Jewish people and their worship of God.

The Living Word of the Living God

The story recorded in the book of Nehemiah is an inspirational account of a man with a dream, who persevered against impossible odds and the ridicule of many of his own people, to begin rebuilding the holy city of Jerusalem. The book records the rebuilding of the city wall. A modern reader might ask, "Why the wall?" In the modern world, we think of stone walls as decorations but not as essential. In the ancient world, walls were the first line of defense against an enemy. A city without a wall was no city at all. It was subject to raids by organized armies and by itinerant bands of thieves and thugs. Therefore, if the Jews wanted to reclaim Jerusalem as the center of worship, culture and national pride, then the first order of business was to rebuild the wall. The example of Nehemiah offers a model for anyone who follows a God-given dream to its conclusion. He had a vision from God and trusted God to provide for every need against overwhelming odds.

1) The Grim Reality – a Ruined City of Jerusalem

"Hannai, one of my brethren came with certain men from Judah; and I asked them concerning the Jews that survived and escaped the exile, and concerning Jerusalem. And they said to me, 'The survivors there in the province who escaped exile are in great trouble and shame; the wall of Jerusalem is broken down and its gates are destroyed.' When I heard these words, I sat down and wept, and mourned for days; and I continued fasting and praying to the God of heaven."

Nehemiah 1:2-4

2) A Vision Founded on the Promises of God

In the midst of Nehemiah's time of despair and prayer, God gave him a vision and his life calling. Nehemiah reminds God of the promises to Moses and pleads that God not forget his people or his promises.

"Remember the word which you commanded to your servant Moses saying 'If you return to me and keep my commandments...I will bring you to the place which I have chosen and make my name to dwell there.' ...O Lord, let your ear be attentive to the prayer of your servant...and give success to your servant today, and grant him mercy in the sight of man."

Nehemiah 1:8-11

3) A Practical Plan To Get the Resources Needed

After praying and receiving the vision, Nehemiah asked God to help him persuade the one person who had the resources to make the vision a reality

— the king of Persia (modern day Iran). He asked the king for permission, protection and building supplies.

> "So I prayed to the God of heaven. And I said to the king... And the king granted what I asked, for the hand of my God was upon me."
>
> Nehemiah 2:4-9

4) Sharing the Vision with Fellow Believers

Nehemiah's next challenge was to convince his fellow Jews to join him in rebuilding the city walls. He reminds the skeptics that his plan is founded on the promises of God.

> "Then I said to them, 'You see the trouble we are in, how Jerusalem lies in ruins with its gates burned. Come let us rebuild Jerusalem, that we may no longer suffer disgrace. And I told them of the hand of God which had been upon me for good, and also the words that the king had spoken to me. And they said 'Let us rise up and build'. So they strengthened their hands for the good work."
>
> Nehemiah 2:17-18

5) Opposition and Ridicule from Others

Nehemiah soon learned two valuable lessons: 1) if you have a mission from God and if your vision seems too large, you can expect opposition and ridicule and 2) if you are sure of your mission, you will never allow opposition to slow you down.

The hecklers:
> "What are these feeble Jews doing? Will they restore things? Will they sacrifice?... Will they revive the stones out of the heaps of rubbish?"

Nehemiah's response:
> "Hear O God, for we are despised; turn back their taunts on their own heads...So we built the wall; and all the wall was joined together to half its height. For the people had a mind to work." ..."For they all wanted to frighten us, thinking 'Their hands will drop from the work and it will not be done'. But now O God Strengthen my hands."
>
> Nehemiah 4:1-2 and 4-6 and 6:9

6) Declare Victory, Give Glory to God and Throw a Party

As the story progresses, more people join in the work, the opposition is silenced and the project is completed. In conclusion, Nehemiah does two important things: gives glory to God and throws a party to say thank you to all his workers.

> "For they (the opposition) perceived that this work had been accomplished with the help of our God."
> Nehemiah 6:15-16

> "Bring them to Jerusalem to celebrate the dedication with gladness, with thanksgivings and with singing, with cymbals, harps and lyres....And they offered great sacrifices that day and rejoiced, for God had made them rejoice with great joy; the women and children also rejoiced. And the joy of Jerusalem was heard afar off."
> Nehemiah 12:27-28 and 43

The heroic work of Nehemiah set the tone, and gave courage to the later rebuilders. Soon Jerusalem was once again a thriving city of God's people. Nehemiah is a powerful role model for all people who trust in God in the face of overwhelming odds. We can hear in his story echoes of Abraham, Moses, David, Elijah and Isaiah. Without a vision, people perish. With a vision from God and trust in God, we can do great things to bear witness to God's kingdom on earth.

IV. New Challenges in The Promised Land

The first Israelis came back to the Promised Land in 539 B.C. There were several waves of immigration after them. But resettling the land proved to be hard. There were many ups and downs, but eventually the Temple was rebuilt and the people of Israel remained more or less faithful to the Covenant and remained a vassal state in the Persian empire for the next two hundred years.

1) Alexander the Great

However, by 334 B.C., another empire was on the rise – the Greek empire. Its king, Alexander the Great conquered the Persian Empire and all of its territories, including the land of Israel. Thus began a new crisis for God's people. Alexander was not just interested in controlling land. He had a mission to spread Greek culture (including polytheistic religion) throughout his empire.

This policy caused several tensions with Jews who wished to remain faithful to God. Several Greek overlords attempted to impose polytheistic worship in the Temple in Jerusalem with mixed success. This caused much tension between different factions in Israel, some of whom wanted to adopt Greek ways and some who regarded such adoption as betrayal of the Covenant with God. Finally, in 167 B.C., this tension came to a head. The Greek-appointed ruler, Antiochus IV Epiphanes robbed and defiled the temple by forcing the worship of Zeus and severely persecuting pious Jews who refused to cooperate. This precipitated a popular revolt among the pious Jews.

2) The Maccabean Revolt

In the Maccabean revolt, pious Jews attacked the Greeks. This revolt was led by the Maccabeus family. After his father was killed in battle, Judas Maccabeus became the leader. The revolt succeeded and Israel regained control of Temple worship. This victory is celebrated in the modern Jewish celebration of Hanukkah. (The Maccabean revolt is recorded in I and II Maccabees in the Apocrypha).

The Hope of Resurrection

During the course of the Maccabean revolt, many pious Israelites were killed in battle with the Greeks. This raised a new question: why did God let these faithful soldiers die at the hands of pagans. In the past God had judged the people of Israel for lack of faith. But why had God allowed those who were fighting to resist paganism die? What would be their destiny?

The answer, discerned by Judas Maccabeus, was that God would vindicate these fallen martyrs by raising them from the dead in the future.

> *"And the noble Judas ...took up a collection, man by man, to the amount of two thousand drachmas of silver, and sent it to Jerusalem to provide for a sin offering. In doing this, he acted very well and honorably, taking account of resurrection. For if he were not expecting that those who had fallen would rise again, it would have been superfluous and foolish to pray for the dead. But if he was looking to the splendid reward that is laid up for those who fall asleep in godliness, it was a holy and pious thought. Therefore, he made atonement for the dead, that they might be delivered from their sin."*
>
> II Maccabees 12:42-45

At the time of the Reformation in the 16th Century, this passage was very controversial because of conflicts between Protestants and Roman Catholics about the appropriateness and efficacy of prayers offered on behalf of the dead

The passage is cited here because it is the most clear and explicit example of the hope and expectation of resurrection in the Old Testament times. This hope of resurrection is a key ingredient in our understating of the salvation that God has made available through Jesus Christ. It is the key which brings together all of the other aspects of God's saving work which we have been discussing throughout the Old Testament. In Chapter 10, we will discuss this hope of resurrection more extensively.

As the Old Testament draws to a close, there are many promises not yet fully realized. From the Christian point of view, Jesus draws together in himself all of the promises that have been prefigured in the saving events of the Old Testament narrative. The Old Testament prepares for the New Testament. The New brings to completion the promises of the Old. In the next chapter, we continue our narrative by considering "What's New in the New Testament?"

V. Time Line of the Old Testament Narrative

Before moving to the New Testament, by way of review, here is an approximate time-line of the Old Testament.

Pre-History	Adam and Eve
	Noah's Ark
1,750 B.C.	Abraham & Sarah
	Isaac & Rebecca
	Jacob & Rachel
	Joseph flees to Egypt
1,200 B.C.	Exodus: Moses leads Israel out of Egypt
1,200-1,000 B.C.	Judges rule
1,000-922 B.C.	Kings Saul, David, Solomon
922 B.C.	Kingdom Divides: North (Israel) and South (Judah)
722 B.C.	Northern Kingdom falls
597 B.C.	Southern kingdom falls; Babylonian Exile begins
538 B.C.	Babylonian Exile ends
334 B.C.	Alexander the Great Conquers Promised land
167 B.C.	Maccabean Revolt

QUESTIONS FOR DISCUSSION AND REFLECTION

1) In the midst of Israel's darkest hour, the prophet Ezekiel declares that God does not desire the death of unfaithful people, but that they "turn and live." How can we claim this promise in times of personal crises and failures? (For example, broken marriage vows, betrayals by friends, recurrent sinful behaviors or compulsions, etc.)

2) The prophet Isaiah declares that Israel is God's "suffering servant" and that God can bring good out of hurtful circumstances. Have you experienced this promise in your own life? Why do you think God allows bad things to happen to us?

Look at the following examples in American history. Do you think that these were times in which God was judging us as a nation? Do you think God was able to bring good out of what seemed at the time to be a really bad thing?

The Civil War
September 11, 2001
Gas costing over $4.00 per gallon

3) In the Exile, the people of Israel were able to renew their faith and trust in God. Ironically, they were able to rediscover their relationship with God when everything else had been taken away. They turned to God when there was nowhere else to turn. Have you had this experience in your own life? Do we need to wait for a major crisis to turn to God for help? What are some "non-crisis" times in which your faith has been renewed and strengthened?

PRAYER EXERCISE

Take a few minutes to reread the first chapter of Nehemiah. Think about a situation in your life that may seem "hopeless", perhaps a relationship, a job or a financial situation. Have you ever asked God for help with this situation? Does the problem seem too big for you (or you with God's help) to handle? Take some time in prayer to ask God to help you see the situation in a new light and to give you a vision for how to deal with it differently. Then ask God to help you in finding a practical way to work on the problem. Then ask God for guidance in seeking other human beings that can assist you with the problem. Then ask God for perseverance and strength to accomplish the vision.

BIBLE MEMORY VERSE

For I know my plans I have for you, says the Lord, plans for welfare and not for evil, to give you a future and a hope. ...I will restore your fortunes and gather you from all the nations and all the places where I have driven you, says the Lord, and I will bring you back to the place from which I sent you into exile."

Jeremiah 29:12-14

Chapter 9

"WHEN THE TIME HAD FULLY COME, GOD SENT HIS SON": WHAT'S "NEW" IN THE "NEW TESTAMENT?"

Main focus of this chapter: A summary of Jesus message, ministry and mission in the social and religious context of his time.

I. What's "new" in the New Testament?

We now begin to study that portion of the Bible known as the "New Testament." As we have observed in chapter 1, the Bible is divided into two main parts: the "Old" and the "New" Testaments. The Old Testament covers the period in time before Jesus Christ. The New Testament covers the life, death and resurrection of Jesus Christ and the work of the Holy Spirit in the early Church.

Many people have asked the simple, yet profound, question: What's "new" in the New Testament? It is true that there is much continuity between the Old and New Testaments. The New tells us of the same God and moral teachings are basically the same. It speaks with great respect for the "Law and the Prophets" and for all of the heroes of the Old Testament. And yet, for all the continuity, there really is something new about the New Testament. God is doing a "new thing." God is revealing His final and complete will and purpose for all humanity. The Old Testament period was a time of preparation and promise. The New Testament is the fulfillment of all of the promises of the Old.

In the Old Testament, God establishes a covenant relationship with the people of Israel. In the New, God establishes a covenant relationship with all the nations. In the Old Testament, the focus of God's salvation is the preservation of a particular group of "Chosen" people in a particular piece of real estate called the "Promised Land." In the New, the focus of salvation is for all humanity (past, present and future) and the "Promised Land" is the whole world, redeemed, restored and reconciled to God.

The Epistle to the Hebrews explains it this way:

> *"In many and various God spoke of old to our fathers by the prophets; but in these last days he has spoken to us through a son, whom he appointed the heir of all things, through whom also he created the world. He reflects the glory of God and bears the very stamp of his nature,..."*
>
> Hebrews 1:1-4

Paul explains it this way:

> *"the (Old Testament) law was our custodian until Christ came, that we might be justified by faith. But now that faith has come we are no longer under a custodian;...when the time had fully come, God sent forth his Son, born of a woman, born under the law, to redeem those who were under the law"*
>
> Galatians 3:24-25 and 4:4-5

These passages (and many others in the New Testament) emphasize one fundamental truth: **God sent Jesus Christ to be the final and complete revelation of God's work of salvation. Jesus is the unique savior of the world.** In the Old Testament, God's saving work with the people of Israel had been real, but incomplete. God had taken all the centuries, from Abraham onward, to shape the religious self-understanding of the people of Israel. God had worked through all of the calamities of Israel's history to prepare an expectation of a coming Messiah. In Jesus, all of the promises of God, prefigured in the events and people of the Old Testament, find their fulfillment.

II. Social Context of the New Testament

Jesus was sent by God at a particular time and place according to God's predetermined plan. ("When the time had fully come, God sent his Son.") The words and symbols which Jesus used to describe his mission, are shaped by the social context of his time and place in history. But his own people had many different ideas about what a Messiah should be. For that reason, many people did not understand what Jesus was talking about and doing. He did not meet their expectations. Many of the false impressions that people (both friend and foe) had about Jesus were also shaped by the social context. So, to understand both Jesus own self-understanding and the misunderstanding of those around him, we need to know a little bit about the social context in which he lived. The following is a brief description of "the life and times" of Jesus Christ.

WHAT'S NEW IN THE NEW TESTAMENT?

1) Judah Ruled by Foreigners

From the time of the return from the Babylonian Exile, the "Promise Land" had been dominated by one foreign empire after another: first the Persians, then the Greeks (under Alexander the Great), then the Egyptians (as a puppet state of the Greeks). At the time of Jesus' birth, the land was ruled by the Roman Empire. There was a puppet Jewish King (Herod), but the real rulers were polytheists from Rome. The Roman governor and army enforced this rule with brutal force if necessary. Before the Romans, there had been a brief period of Jewish independence from 167 B.C. to 63 B.C.

2) Expectation of a Messiah-King

Jesus was born about 60 years after the Jews had lost their freedom and been conquered by the Romans. Therefore, many people at the time of Jesus had a living memory of a free land, ruled by Jews and for Jews, as God had promised to Abraham and Moses. Many devout Jewish people expected God to send a Messiah to free the land of the evil Roman rulers and reestablish an earthly Kingdom ruled by God's Messiah-King.

3) Hope of Resurrection

This hope for a Messiah – King was also coupled with a hope for resurrection of those who had been killed defending their land against foreign domination. (Remember the Maccabean martyrs discussed in chapter 8.) This hope of resurrection was especially prevalent among the Pharisees and the lower classes in Jewish society. We will discuss this in greater depth in Chapter 10.

4) Religious Factions

There were several religious factions in the Jewish faith at the time of Jesus. These groups were similar to modern day "denominations" of Jews and Christians. They had a common allegiance to the basic teachings of Judaism, but each group emphasized different aspects of the Jewish faith.. They were: Pharisees, Sadducees, Essenes and Zealots.

Pharisees had their beginnings in the Maccabean revolt (which we discussed in chapter 8). They expected a Messianic King and a resurrection of the fallen Maccabean martyrs and a general resurrection of all faithful Jews. The Pharisees wanted to purify Jewish religion from all polytheistic influences which were added during the period of Greek domination. To accomplish these reforms, they strongly emphasized education of the people through the study, and correct interpretation, of God's Word. They organized a network of fellowships (called "havurahs") throughout the countryside to enable poor and uneducated people to pray and study God's Word. The Pharisees were very critical of the Sadducees whom they considered to be collaborationists with the Romans and illegitimate spokesmen for the Jewish people.

Sadducees were the wealthy land owners and the priestly aristocracy. It was from their ranks that the temple priests, the High Priest and the Sanhedrin were chosen. They were happy with the Roman occupation because it provided stability and allowed them to retain their land and a privileged place in society. They were very nervous about the lower classes starting a rebellion, making the Romans unhappy, risking a military crackdown and thus upsetting the *status quo*. They disapproved of any religious group in Judaism which questioned their right to speak as unquestioned leaders of the Jewish people. They were especially nervous about anyone claiming to be a Messiah (of which there were many at the time) because they tended to rally the radical elements of society and start ill-fated rebellions. The Sadducees did not have any hope for a restored Israel independent of Roman rule. Indeed, they hoped that this would not happen because they would lose control. They also rejected any belief in the resurrection. Considering all these factors, it is easy to see why these people were so eager to get rid of Jesus when he became popular with the lower classes. They were afraid that he would encourage a revolt which would be brutally suppressed by the Romans.

Essenes were radical separatists who believed in having nothing to do with the Roman occupation arrangement. They believed that their function was to wait and pray for God to reestablish the kingdom of Israel. They lived in the desert in caves and adhered to very strict moral rules and ritual practices. John the Baptist may have come from one of their communities. The Dead Sea Scrolls (discovered between 1947 and 1960) were written by different Essene communities and tell us much about their beliefs and practices. There are many similarities between the ethical teaching of Jesus recorded in Matthew's gospel and the teachings of the Essenes.

Zealots were radical revolutionaries who believed in the sudden and violent overthrow of the Romans. They lead many suicidal revolts against the Romans in an attempt to establish God's Kingdom. They were similar to many groups (both Jewish and Islamic) which are active in modern Middle East politics.

All of these groups (except the Essenes) are mentioned by name several times in the gospel accounts. Their ideas and expectations formed the social/religious context in which Jesus lived and died. They contributed to many of the false understandings and expectations of what kind of Messiah Jesus was, what kind of Kingdom he came to proclaim and what kind of salvation he came to deliver.

III. A Brief Biography of Jesus Christ

1) A Miraculous Birth

Jesus was born in a small village (Bethlehem) to parents of low social standing. Prior to her marriage, Jesus' mother, Mary received a visitation from an angel who told her that she would conceive a child in a miraculous way. The child would be conceived "of the Holy Spirit" without having sexual relations with her husband. She did not understand what this meant, but agreed to God's plan and became pregnant with Jesus. Mary's husband Joseph also received a message from God on this miraculous conception and agreed to take Mary as his wife and raise Jesus as his son.

2) Early Formation in the Jewish Faith

Shortly after Jesus was born, he and his parents had to flee to Egypt to escape the Israelite king (Herod) who was threatened by the possibility of a new king being born and had ordered all male babies to be killed.

After Herod's death, they returned and lived in their native village of Nazareth. During this time, Jesus learned and observed the religious faith of his parents (the Jewish faith as described and lived in the Old Testament). During this time, Jesus formed some very strong convictions about his faith and had discussions with religious teacher who were impressed with his knowledge. It is very important to remember that Jesus was, from beginning to end, a faithful Jew. He never repudiated the faith of his people, although he had some very negative opinions about those who distorted this faith for their own selfish purposes.

3) Public Ministry

At about age 30, Jesus began his public career. After a period of intense fasting and prayer in the wilderness, Jesus began to preach and teach in synagogues and in the countryside. The focus of his teaching was on the coming kingdom of God and on attitudes and behavior which prepared for that kingdom. Jesus especially emphasized the need for all people to prepare for this Kingdom by repentance, acts of mercy, justice and love to all people and devotion to God.

Jesus' teaching was accompanied by many miracles which demonstrated the power of God at work in his life. Many people were impressed by his miracles and teachings and he gathered large crowds wherever he went. Many people were convinced that he was the promised "Messiah" who would lead a military revolution, defeat the Romans who ruled the people of Israel, and establish God's kingdom on earth. Jesus repeatedly told the people that God's kingdom was different than they expected and that he was a different kind of Messiah than they expected, but most people did not understand him.

Jesus gathered several close followers (called "disciples") whom he taught and with whom he developed a very close relationship. Among these disciples he chose twelve special leaders (called "apostles") whom he designated to carry on his work and message after he ascended into heaven.

4) Growing Popularity and Persecution

As time went on, Jesus' popularity with the common people became a source of great fear for the Jewish religious leaders. The Sadducees feared that he would cause a revolt and that the Romans would retaliate and their privileged positions would be lost. The Pharisees were fearful that Jesus would undermine their teaching authority because he called attention to, and denounced, their scrupulous moralizing and hypocrisy in matters of the Law. For these reasons, the Jewish religious leaders (Pharisees as well as Sadducees) plotted to find a way to put Jesus to death. Jesus knew that his life was in danger, but also knew that God wanted him to proclaim the Kingdom without compromise and without fear. He also trusted in God's love for him and refused to back down from his mission.

5) Trial and Death

Finally, the Jewish religious authorities arrested Jesus and put him on trial for blasphemy, claiming that he had dishonored God by claiming to be God's Son and calling God his "Father."

After condemning Jesus on religious grounds, the Jewish leaders handed him over to the Roman governor (Pontius Pilate) to be tried on the charge of treason. They said that Jesus, was in rebellion against Caesar by proclaiming his allegiance to God's Kingdom and by claiming to be its King. Jesus explained to Pilate that his Kingdom was "not of this world." Pilate was not inclined to condemn Jesus, but feared a mob insurrection led by the Jewish religious authorities. To please the mob, Pilate condemned Jesus to death, even though he knew that Jesus was not guilty of treason.

Jesus was executed in the normal Roman style – crucifixion. After beating and public humiliation by the Roman soldiers, Jesus was nailed to the cross. He died after three hours and was taken down for burial before sundown on Friday.

Up to this point in the story, most of what we have said about Jesus' life and death would not have been very different from hundreds of other popular Jewish leaders. There were many would-be Kings and would-be Messiah's; many martyred prophets who were persecuted by the Jewish religious authorities; many zealous believers who were faithful to God even unto death; many Jewish patriots crucified by the Romans for real or suspected treason. In all of these aspects Jesus was not unique and would not have been remembered for more than a few years by anyone other than his friends and relatives. But the story does not end with his death.

6) Resurrection

Jesus died on Friday. The Sabbath began at sundown on Friday and extended to sundown on Saturday. There had not been time on Friday to finish preparing his body for a proper burial. Early on Sunday morning, before dawn, some women who were friends of Jesus went to the tomb to complete the job of burying their dead hero. But when they got to the tomb, their hero could not be found. Instead, they saw angels who told them that he had risen from the dead.

Later, Jesus appeared to them, as individuals and in large groups. In those encounters, they slowly came to know and understand that wonderful thing that had happen. Jesus was not a resuscitated corpse – not returned from a "near death experience." He really died and he was really alive again – but alive in a new and wonderful way. Alive in a way that demonstrated that God's kingdom was triumphant over the powers of sin and death. He was alive to complete the work of salvation begun by God when Adam and Eve destroyed the harmony between themselves and God. He was alive with the power to impart new and everlasting life to all who believed in God through him. He was alive to become the source of eternal salvation for all humanity.

7) The Great Commission: Tell the Good News to the Whole World

This indeed was "good news" (gospel) for all of Jesus' followers. They had put all of their hope in him. They had seen their hopes dashed when he died. And now, they had happiness beyond their wildest dreams. But that was not all. Jesus rose from death for all humanity. This was God's final and complete work of salvation – not just for the immediate followers of Jesus, not just for the Jewish people – but for every human being. For that reason, Jesus sent his followers to tell the "good news" of his resurrection – and of God's victory over sin and death – to the whole world. This is called the Great Commission. (All future followers of Jesus have a duty to carry out this Great Commission. No Christian is ever excused from telling others the good news of Jesus' triumph over sin and death and inviting others to share in His Kingdom.)

8) The Holy Spirit is Sent

Jesus appeared to his followers for a period of forty days. Then he promised to send the Holy Spirit who would empower them to complete the world-wide mission and who would call to their memory all Jesus had taught them and who would lead them into all truth. He told them to wait in Jerusalem until he Holy Spirit had been sent to them.

They waited in prayer for ten days. On Pentecost, the fiftieth day after Jesus had risen from the dead, the Holy Spirit descended on the disciples and apostles and gave them the necessary power and gifts to preach the gospel effectively. From that day forward, the mission of the Church began. Through the activity of the Holy Spirit, the Risen Lord Jesus continues to proclaim the Kingdom of God. Jesus is alive and active through the Church offering forgiveness of sins and eternal salvation to all who will receive Him.

This "brief biography of Jesus Christ" is, in a nutshell, the message of the New Testament. In the next several chapters, we will study the message in much greater detail. For now, let's look at the basic structure of the New Testament (which is quite different from that of the Old Testament).

IV. One Gospel: Many Reporters

The New Testament is made up of four different kinds of writing: Gospels, Epistles, Acts and Revelation.

1) The "Gospels": Matthew, Mark, Luke and John.

These are the four different accounts of the life, death and resurrection of Jesus Christ. At first glance, these accounts seem to be repetitive. They tell the same basic story. However, on closer inspection, they each give us a different portrait of who Jesus was and what he came to accomplish. Like different portraits of a famous person (for instance George Washington) each gospel portrays the same person, but reflects a different perspective, a different set of emphases and priorities. It is only in reading each of the gospel accounts as a separate portrait that we see the complete picture of the meaning and purpose of Jesus' life.

2) The Epistles: Paul, (Unknown), James, Peter, John and Jude

The Epistles are letters written by the apostles to the early Christian communities. When we read the Epistles, we are reading "other people's mail." These were not intended to be orderly works of literature (as the Gospels were). They usually focus on questions, problems and challenges in the early Church.

The Epistles attributed to Paul are the most numerous and have been the most influential in shaping later Christian theology. They are: Romans; I and II Corinthians; Galatians; Ephesians; Philippians; Colossians; I and II

Thessalonians; I and II Timothy; Titus; Philemon.

The Epistles to the Hebrews was once generally thought to have been written by Paul, but modern scholars no longer think so. The author is unknown.

The Epistle of James is attributed to James "the Just" who was the first bishop of Jerusalem.

The Epistle of I and II Peter are attributed to Peter, the apostle who was later martyred in Rome.

The Epistles of I, II and III John are attributed to the apostle John (also author of the gospel of John).

The Epistle of Jude is attributed to the apostle Jude who was the brother of James.

3) The Acts of the Apostles ("Acts" for short)

Some scholars have called this book "the gospel of the Holy Spirit." Acts is an account of the life of the early Church from the time Jesus ascended into heaven and the Holy Spirit descended on the apostles at Pentecost. Acts tells the story of the mission and growth of the first generation of the Church. Peter and Paul are the main human characters in Acts, but the real mover and shaker is the Holy Spirit. The Holy Spirit is portrayed as the power and inspiration for every decision, insight, prayer and mission initiative.

4) The Book of Revelation

The title of this book is derived from the first word of the first verse (in the original Greek): "Revelation of Jesus Christ…" The English word "revelation" is a translation of the Greek word "apocalypse" (which is roughly translated "the unveiling of that which is hidden"). Revelation is a mystical vision of the final consummation of God's kingdom in "a new heaven and a new earth." Its imagery is wild and colorful. It is hard to understand and has been subject to many diverse interpretations. It has always been, and continues to be, a source of great controversy in the Church. However, when interpreted in harmony with other books in the New Testament and within the Church's normative historical interpretation, Revelation is a source for awe-inspiring imagery, poetry and hymnody. Christian devotional life, liturgical practice, music, art and architecture would be greatly impoverished without the beauty and majesty of the book of Revelation.

In the next several chapters, we will look more closely at the Four Gospels, the Epistles, Acts and Revelation. Each provides a unique portrait of who Jesus is, what God has done (and is now doing) through Jesus, and how we are called to live our lives in response to God.

QUESTIONS FOR DISCUSSION AND REFLECTION

1) Many pious and devout Jewish people did not recognize Jesus as the Messiah. Why do you think this was so? If Jesus was to return in bodily form today, do you think you would recognize him?

2) Try to play the part of a Pharisee, Sadducee, Essene or Zealot as sympathetically as you can. What kind of motivations might they have had to reject Jesus and his message? How might they have thought that they were honoring God while rejecting Jesus?

3) Are there any religious groups (or personality types) today that resemble the Sadducees, Pharisees, Essenes, or Zealots? Try to play the part of one of these modern groups as sympathetically as possible. How do they see Jesus and his message? How do they interpret it differently than you do?

4) The New Testament portrays Jesus from many points of view. Discuss with others their particular picture of image of Jesus and what he means to them. After sharing each person's image of Jesus, how has your understanding of him been changed or enhanced?

PRAYER EXERCISE

Sit quietly and close your eyes. Reflect on the different images of Jesus that have come up in your group discussion or individual reflection. Choose one of these images and form a picture in your mind. With that picture as a focus, repeat quietly the "Jesus Prayer": "Lord Jesus Christ, Son of the Living God; Have Mercy on me a sinner." Repeat this prayer several times and then focus in silence on the presence of Jesus in your life. Remain in silent prayer for 5 or 10 minutes.

BIBLE MEMORY VERSE

"In many and various God spoke of old to our fathers by the prophets; but in these last days he has spoken to us through a son, whom he appointed the heir of all things, through whom also he created the world. He reflects the glory of God and bears the very stamp of his nature,..."

Hebrews 1:1-4

Chapter 10

JESUS' RESURRECTION: WHAT HAPPENED? AND WHAT DIFFERENCE DOES IT MAKE?

Main focus of this chapter:
An in-depth look at the central event of the New Testament.

Before discussing the specific books of the New Testament, we need to consider the motivation of its writers. Even though the books of the New Testament were written by several different authors with differing priorities and points of view, they all had one thing in common. They were convinced that God had done something radically new and decisive in the raising Jesus from the dead. In this chapter, we will summarize what the New Testament teaches about the resurrection. To do that, we need to look back to the Old Testament which "sets the stage" for the final act of the drama of salvation found in the New Testament.

I. Old Testament Preparation: Hope of Resurrection

In a human friendship, we get to know another person better over a long period of time. The longer we know another person, the better we can anticipate his or her thoughts, intentions and actions. Furthermore, our perception of another person's character grows over time. Early in a friendship, we may see small signs which give us some hints about a person's character (either good or bad). Over time, early intuitions develop into deeper convictions. Similarly, in the Bible, God reveals more of his character and purpose over time. Concurrently, we see the people of Israel come to understand God better over time. Early intuition develops into strong conviction. Thus, the Bible contains many examples of what we might call "emergent beliefs" about God's character and intentions. As we have discussed in previous chapters, we find many examples of "prefiguration" in which God's people learn from the past to anticipate God's thoughts, intentions and actions in the future. The Old Testament creates a "horizon of expectation" for the resurrection which is the central "emergent belief" of the Bible. We will now briefly summarize how this expectation developed.[5]

5 This summary in the first section of this chapter is a condensation of an extensive

1) Prolonged Earthly Life

In much of the Old Testament, there is an expectation that physical death is the end and we all go to "Sheol" (the abode of the dead). *"Enjoy life… for there is no work, or thought, or knowledge or wisdom in Sheol to which you are going."* (Ecclesiastes 9:9-10)   In many instances, prayers seem to be asking God for protection in, and extension of, this earthly life, but nothing more. For example: *"Turn, O Lord, save my life; deliver me for the sake of your steadfast love. For in death, there is no remembrance of thee; in Sheol, who can give thee praise?"* (Psalm 6:4-5) However, in many of these prayers, there is an implied hope that the living God will give more than a brief extension of earthly life. There is an expectation that the Creator's superabundant life-giving power will overrule the power of Sheol, available to those who put their ultimate trust in God and not in themselves. The following Psalm begins with the pessimism of Ecclesiastes, but holds out hope for those who trust in God rather than themselves.

> *"Truly no man can ransom himself, or give back to God the price of his life…that he should continue to live on forever and never see the Pit….This is the fate of those who have foolish confidence, the end of those who are pleased with their own portion. Like sheep they are appointed for Sheol; Death shall be their shepherd; straight to the grave they will descend and their form shall waste away; Sheol shall be their home. But God will rescue my soul from the power of Sheol, for he will receive me."*
>
> Psalm 49:7-9 and 13-15

The following psalm expresses hope that the benefits of a relationship with God will extend "for evermore."

> *"Therefore my heart is glad, and my spirit rejoices; my body also rests secure.*
>
> *For thou dost not give me up to Sheol, or let thy godly one see the Pit.*
>
> *Thou dost show me the path of life; in thy presence is fullness of joy,*
>
> *and in thy right hand are pleasures for evermore."*
>
> Psalm 16:9-11

---

study in *The Resurrection of The Son of God* by N.T. Wright, Fortress Press, Minneapolis, 2003 pp.85-127

2) The Hope of National Resurrection

As we have noted in chapters 6 and 8, the Hebrew prophets spoke in times of national calamity both warning the people of Israel to repent and consoling them with the promise of God's power to save and redeem the people when they returned to the Covenant. And as we also have noted previously, the words of the prophets carried meaning for their own time and potential for God's future intentions and actions. In the following prophets, we see the promises which, according to the New Testament, reach their ultimate fulfillment in Jesus.

Hosea

The prophet Hosea lived in the north during the war with the Assyrians in 732 B.C. and during the chaos and destruction that followed. As did all of the other prophets, he saw national calamity as God's appropriate judgment on a wayward people and he promised God's restoration if the people would return to their God.

> *"Come, let us return to the Lord; for he has torn, that he may heal us; he has stricken and he will bind us up. After two days, he will revive us; on the third day, he will raise us up, that we may live before him. Let us know, let us press on to know the Lord; his going forth is sure as the dawn; he will come to us as the showers, as the spring rains watering the earth."*
>
> Hosea 6:1-3

Later, in the same book God asks himself a rhetorical question after observing the continuing unfaithfulness of (at least some) of the people of Israel.

> *"Shall I ransom them from the power of Sheol? Shall I redeem them from Death? O Death, where are your plagues? O Sheol, where is your destruction?"*
>
> Hosea 13:14

In this case, God seems to have answered his own question in the negative. However, in asking the question, God indicates that he has the power to ransom from death. In the New Testament, Paul asserts that God has answered this rhetorical question positively in the resurrection of Jesus and of all who trust in God's willingness and power to save. (See I Corinthians 15:54-57)

Ezekiel

Ezekiel lived in Jerusalem at the time of its destruction by Nebuchadnezzar and in Babylon with the exiles. He saw the absolute destruction of his nation and his people. And yet, in the midst of this destruction, when things seemed to be beyond any hope of renewal, he promised that God would miraculously rebuild his people. The following is an excerpt from chapter 37 (which the reader is encouraged to read in its entirety before proceeding).

> *"The hand of the Lord was upon me, and he brought me out by the Spirit of the Lord, and set me down in the midst of the valley; it was full of dry bones. And he led me around them and they were very dry. And he said to me 'Son of man, can these bones live?' And I answered 'Lord you know'. Again he said to me 'Prophesy to these bones, and say to them, O dry bones, hear the word of the Lord. Thus says the Lord God to these bones: Behold, I will cause breath to enter you and you shall live. ...And you shall know that I am the Lord.*
>
> *"Then he said to me 'Son of man, these bones are the whole house of Israel. Behold they say, 'Our bones are dried up, and our hope is lost; we are clean cut off.' Therefore prophesy to them and say to them, Thus says the Lord God: Behold I will open your graves, and raise you from your graves, O my people; and I will bring you home to the land of Israel. And you shall know that I am the Lord, when I open your grave, and raise you from your graves, O my people'."*
>
> Ezekiel 37:1-6 and 11-14

In this passage Ezekiel is drawing a dramatic picture that none of his contemporaries could have misunderstood. He is saying that the state of his people is as bad as it could possibly be. Humanly speaking, there is absolutely no hope. But the Creator God who breathed life into earth to create humans will miraculously redeem his people from the grave of national destruction. In this passage, Ezekiel's immediate concern was the redemption of his people and their return to the promised land. But in the teaching and interpretation of the rabbis after his life, this passage came to be understood as a promise of future resurrection at the end of time. As we have seen in chapter 9, this was a central belief of the Pharisees at the time of Jesus. And the New Testament writers saw the resurrection of Jesus as the fulfillment of this promise.

Isaiah

Isaiah lived and wrote in Jerusalem in the time before, during and after the Exile to Babylon in 597 B.C. As with the other prophets, his immediate concern was the chaos and destruction of his society and his immediate hope, the rebuilding and restoration of his nation. However, many of his words point to a grander and more complete work of God that will extend to all people from a redeemed Jerusalem. "This mountain" refers to Mt. Zion – just outside Jerusalem.

> *"On this mountain, the Lord will make for all people a feast of fat things, a feast of wine on the lees, of fat things full of marrow, of wine on the lees well refined. And he will destroy on this mountain the covering that is cast over all peoples, the veil that is spread over all nations. He will swallow up death forever, and the Lord God will wipe away tears from all faces, and the reproach of his people he will take away from all the earth; for the Lord has spoken. It will be said on that day, 'Lo this is our God we have waited for him that he might save us. This is the Lord; we have waited for him, let us be glad and rejoice in his salvation."*
>
> Isaiah 25:6-9

Furthermore, Isaiah tells his people that God has a redemptive purpose in their national tragedy. As we saw in our discussion of Job in chapter 7, the reality of suffering is hard to reconcile with trust in a just and loving God. Isaiah is unsparing in his condemnation of false kings and prophets, but he sees many of his fellow citizens who are faithful to God and yet who are suffering. He tells them that God has a redemptive purpose in their national nightmare. He identifies the people of Israel as a **"Suffering Servant"** in **chapter 53** (which the reader is encouraged to read before proceeding). The following is a brief excerpt.

> *"Surely he has borne our griefs and carried our sorrows; yet we esteemed him stricken, smitten by God and afflicted. But he was wounded for our transgressions, he was bruised for our iniquities; upon him was the chastisement that made us whole....*
>
> *Yet it was the will of the Lord to bruise him; he has put him to grief; when he makes himself an offering for sin...the will of the Lord will prosper in his hand; he shall see the fruit of the travail of his soul and be satisfied. ...Therefore, I will divide*

> *him a portion with the great and he shall divide his spoil with the strong; because he poured out his soul to death, and was numbered among the transgressors, yet he bore the sin of many, and made intercession for the transgressors"*
>
> Isaiah 53:4-5 and 10-12

We see in this passage the nation personalized in "the Suffering Servant" and God uses the suffering of the nation to bring redemption for the sins of "many ...transgressors." In other words, many people (Jews and non-Jews) will benefit from the continued faithfulness of those who suffered through the exile and returned and rebuilt Jerusalem. The New Testament writers take this interpretation a step further. The personal suffering of Jesus (on the cross) and the personal vindication of Jesus (in the resurrection) extend the forgiving and saving power of God to all humanity.

3) Resurrection as the Reward for Righteousness

In contemporary American culture, we place a strong emphasis on individual rights, identity and autonomy over against cultural and societal norms. The Bible's emphasis is just the opposite. God relates to *the people of Israel as a whole*. God calls individuals only for the purpose of calling the whole community of faith back to God. There are, however, passages which promise future reward to righteous individuals who have been faithful to God's call to the people in times of distress.

> *"O Lord, in distress they sought thee, they poured out a prayer when the chastening was upon them. Like a woman with child, who writhes and cries out in her pangs, when she is near her time, so were we because of thee O Lord. ... Thy dead shall live, their bodies shall rise. O dwellers in the dust, awake and sing for joy!*
>
> Isaiah 26:16-19

4) Resurrection as Reward for Good and Punishment for Bad Guys

The prophet Daniel lived in Jerusalem during the reign of the Greek king Antiochus Epiphanes and the Maccabean revolt in 167 B.C. (which we briefly summarized in chapter 8). In the other resurrection passages we have discussed so far, resurrection is God's final reward for his faithful people and there is no mention of the enemies of God's people (who presumably remain dead.) In the following passage Daniel speaks of a general resurrection in which good people are rewarded and evil people are further punished.

"At that time shall arise Michael, the great prince who is in charge of your people...but at that time your people shall be delivered. ...And many who sleep in the dust of the earth shall awake, some to everlasting life, and some to shame and everlasting contempt. And those who are wise shall shine like the brightness of the firmament; and those who turn many to righteousness, like the stars forever and ever."

Daniel 12:1-3

Summary: Resurrection Hope: A Three-Stage Development

All of the Old Testament passages that we have summarized here have one thing in common. They believe that the same God who created the world, who led Israel out of slavery, who preserved Israel in the promised land, who brought Israel back from utter destruction in the Babylonian exile – this powerful God would win the final battle against Israel's every enemy. As we have seen, this hope developed over many centuries and expanded from 1) a hope for a long natural life, to 2) national survival and renewal, to 3) a hope for God's triumph in a different order of being at the end of history. As we shall see in the next section, all of these hopes came to fulfillment in the life, death and resurrection of Jesus Christ.

II. Jesus Resurrection: What Happened?

The "Jesus movement" in Judaism (which only later became known as "Christianity"), began very small: eleven frightened men and a few bewildered women hiding together and mourning the death of their leader. Within a very few years, the "Jesus movement" had spread to every major city on the Mediterranean seacoast. Within three hundred years, it became the official religion of the Roman Empire. For the next fifteen hundred years, it was the defining moral, cultural and intellectual institution of the West. It now comprises more than two billion people on every continent on earth. Its most rapid growth in history was in the 20th century, primarily in Africa and Asia. It now appears to be growing fastest in China – an officially "atheist" nation.

What accounts for this amazing growth, resilience and near universal appeal? The heart of the matter for those first frightened followers of Jesus, and for millions today, is this core conviction: God raised Jesus from the dead and that those who believe in Christ will share in this victory over death. We will now summarize what the Bible teaches about the resurrection of Jesus and its implications for those who believe in him. To do so we will look at the most extensive biblical passage on the subject, I Corinthians chapter 15 (which the reader is encouraged to read before continuing).

1) "I Delivered To You As Of First Importance"
I Corinthians 15:1-3

Many Christians recite a "creed" as part of their normal worship service. For many, it is the Apostles Creed or the Nicene Creed. For others, it may be a statement of faith written by their denomination or congregation. The purpose of repeating these creeds is to remind everyone, in a short summary form, what we believe about God and ourselves. Many Christian communities repeat these creeds regularly as a constant reminder and reinforcement of what is most important. What we have here in **I Corinthians 15:3-8** is the **earliest form of a Christian creed**. Paul is reminding everyone of the basic summary of faith that he himself received from others and passed on to the new believers in Corinth. He evidently also believes in the value of regular repetition and reinforcement.

> *"Now I would remind you brethren, in what terms I preached to you the gospel, which you receive and in which you now stand, by which you were saved, if you hold it fast – unless you believed in vain. For I delivered to you as of first importance that which I also received."*

2) "In accordance with the Scriptures"
I Corinthians 15:3-4

"The scriptures" in this case means "the Old Testament" because the New Testament was just being written and not yet considered "scripture." Here we see the fulfillment of the Old Testament emergent belief in the resurrection.

> *"that Christ died for our sins in accordance with the scriptures, that he was buried, that he was raised on the third day in accordance with the scriptures"*

It is the earliest Christian conviction that God has done something radical and new in raising Jesus from the dead, but it is the fulfillment and culmination of God's purposes which had been revealed throughout the Old Testament. That Christ died for our sins is a fulfillment specifically of "the Suffering Servant" song of Isaiah 53 with its reference to the atoning sacrifice "for the sins of many." More generally, it is a fulfillment of the passages referring to the sacrifice of Isaac, the Passover Lamb and the priestly sacrifices of the Temple all of which prefigure the ultimate sacrifice of Christ. (This theme is further developed in the New Testament letter "Hebrews.") That Christ was raised "on the third day" is the fulfillment of the specific promise of Hosea 6 "on the third day he will raise us up that we may live before him", but also more generally of the resurrection hope based on the passages from Isaiah, Ezekiel, Hosea, Daniel and others.

3) "That he appeared to Cephas, then to the twelve…"
I Cor. 15:5-9

> *"That he appeared to Cephas, then to the twelve. Then he appeared to more than five hundred brethren at one time…Then he appeared to James, then to all of the apostles. Last of all, as to one untimely born, he appeared also to me."*

According to this earliest Christian creed, it is absolutely essential to believe that Jesus appeared in his resurrection body to his followers. To say the God raised Jesus from the dead is not a pious way of saying "Jesus died, his body is buried and his soul went to heaven." It means that God did something radical and unprecedented and ultimate to demonstrate the Jesus had defeated death. That the early followers of Jesus met him alive after his death, talked with him, ate with him and were scolded by him is the bedrock of the conviction that Jesus is risen and alive and present with his followers. The tomb was empty. His body was not there. He was raised and has power to give death-destroying life to all who trust in him.

4) "How Can You Say There Is No Resurrection?"
I Corinthians 15:12-19

In this section, Paul is correcting a distortion of the Christian hope which has arisen in the church in Corinth. Some evidently believed that their own personal resurrection had already happened when they began to believe in Jesus. They believed that their heightened spiritual awareness of Jesus presence was evidence that they were already living in a different dimension. On this matter, Paul wants to make it clear that their expectations are too low. They do not appreciate the full picture of what God has done in raising Jesus from the dead. What is promised is not just a heightened spiritual awareness on this earth, but a completely new order of being, beyond our imagining and extending to eternity.

> *"Now if Christ is preached as raised from the dead, how can some of you day that there is no resurrection from the dead? But if there is no resurrection from the dead, then Christ is not raised; if Christ has not been raised, then our preaching is in vain and your faith is in vain. We are found to even be misrepresenting*

God. ...If it is for this life only we have hoped in Christ, we are of all men most to be pitied."

5) "First Fruits" of a New Creation
I Corinthians 15:20-28

Now, after having scolded those with low expectations, Paul gives a full picture of appropriately high expectations. In these eight verses, Paul connects the resurrection of Jesus to the whole history of salvation, to every human being, to the whole universe, to the end of time and beyond time. The God who created the world, who loved us even when we rejected his love, who raised Jesus from death is the same God who will refashion a new creation in the fullness of time. The resurrection of Jesus is the "first fruits" of God's universal harvest of all creatures, all spiritual forces and all creation,

> *"But in fact Christ has been raised from the dead, the first fruits of those who have fallen asleep. For as by a man came death, by a man has come also the resurrection from the dead. For as in Adam all die, so also in Christ shall all be made alive. But each in his own order: Christ, the first fruits, then at his coming those who belong to Christ. Then comes the end, when he delivers the kingdom to God the Father after destroying every rule and authority and power. For he must reign until he has put all his enemies under his feet. The last enemy to be destroyed is death. ... When all things are subjected to him, then the Son himself will also be subjected to him who put all things under him, that God may be everything to everyone."*

In light of this vision of what God has done in the death and resurrection of Christ, and what God intends to do with the whole created order, we can see why the diminished Christian vision "for this life only" is just not enough. The promise is of a redeemed creation in which God's sublime love, perfected justice, and unfailing mercy will be "everything to everyone."

6) "How Are The Dead Raised? What Kind of Body?"
Cor. 15:35-44

All of the New Testament writers grope for the right words to explain an inexplicable mystery. The resurrection can never be adequately explained in ordinary human language because it is outside of normal human language and experience. In this passage, Paul uses the language of agriculture. He uses the analogy of the seed buried in the ground which gives life to the plant. (Please note that this passage is symbolic and not intended to be a textbook statement of scientific truth.)

Jesus' Resurrection

> *"But someone will ask, 'How are the dead raised? With what kind of body will they come? ...What you sow does not come to life until it dies. What you sow is not the body that is to be, but a bare kernel, perhaps of wheat or some other grain. But God gives it a body as he has chosen, and to each kind of seed its own body."*

The point here is that there is dissimilarity between the seed that is sown (and dies) and the glorious plant that arises. One is a seemingly lifeless shell, the other a life-giving plant infinitely more beautiful and vibrant than the seed. At the same time, there is a distinct similarity between the specific plant and the originating seed "which God has chosen." He then connects the seed/plant analogy to the resurrection.

> *"So it is with the resurrection from the dead. What is sown is perishable. What is raised is imperishable. It is sown in dishonor. It is raised in glory. It is sown in weakness. It is raised in power. It is sown a physical body. It is raised a spiritual body.*

He then applies this physical/spiritual contrast to Adam as "the man of dust" and Christ as the "man of heaven."

> *"Just as we have borne the image of the man of dust, we shall also bear the image of the man of heaven. I tell you this brethren, flesh and blood cannot inherit the kingdom of God, nor does the perishable inherit the imperishable.*
>
> *Lo, I tell you a mystery. We shall not all sleep, but we shall be changed, in a moment, in the twinkling of an eye, at the last trumpet. For the trumpet will sound, and the dead will be raised imperishable, and we shall be changed. For the perishable nature must put on the imperishable, and this mortal nature must put on immortality."*
>
> I Corinthians 15:49-53

The resurrection body (of Jesus and of everyone else whom God will raise from the dead) is a "spiritual body." In other words, there is some similarity of character (and perhaps of shape and features) between the "earthly" body and the "spiritual" body, but the spiritual body will be of infinitely greater "glory." It will not be subjected to the trials, pain, diseases and limitations of the earthly body. At the same time, it will be a distinct and personal "somebody." The promise is of a "communion" with God – a fellowship of individual spiritual persons with a personal God. We shall be changed into something infinitely greater than we are now – not as drops of water dissolved into an impersonal ocean of "Being." Resurrection is eternal "somebody-ness" – not eternal "nobody-ness."

7) "Death Is Swallowed Up In Victory"
I Corinthians 15:54-58

Paul then concludes by again connecting the resurrection of Jesus (and of all others whom God will raise) to the Old Testament prophets, Isaiah 25:8 and Hosea 13:14.

> *"When the perishable puts on the imperishable, and the mortal puts on immortality, then shall come to pass the saying that is written: 'Death is swallowed up in victory,*
>
> *O death, where is thy victory? O death, where is thy sting?' The sting of death is sin, and the power of sin is the law. But thanks be to God who gives us the victory through our Lord Jesus Christ."*

The heart of the Christian faith, then and now, is the unshakable conviction that God has overcome sin and death and that we have a share in God's victory. Trusting in this victory of God, we can have the strength, courage and hope to face every challenge and trial on this earth. In the concluding section of this chapter, we will explore this further.

III. What Difference Does The Resurrection Make?

What difference does Jesus life, death and resurrection have with my living and dying? If we believe that God has defeated sin and death in the resurrection of Jesus, and that we can share in God's victory over sin and death, then how shall we respond? In fact, the entire New Testament is an extended answer to this question. The general purpose of the New Testament is summarized in one verse from the Gospel of John (20:31): ***"These things are written that you may believe that Jesus is the Christ, the Son of God, and that believing you may have life in his name."*** The following is a brief summary of what kind of life we should have, and live, "in his name."

1) Courage in the Face of Death

The immediate effect of Jesus' resurrection was the transformation of his followers. After his death, they huddled together in fear – fear of being killed like their leader. But their fear was turned to joy, and then courage.

Jesus' Resurrection

"But the angel said to the women, 'Do not be afraid; for I know that you seek Jesus who was crucified. He is not here. He is risen as he said'." Matthew 28:5-6

"And behold, Jesus met them and said 'Hail!' And they came and took hold of his feet and worshipped him. Then Jesus said to them 'Do not be afraid.'" Matthew 28:9-10

"On the evening of that day (Easter) the first day of the week, the doors being shut for fear of the Jews, Jesus came and stood among them and said 'Peace be with you'." John 20:19

"And Jesus himself stood among them. But they were frightened... And Jesus said to them "why are you troubled? And why do questionings arise in your hearts? See my hands and my feet, that it is I myself. ...and they disbelieved for joy."
Luke 24:36-40

When reading the accounts of the resurrection, we see that the disciples are slow to "get it." It takes them some considerable time for their minds and hearts to catch up with what their eyes see. But after they did "get it", their fear turned into a miraculous courage as they told anyone who would listen about the wonderful thing that God had done. The book of Acts has several accounts of the disciples willingly face beating, imprisonment and death to bring the good news to the whole world. In Acts 2, we see Peter boldly proclaiming the resurrection to large crowds in Jerusalem – the same crowds and leaders who put Jesus to death a few weeks earlier. In Acts 4 and again in Acts 5, Peter and others are arrested and imprisoned but refuse to abandon their mission. In Acts 7, Stephen willingly suffers death to tell others about the risen Christ. Similarly, Paul willingly faced prison, beatings and death rather than fail to tell others the wonderful truth of the Resurrection. (See Acts chapters 18 through 21 and 23 through 28.) Although not recorded in the Bible, we know from early Church historians that Peter, Paul, James and most of the first apostles willingly suffered a martyr's death. What motivated this courage? It is best summarized in the following eloquent and powerful passage from Paul's letter to the Romans:

"If God is for us, who can be against us? He who did not spare his own Son but gave him up for us all, will he not also give us all things with him? ... Who shall separate us from the love of Christ? Shall tribulation, or distress, or persecution, or famine, or nakedness or peril or sword? ... No, in all these things we are

> *more than conquerors through him who loved us. For I am sure that neither death, nor life, nor angels, nor principalities, nor things present, nor things to come, nor powers, nor height, nor depth, nor anything else in all creation, will be able to separate us from the love of God in Christ Jesus our Lord."*
>
> Romans 8:31-32,35,37-39

This powerful passage has been on the lips of countless Christians as they looked in to face of death – either their own or the death of someone they love. If we trust in the God who raised Jesus from the dead, we have nothing to fear from death – or "anything else in all creation." To those without faith in Christ, death seems like the ultimate enemy. But for those who believe in God's power and intention to raise the dead, death is never the last word. Resurrection life is the last word.

2) Hope in the Face of Adversity

Every human being faces adversity in this earthly life: some of us more than others; some sooner and some later. We are plagued by losses of every kind, personal and material; mental and physical diseases for which there is no cure; violence from other individuals and the organized violence of war; relationships that bring more pain than pleasure; insurmountable obstacles to our hopes and dreams, economic setbacks and so on. The question is not "if" we will experience adversity, but "when" and "how" we will face it and deal with it. Paul was very familiar with adversity, as he relates in the following passage in which he is engaged in a bragging contest with others who have cast doubts on his seriousness.

> *"Five times I have received at the hands of the Jews, the forty lashes less one. Three times I have been beaten with rods; once I was stoned. Three times I have been shipwrecked; a night and a day I have been adrift at sea; on frequent journeys, in danger from rivers, danger from robbers, danger from my own people, danger from the Gentiles, danger in the city, danger in the wilderness, danger at sea, danger from false brethren; in toil and hardship, through many a sleepless night, in hunger and thirst, often without food..."*
>
> 2 Corinthians 11:24-27

Even though Paul was very familiar with adversity, he was never undone by it. His unswerving conviction was that all adversity provided a context in which God's mercy and strength could be known more deeply. Through our connection to Jesus Christ, the power of resurrection hope is able to strengthen us to meet any adversity. And therefore, while no one should seek out adversity, when it comes we should see it as an opportunity to trust God more deeply.

> *"Therefore, since we are justified by faith, we have peace with God through our Lord Jesus Christ. Through him we have obtained access to this grace in which we stand, and we rejoice in the hope of sharing the glory of God. More than that, we rejoice in our sufferings, knowing that suffering produces endurance; and endurance produces character, and character produces hope, and hope does not disappoint us, because God's love has been poured into our hearts through the Holy Spirit which he has given us."*
>
> Romans 5:1-5

3) Forgiveness in the Face of Crippling Guilt and Shame

Every human being has a conscience; and therefore every one of us experiences guilt. Some apparently have more (or less) sensitive consciences than others. And frankly, some of us have more good reasons for feeling guilty than others. Guilt is good and healthy to the extent that it helps us to recognize when we have done something wrong and to want to change our behavior in the future. But guilt can also be unhealthy and debilitating as well. Any pastor, psychiatrist, bar-tender or member of Alcoholics Anonymous can tell a hundred stories of people crippled by guilt and shame.

Another immediate effect of the resurrection of Jesus was the (delegated) power to proclaim God's forgiveness of sins. The miracle of the resurrection is God's victory over death and a sign of God's willingness to forgive our sin. On Easter night, the risen Jesus appeared to the disciples in their hiding place. *"Jesus said to them again 'Peace be with you. As the Father has sent me, even so I send you'. And he breathed on them and said, 'Receive the Holy Spirit. If you forgive the sins of any, they are forgiven. If you retain the sins of any, they are retained'."* (John 20:21-23)

Sometime later, Jesus applies this forgiveness to Peter in a direct and personal way. Peter was someone who had at least three good reasons to feel guilty. He had denied Jesus three times on the night of Jesus death. He was a coward of the worst sort and he knew it. He was unworthy to lead his fellow disciples. In the Gospel of John (chapter 21) Jesus gives him three opportunities to receive the forgiving love of God and to rebuild the relationship with Jesus. At the end of each of three exchanges, Jesus tells him:*"Feed my lambs"*, *"Tend my sheep" "Feed my sheep."* In other words, "Peter, your failures are forgiven. Now go do what I have called you to do."

The letter to Hebrews makes a similar point by connecting Jesus' resurrection to priest's role in the Old Testament "Day of Atonement": *"Since then we have a great high priest who has passed through the heavens, Jesus the Son of God, let us hold fast to our confession. For we have not a high priest who is unable to sympathize with our weaknesses, but one who was tempted in every way as we are yet did not sin. Let us then with confidence draw near to the throne of grace, that we may receive mercy and find grace to help in time of need."* (Hebrews 4:14-16)

The point of all of these passages, and many more in the New Testament, is that God has forgiven sin and defeated death in the resurrection of Jesus. All who believe in, and trust, God's power and willingness to forgive should receive the gift for themselves and live accordingly. This does not mean we should never feel guilty. There are many times when guilt is helpful (in the same way that physical pain helps us to identify, and hopefully eliminate, the harmful source. When we feel appropriate guilt for wrongs we have done, we can and should admit our sins, ask for God's forgiveness and for the courage and strength to change. Then (like Peter) we should get on with the mission God has given us to do.

4) Life in Christ – A New Creation

The story of the Bible is the story of redemption. The God of the Bible is a redeeming God. The world is created "very good", but we have made a mess of it and God is cleaning up the mess. The resurrection of Jesus is the ultimate sign of God's intention to redeem fallen humanity and re-create a broken world. Those who believe in, and attach themselves to, Jesus Christ in faith share in God's recreating power.

> *"From now on therefore, we regard no one from a human point of view; even though we once regarded Christ from a human point of view, we regard him thus no longer. Therefore if anyone is in Christ, he is a new creation; the old has passed away, behold, the new has come."*
>
> 2 Corinthians 5:16-17

When a person commits herself (or himself) to Christ in faith, there is a "marriage of spirits" so to speak. We are "in Christ" – wrapped up in his arms forever. Jesus makes his home in our soul. His life becomes our life, and our life becomes his. His defeat of death and eternal destiny become ours. His personality infuses ours with a new life and a new set of priorities. Christ is alive in heaven and he is also alive on earth in the people who have received him in faith. This "new creation" reality is a great joy, a lifelong vocation and a source of profound humility.

> *"For what we preach is not ourselves, but Jesus Christ as Lord, with ourselves as your servants for Jesus' sake. For it is the God who said 'Let light shine out of darkness', who has shone into our hearts to give the knowledge of his glory in the face of Christ. But we have this treasure in earthen vessels to show that the transcendent power belongs to God and not to us. ...always carrying in our body the death of Jesus, so that the life of Jesus may also be manifested in our bodies.*
> 2 Corinthians 4:5-7,10

Living this "new creation" reality is a matter of "already – but not yet." We begin to experience something of the life of heaven on this earth, but we have to wait for the final consummation. We begin to see the evidence of God's redeeming work on this earth, but we have to wait for the completion of it in the fullness of God's time.

> *"For this slight momentary affliction is preparing us for an eternal weight of glory beyond all comparison, because we look not to the things that are seen but to the things that are not seen; for the things that are seen are transient, but the things that are unseen are eternal. For we know that if this earthly tent we live in is destroyed, we have a building from God, a house not made with hands, eternal in the heavens.*
> 2 Corinthians 4:17 – 5:1

IV. Modern Criticisms of the Resurrection Accounts

As we have seen in this chapter, the resurrection of Jesus is the foundation of the New Testament and fulfills the expectation of the Old Testament. Several contemporary authors have challenged the centrality of the resurrection. Few publicly deny the resurrection, but many downplay its importance to the point of *de facto* denial. In conclusion, let us briefly consider three modern criticisms found in several scholarly and popular books.

Criticism # 1: The resurrection is really not that important. It's controversial. It can't be proven. Focusing on the resurrection encourages a "pie in the sky" escapist spirituality. Therefore, we should focus on Jesus' teaching and example instead. The important thing about Jesus was his teaching and his example of inclusive love; and by following his teaching and imitating his example we experience an elevated spiritual awareness in this earthly life. Beyond that, we shouldn't expect much. If the resurrection happened, it's "icing on the cake", so to speak, but we should pay more attention to the cake.

Response to Criticism # 1: While it is a very good thing to follow the teaching and example of Jesus and to become more spiritually aware in so doing, this minimalist approach is a serious distortion of history and of Christian belief. If Jesus had not risen from the dead, and if his followers had not seen him alive "by many proofs" after his resurrection, and if their lives had not been irreversibly changed by this experience, then no one would have bothered to write down what Jesus taught and how he behaved. The several New Testament writers are unanimous in their conviction that God raised Jesus from the dead. They wrote their gospels and epistles because they believed that this teacher and lover of outcasts was raised from death by God and was therefore the fulfillment of all of the promises of God. They believed that his resurrection reinforced and vindicated his teaching and his example. Therefore, we must reject any false "either/or" dichotomy between believing the resurrection of Jesus and following the teaching and example of Jesus. Paul's ancient admonition is as relevant today as it was then: *"If it is for this life only we have hoped in Christ, we are of all men most to be pitied."*

Criticism # 2: There were many self-proclaimed Jewish "messiahs" in Jesus' time. They were all martyrs for Israel's national autonomy. Jesus was no more, or less, important than any of them. He was a good man who died for a good cause, and nothing more.

Response to Criticism # 2: The first Christians also believed that Jesus was the Messiah because they saw him alive after they saw him die. There were scores of self-proclaimed Jewish "messiahs" before, during, and immediately after, the lifetime of Jesus. Each of them had an enthusiastic group of followers. Many of them were also crucified by the Romans. In every case, their movement died when the leader died. Why? Because a crucified messiah is a failed messiah. Only one crucified Messiah was remembered after his death. Only one attracted more followers immediately after his death than during his lifetime. Only one inspired his followers to go throughout the world to tell others. The resurrection is central and essential to the biblical witness of who Jesus is, why he came and what God has done in and through him.

Criticism # 3: The New Testament authors invented the resurrection accounts to bolster Jesus' reputation as the true Messiah and promote themselves and their own claim to authority in the early Christian movement. The resurrection stories are self-promoting propaganda and nothing more.

Response to Criticism # 3: In response to this assertion of self-aggrandizement, one needs to ask, "If the early disciples were propagandists seeking to build their own authority, why didn't they do a better job of self-promotion?" When we read Paul's epistles, his several unattractive personality quirks are vividly on display, and from them we learn about more early church "dirty laundry" than most of us really want to know. Why didn't some propagandist editor remove these unedifying passages? When we read the gospels, the apostles do not look like super-heroes of faith. Peter is portrayed as bombastic and impetuous, always promising more than he can deliver. Worse, he is a three-time coward when he faces the real test of faith. James and John, whom Jesus calls "sons of thunder", are often portrayed as narcissistic knuckleheads. Jesus often scolds the apostles for being so slow to "get it" when he's trying to teach them. This is especially true in the resurrection accounts. In Luke, Jesus scolds them for being "foolish men and slow of heart to believe all that the prophets have spoken" (about the resurrection). In Mark, Jesus "upbraids them for their unbelief and hardness of heart because they did not believe those that saw him after he had risen." In Matthew, "some doubted" when they saw him raised from the dead. If the authors and editors of the New Testament were self-serving and self-promoting propagandists, why didn't someone clean up these passages to make the disciples look more heroic and faithful?

Finally and most importantly, the gospels all tell us that it was the women who were the first witnesses to the resurrection. This is significant because, in the ancient Roman and Jewish culture, women were considered unreliable witnesses and their testimony was not admissible in a court of law. If the New Testament authors were seeking to write propaganda to bolster Jesus' reputation and their own authority, why didn't they give men (instead of women) the central role in telling the most important truth of all? Why admit that the women were the first to "get it" and that the men were slow to believe? The only possible answer is that they were telling the truth, as embarrassing as it was. In sum, the New Testament has the ring of truth because it is obviously not a polished propaganda piece. The first disciples were as frail, fickle and fallible as we are. They were just as confused and bewildered as most of us are when we try to understand, believe and explain the resurrection. And they weren't ashamed to admit it.

Summary

The expectation of God raising the dead was an "emerging belief" in the faith of the people of Israel throughout the Old Testament period. It was embedded in, and grew out of, several converging beliefs about God's purpose in history, his creative and life-giving power and his promise to protect, deliver and redeem his chosen people. Jesus' resurrection is the culmination of God's purpose in redeeming Israel and all humanity. Those who believe in Jesus' resurrection are connected to him in faith and are part of God's new creation. Belief in the resurrection is essential to what we believe God was doing with Israel all along, what he was doing through Jesus, and what he will do with us, now and in eternity. While it is a good and holy thing to obey the teaching of Jesus and to follow his example, this is not the full picture. Christianity without the resurrection is an impoverished substitute for the real thing.

QUESTIONS FOR DISCUSSION AND REFLECTION

1) During the Iraq war of 1991 (called "Desert Storm") there were news reports of a mother who received notice that her son (an American soldier) had been killed in battle. A month later, she received a phone call from her son. When she first heard his voice, she refused to believe it was really her son. She thought that someone was playing a cruel joke. Only after an hour's conversation, during which time the son told her the exact details of family events that only he could have known, did she begin to allow herself to believe that her son was really alive. Try to get inside this woman's heart and mind. Why would she have been so slow to believe?

In Luke 24:41, the disciples "disbelieved for joy and wondered" when they met the risen Lord. In Mark 16:14, Jesus scolds the disciples for "their unbelief and hardness of heart because they did not believe those that saw him after he had risen." What are the similarities between these gospel stories and the woman who lost her son? How does this relate to your own life? Have there been times when you thought something was "too good to be true"? Times when you "disbelieved for joy"? Times when you have had a very hard time believing in the resurrection of Jesus (or of anyone else)?

2) Paul says, *"(W)e rejoice in our sufferings, knowing that suffering produces endurance; and endurance produces character, and character produces hope, and hope does not disappoint us, because God's love has been poured into our hearts through the Holy Spirit which he has given us."* (Romans 5:3-5)

Have there been times in your life when things seemed so bad that you lost all hope? How did you get through it? How do you respond to the statement that we should "rejoice in our sufferings"? Do these words seem delusional? ... realistic?

JESUS' RESURRECTION

Now read the two verses that immediately precede these verses quoted above: *"Therefore, since we are justified by faith, we have peace with God through our Lord Jesus Christ. Through him we have obtained access to this grace in which we stand, and we rejoice in the hope of sharing the glory of God."*

What difference does belief in the resurrection make in your understanding of suffering, endurance, character and hope?

3) Every construction site in the world has a fence built around it. Why? To keep curious observers from getting hurt and interrupting workers. People of every age are fascinated by new buildings being built. It is awe-inspiring to see something new rising from the ground – a new creation.

Paul says *"If anyone is in Christ, he (or she) is a new creation, the old has passed away, behold the new has come."* (2 Corinthians 5:17) Have you ever experienced this reality of something new being created in you? In another person? Have you ever experienced the power of another person changing your perspective and priorities – a friend, a teacher or someone you love? Have you ever considered Jesus to be a formative person in your own life?

PERSONAL REFLECTION

Read the story of "doubting Thomas" in John 20:24-29. What were his objections to believing in Jesus? What caused him to begin to "doubt his doubts"? What changed him from "doubting Thomas" to "believing Thomas"? Reflect on his journey of doubt and faith. How does it relate to your own doubts, fears and moments of clarity?

The passage closes with the words "Blessed are those who have not seen and yet believe." Take some time in prayer to visualize the risen Lord appearing to you as he did to Thomas. Ask him in prayer for the grace to extend your hand to his hand and to receive the experience his presence in your life.

BIBLE MEMORY VERSE

"For this slight momentary affliction is preparing us for an eternal weight of glory beyond all comparison, because we look not to the things that are seen but to the things that are not seen; for the things that are seen are transient, but the things that are unseen are eternal. For we know that if this earthly tent we live in is destroyed, we have a building from God, a house not made with hands, eternal in the heavens."

2 Corinthians 4:17 – 5:1

Chapter 11

MATTHEW: THE MESSIAH-KING

Main focus of this chapter: Matthew's unique portrait of Jesus as the one who fulfills Old Testament expectations

Introduction

Each of the four gospels has a three-fold purpose:

1) To tell the story of Jesus in order to enable later generations of Christians to pass on the faith throughout the world.

2) To teach believers apostolic norms for following Christ and living the true Christian life.

3) To persuade non-Christians that Jesus is the Savior of the world.

As we noted in Chapter 9, each of the four gospel accounts (Matthew, Mark, Luke and John) portrays a different aspect of who Jesus is and what his mission means for us.

The Gospel according to Matthew portrays Jesus as the long-awaited Messiah-King. After many centuries of foreign domination, the Jewish people were expecting a Messiah to cast out the Romans occupation army and reestablish the earthly kingdom of Israel and the dynasty of King David. More than any of the other accounts of the gospel, Matthew was intent on persuading Jewish people that Jesus is the One they have been waiting for.

Matthew continually emphasizes that Jesus is the fulfillment of Israel's hopes. He cites Old Testament references twenty-nine times. On thirteen occasions, he uses the following expression to refer to some events in Jesus' life: *"This was to fulfill what the Lord has spoken by the prophet...."*

But Matthew also wants the followers of Jesus (whether Jew or non-Jew) to understand that Jesus is a different kind of King than many were expecting. He did not come to conquer with military might, nor to reestablish Jewish sovereignty over a small piece of real estate. Instead, he came to teach about, and make available, God's eternal and heavenly kingdom. He came to establish a kingdom of love and justice which begins in the human heart and is to be lived out "on earth as it is in heaven." This kingdom will be completely fulfilled only at the end of time. But believers are called to make this kingdom visible in their own lives here and now.

Matthew's purpose is three fold:

1) to persuade Jewish people that Jesus is the promised Messiah-King.
2) to tell the story of the King who will judge and rule all creation for all eternity.
3) to teach believers how to live faithfully in the kingdom in which Jesus is King.

I. Birth of the Messiah-King

1) Genealogy
(read Matthew 1:1-17)

> "Abraham was the father of Isaac' and Isaac the father of Jacob, and Jacob the father of Judah, and Judah the father of Perez and Zerah by Tamar, and Perez the father of Hezron, and Hezron the father of Ram..... and Matthan the father of Jacob, and Jacob the father of Joseph the husband of Mary, of whom Jesus was born who is called Christ."

> "So all of the generations from Abraham to David were fourteen generations, and from David to the deportation to Babylon fourteen generations, and from the deportation to Babylon to the Christ fourteen generations."

Many modern readers find this section extremely boring and wonder why Matthew bothered to write it down. Why spend all that space discussing dead relatives? However, Matthew is making a very important point about Jesus' identity: He is "the son of David, the son of Abraham." In other words, Jesus is the fulfillment of the promises made to both (Abraham, a "blessing to all peoples of the earth"; David, and "everlasting kingdom"). Next Matthew tells us (verse 17) that Israel's history is divided into three sections (Abraham to David, David to the exile in Babylon, the exile in Babylon to Christ) each consisting of fourteen generations. This is another way of saying that Jesus came according to the definite prearranged plan of God. Jesus is the final chapter in the drama of God's work of salvation.

2) A Notable Birth
(read Matthew 1:18-2:23)

Here we have information recorded only in Matthew.

1) His Name: (1:21) *"you shall call his name Jesus (in Hebrew: "Jeshua" or "Joshua") for he will save his people from their sins."* This recalls Joshua (the successor of Moses) who conquered the promised land. Jesus who provided entrance into the greater promised land – eternal life in the kingdom of heaven.

2) Visit of the Wise Men (2:1-12) His kingship was recognized by (non-Jewish) "wise men from the East" emphasizing that Jesus came to bring salvation to all people - not only to the Jews.

3) Persecution by Herod, Exile and Return from Egypt: (2:13-23) This emphasizes Jesus' identity with Moses and with Israel as a whole (persecuted by Pharaoh, exiled and returned to promised land). This fulfills the prophecy, *"out of Egypt I have called my son."*

II. The Five Teachings of the Kingdom

There are five separate sections in Matthew's gospel in which Jesus teaches at length about some aspects of the kingdom of heaven. (Note that, unlike the other gospel authors, Matthew almost always uses the term "kingdom of heaven" rather than "kingdom of God." This reflects his sensitivity to his intended Jewish readers who would have been reluctant to speak the name of God directly, and preferred the more circumspect way of speaking about the divine reality.)

1) The Sermon on the Mount (chapters 5, 6 and 7)
2) The Instruction of the Twelve Apostles (chapter 10)
3) The Parables of the Kingdom (chapter 13)
4) The Teaching on Forgiveness (chapter 18)
5) The Teaching on the End of The Age (chapters 24 and 25)

1) The Sermon on the Mount
(read Matthew chapters 5, 6 and 7)

The most widely known portions of this first teaching are "The Beatitudes" and the "Lord's Prayer." The word "Beatitudes" takes its name from the first line in each of the statements: "blessed are you when...."

Matthew: The Messiah-King

The Beatitudes (5:2-12)

Blessed are the poor in spirit, for theirs is the kingdom of heaven.
Blessed are those who mourn, for they shall be comforted.
Blessed are the meek, for they shall inherit the earth.
Blessed are those who hunger and thirst for righteousness, for they shall be satisfied.
Blessed are the merciful, for they shall obtain mercy.
Blessed are the pure in heart, for they shall see God.
Blessed are the peacemakers, for they shall be called sons of God.
Blessed are those who are persecuted for righteousness sake,
for theirs is the kingdom of heaven.
Blessed are you, when men revile you and persecute you and utter all kinds of evil against you falsely on my account. Rejoice and be glad, for your reward is great in heaven, for so men persecuted the prophets who were before you.

The Beatitudes have three dimensions. They are:

1) Attitudes, or dispositions of the spirit, which are needed to make oneself available to the kingdom of heaven.

2) Actions and ways of relating to others which help to make God's kingdom visible and tangible in our day to day life.

3) Promises of happiness which we can experience to a certain degree in this life, but which are completely fulfilled in heaven.

The Lord's Prayer (6:9-13)

Our Father who art in heaven, hallowed be thy name.
Thy kingdom come, thy will be done, on earth as it is in heaven.
Give us this day our daily bread; and forgive us our debts as we forgive our debtors.
And lead us not into temptation, but deliver us from evil.

The Lord's Prayer is short and simple, yet profound. In saying it, we acknowledge the sovereignty and holiness of God, our responsibility to make God's kingdom come alive in our daily life, and we ask God to give us the strength to do so. It is a daily reminder that we are to be dedicated to God's kingdom "on earth (in my life) as it is in heaven."

2) Instructions of the Twelve Apostles
(Read chapter 10)

In this chapter, Jesus teaches his "inner circle" of twelve apostles and sends them out to be heralds of the kingdom. He gives the apostles authority over unclean spirits and the ability to heal diseases. In so doing, he has given them a portion of his own miraculous power to demonstrate the kingdom of heaven.

> " Go nowhere among the Gentiles, and enter no town of the Samaritans, but go rather to the lost sheep of the house of Israel. And preach as you go saying, 'The kingdom of heaven is at hand'. Heal the sick. Raise the dead, cleanse lepers, cast out demons... Behold I send you out as sheep in the midst of wolves; so be wise a serpents and gentle as doves."
>
> Mt. 10:5-8 and 16

In this passage, Jesus instructs the apostles not to go to the Samaritans or the Gentiles but only to the lost sheep of the house of Israel." It was only after his resurrection that he told them to "go into all the world and preach the gospel to all nations." Evidently, he wanted them to concentrate their efforts on their own people in this early stage of his ministry. He did not feel that they were yet ready, or able, to effectively communicate the message of the kingdom until after the resurrection. Then, they had the full understanding of what God would accomplish through Jesus and the power of the Holy Spirit to enable them to preach effectively to the Gentiles.

3) The Parables of the Kingdom
(Read chapter 13)

"The kingdom of heaven is:

Like a man who sowed good seed in his field; but while he was sleeping, his enemies came and sowed weeds between the wheat. ...

Like a grain of mustard seed...the smallest of seeds, but when it is grown it is the greatest of shrubs and becomes a tree...

Like leaven which a woman took and hid in three measures of flour...

Like a treasure hidden in a field...

Like a merchant in search of fine pearls...

Like a net which was thrown into the sea and gathered fish of every kind..."

Most of the people whom Jesus taught were not educated in abstract thinking. They were simple farmers and fishermen. Therefore, Jesus taught them about God's kingdom in terms and symbols they could understand. In these "parables of the kingdom", Jesus uses the language of planting seeds, harvesting crops and catching fish to teach about the need to make a decision to respond to the kingdom of heaven. People are like soil into which seeds are planted, some are receptive to the kingdom of heaven and some are not. Some are like good crops and some are like weeds. Some are like good fish and some like bad. Those who reject or neglect the Kingdom of God will be rejected at the close of the age – thrown into a furnace of fire. There is nothing delicate about these images and nothing that a simple farmer would not have understood. The point is, we need to make a decision for or against the kingdom of heaven and the decision has serious consequences. It should also be pointed out that the parable of the vineyard (in chapter 20) is in tension with the severity of the parables in chapter 13. It emphasizes the unbounded mercy of God who is always ready to receive someone into the kingdom, even if they come at the eleventh hour.

4) **Teaching on Forgiveness**
   (read chapter 18)

> *Peter said "Lord, how often shall my brother sin against me and I forgive him? As many as seven times?' And Jesus said to him, "I do not say seven times, but seventy times seven. Therefore the kingdom of heaven may be compared to a king who wished to settle accounts with his servants. ... The servant fell on his knees, imploring him, 'Lord have patience with me, and I will pay you everything'. And out of pity for him the lord of the servant released him and forgave him the debt. But that same servant, as he went out, came upon one of his fellow servants who owed him a hundred denrii; and seizing him by the throat he said, 'Pay what you owe'. ... (When the king heard of this) he said "you wicked servant! I forgave you all that debt because you besought me; and should you not have had mercy on your fellow servant as I had mercy on you? And in his anger, the lord delivered him to the jailers until he should pay all his debt. So also my heavenly Father will do to every one of you if you do not forgive your brother from your heart."*

This teaching focuses on relationships between believers in the kingdom of heaven. It is especially clear on the need for forgiveness. Peter asks how many times one may reasonable ask to forgive a fellow believer who has harmed you and repented. Jesus responds with an outlandish number ("Seventy times seven") and reminds us (with another parable) that the foundation of the kingdom is God's unmerited forgiveness of us sinners. Therefore, we must be imitators of God and "forgive your brother from the heart." This parable illustrates the short phrase in the Lord's Prayer "forgive us our debts as we forgive our debtors."

5) Teaching on the End of the Age and Final Judgment
(Read chapters 24 and 25)

> *"But at midnight, there was a cry, 'Behold, the bridegroom! Come out to meet him!' Then all of those maidens rose and trimmed their lamps. (But the foolish maidens ran out of oil and...) while they went to buy, the bridegroom came, and those who were ready went with him into the marriage feast; and the door was shut. ...Watch, therefore, for you know neither the day nor the hour."*

The emphasis of this teaching is on the end of the world as we know it and the fullness of the kingdom of heaven. We are to live as if this were to happen at any moment and not be caught unprepared like the foolish maidens who were unprepared at the moment of truth.

We are challenged to live every moment of our lives as if the kingdom were coming today. We are to pray and work, for God's kingdom come, and God's will to be done in our lives, in our family, our nation and our global community as it is in heaven. And then, he gives us a picture of what heaven on earth looks like:

> *"When the Son of man comes in his glory, and all the angels with him, then he will sit on his glorious throne. Before him will be gathered all the nations, and he will separate them one from another as a shepherd separates the sheep from the goats, and he will place the sheep at his right and the goats at the left. Then the King will say to those at his right hand, 'Come, O blessed of my Father, inherit the kingdom prepared for you from the foundation of the world; for I was hungry and you gave me food, I was thirsty and you gave me drink, I was a stranger and you welcomed me, I was naked and you clothed me, I was in prison and you came to me. Then the righteous will answer him, 'Lord, when did we see thee hungry and feed thee, or thirsty and give thee drink? And when did we see thee a stranger and welcome thee, or naked and clothe thee? And when did we see thee sick*

and in prison and visit thee? And the King will answer them, 'Truly, I say to you, as you did it to one of the least of these my brethren, you did it to me.'"

Matthew 25:31-40

And then a picture of what hell on earth looks like:

"Then he will say to those on his left hand, 'Depart from me, you cursed, into the eternal fire prepared for the devil and his angels; for I was hungry and you gave me no food, I was thirsty and you gave me no drink...Truly I say to you, as you did it not for one of the least of my brethren, you did it not to me."

Matthew 25:41-46

In these passages, Jesus identifies himself in a dual role. He is, first of all the judge of history and king of heaven. But paradoxically, he is also uniquely present among the outcasts of history. Where can we find the master of the universe, the King of all kings, the Judge of all judges? We can find him in the faces of the hungry, the naked, the lonely, those who are sick and in prison. How can we serve to the King of all kings? By serving the lowliest of the lowly in his kingdom. How can we most deeply offend the Judge of all humanity? By denying the humanity of the "least of these, my brothers."

III. The Last Supper: Meal of the Coming Kingdom

The Last Supper was a Passover meal. Recall (from chapter 5) that the original Passover meal was:

1) Part of the substitutionary sacrifice – the Passover lamb was sacrificed to save the people from death

2) To initiate the act of salvation that God was about to perform – delivering the people of Israel from slavery to freedom

3) A commemoration for future generations of what God had done

When Jesus celebrated the Passover with his disciples on the night before he died, he gave the Passover a new meaning:

1) This meal would precede a new substitutionary sacrifice – Jesus died on the cross for the sins of all humanity; He is the "lamb of God that takes away the sins of the world.

2) This meal would initiate a new act of salvation – God would deliver us from sin and death and grant eternal life to all who believe in and follow Jesus Christ.
3) This meal would be a commemoration for future generations of Christians of what God had done for us through Jesus Christ.

(Read chapter 26:17-29)

Each one of the gospels gives an account of the Last Supper. Yet each one reports different details and gives a slightly different emphasis on this meal that was to become the central act of Christian worship – the Holy Eucharist.

Matthew emphasizes the future aspect of the Last Supper – Holy Eucharist.

> "Now as they were eating, Jesus took bread, and blessed, and broke it, and gave it to the disciples and said, 'Take, eat; this is my body.' And he took the cup, and when he had given thanks he gave it to them saying, 'drink of it, all of you; for this is my blood of the covenant, which is poured out for many for the forgiveness of sins. I tell you I shall not drink again of this fruit of the vine until that day when I drink it new with you in my Father's kingdom.'"

In this meal, Jesus is giving his friends a foretaste of the future. Those who participate in the Last Supper (and Holy Eucharist) are partaking of the banquet with the king of the future kingdom of heaven. (See Matthew 22:1-10 for a parable on a related theme.)

IV. Death of the Messiah King

For most people, death is the end of a career. For Jesus, it was the fulfillment of his career. Jesus' suffering (traditionally called "the passion") and his death and resurrection are the climax of his mission on earth. They demonstrate the power of God at work through Jesus. Again, each of the gospel authors gives us different details and a different emphasis on the passion, death, and resurrection of Jesus Christ.

Matthew's emphasis is on Jesus' authority as king and judge of all human history. His death (and resurrection) demonstrate that the powers of the kingdoms and governments of this world have no final authority over him.

(Read 26:30 – 27:54)

Matthew: The Messiah-King

After the Last Supper Jesus experiences what is traditionally called "the Agony in the Garden" (26:36-46). During this time, he asks the Father that he be spared of the coming ordeal ("if possible, let this cup pass from me"), but through prayer, he knows that this is the Father's will and the fulfillment of his mission. He willingly consents to go to his death ("but nevertheless, not as I will, but as thou wilt"). From this point on, Jesus knows that the kingdom of God will be triumphant in his death and goes forward trusting in his Father's love.

In the scenes that follow, the power of this world cannot undo Jesus' confidence in the Father. When confronted with the soldiers, he shows no fear (26:53-56). When threatened by the Jewish religious authorities, he speaks of his relationship to the Father and of his authority in the coming kingdom (26:57-68). When taken before the Roman governor (who has power to sentence him to death) he shows no fear and refuses to be intimidated by the world's highest human authority, knowing that a greater power was behind him. After many humiliations and having been nailed to the cross with a sign announcing "the King of the Jews", Jesus hung between life and death for three hours.

And then, the moment of climax:

> *"Jesus cried out with a loud voice and yielded up his spirit. And, behold, the curtain of the temple was torn in two, from top to bottom; and the earth shook, and the rocks were split; and the tombs opened, and many bodies of saints who had fallen asleep, were raised and coming out of the tombs after his resurrection they appeared to many. When the centurion and those who were with him, keeping watch over Jesus, saw the earthquake and what took place, they were filled with awe, and said, 'Truly this was the Son of God.'"*
>
> Matthew 27:50-54

In his death, a substitutionary sacrifice offered for all humanity, the king demonstrates his power over death. The curtain in the temple (separating the "Holy of Holies" – God's Presence from the people) was torn in two. Through the death of Christ, we all have access to the holiness of God. In his death, the power of death is destroyed and the saints of the Old Testament are raised (remember the hope of resurrection for the Maccabean martyrs whom we discussed in chapter 8). Through his death, bystanders and even the pagan soldier recognize that the power of God's kingdom is at work ("Truly this was the Son of God").

V. Resurrection of the Messiah – King: "All Authority On Heaven And Earth Has Been Given To Me"

The resurrection is the final and complete triumph and vindication of Jesus' ministry. In portraying its significance, the gospel writers give different emphases. Matthew emphasizes Jesus' authority.
(Read chapter 28)

All through the gospel of Matthew, we have been reading about a King and Judge. Every king and judge has authority from some governmental power. Who or what gives Jesus the authority to rule and judge all humanity? His resurrection from the dead. Every powerful person, whether king, emperor, warrior or multi-millionaire, must come face to face with a power greater than himself or herself – death. Every earthly empire, no matter how great, must one day be "swept into the dust-bin of history." In Jesus, a greater power has been shown: the power of God over sin and death; the power of God's eternal kingdom.

The Great Commission

Jesus, in his final earthly pronouncement, delegates the authority of that kingdom to his followers.

> *"All authority on heaven and earth has been given to me. Go therefore and make disciples of all nations, baptizing them in the name of the Father, and of the Son, and of the Holy Spirit, teaching them to observe all that I have commanded you; and lo, I am with you always, to the close of the age."*
> Matthew 28:18-20

Jesus followers (then and now) have the privilege and responsibility to proclaim his eternal kingdom, to invite others into it through baptism and faith and to make disciples of all baptized persons in all nations. Jesus is a "king of hearts." He enters every willing heart and dwells there. He transforms individuals, not by external threats, but from the "inside out." He transforms the world, not by force of arms, but by the force of love. We have the promise of Jesus' presence with us and we have the authority of knowing that nothing in this world can separate us from the triumphant love of God. This passage is often called "The Great Commission." It is the "job description" of the Church for all time. When the Church neglects or forgets the Great Commission, it ceases to be what Jesus desires and commands it to be.

The Great Commission tells us:

1) Spiritual authority has been given to Jesus through his death and resurrection
2) He delegates his authority to us to do the following three things:
   a. Make disciples (followers of Jesus)
   b. Baptize people into the faith
   c. Teach all that Jesus taught
3) That he will be with us to protect, empower and guide us

QUESTIONS FOR DISCUSSION AND REFLECTION

1) The "beatitudes" (Matthew 5:1-11) are attitudes and dispositions of the spirit, which open a person to the reality of the kingdom. Try to think of a specific area of conflict or tension in your immediate experience (family, friends, co-workers, neighbors). What would it mean for you to be a "peacemaker" in that situation? What would you need to change in your attitudes and behavior to make it possible for you to be an agent of God's peace? What would it cost you to do so?

2) The Beatitudes are: attitudes of the heart, actions to others, and promises of reward in God's kingdom. A modern proverb (author unknown) teaches a similar lesson:

> Watch out for your **thoughts**, because your thoughts become your **attitudes**.
> Watch out for your **attitudes**, because your attitudes become your **words**.
> Watch out for your **words**, because your words become your **actions**.
> Watch out for your **actions**, because your actions become your **habits**.
> Watch out for your **habits**, because your habits become your **character**.
> Watch out for your **character**, because your character becomes your **destiny**."

Discuss how this proverb has been worked out in your life experience, both in positive and in negative ways.

3) Read each of the beatitudes slowly and reflect, as honestly as you can, about your own attitudes and behavior patterns. How many of the beatitudes can you recognize as being at work in your own life? Do you think it is humanly possible for anyone to live the beatitudes every day in every aspect of their lives?

4) Jesus teaches that his followers must be willing to forgive others who have hurt us as many as "seventy times seven." Do you think he is really serious about this? Does he mean that we should allow people to repeat destructive and abusive behaviors to us and others? Do you think he wants us to forgive someone even if they show no regret or do not ask for forgiveness? Why is it so difficult to forgive someone who has hurt you? Does prayer help us to do so?

PRAYER EXERCISE

Read again the parable of the king and the debtors (Matthew 18:23-35). Now think about your own life. How many times have you been unwilling to forgive someone who has hurt you. How many times have you been forgiven for similar hurts that you have inflicted on others. Take some time praying for God to help you look at your life honestly. And ask for God's help to forgive those who have hurt you.

BIBLE MEMORY VERSE

"When the Son of man comes in his glory, and all the angels with him, then he will sit on his glorious throne. Before him will be gathered all the nations, and he will separate them one from another as a shepherd separates the sheep from the goats, and he will place the sheep at his right and the goats at the left. Then the King will say to those at his right hand, 'Come, O blessed of my Father, inherit the kingdom prepared for you from the foundation of the world; for I was hungry and you gave me food, I was thirsty and you gave me drink, I was a stranger and you welcomed me, I was naked and you clothed me, I was in prison and you came to me. Then the righteous will answer him, 'Lord, when did we see thee hungry and feed thee, or thirsty and give thee drink? And when did we see thee a stranger and welcome thee, or naked and clothe thee? And when did we see thee sick and in prison and visit thee?' And the King will answer them, 'Truly, I say to you, as you did it to one of the least of these my brethren, you did it to me.'"

Matthew 25:31-40

Chapter 12

MARK:
TRIUMPH OF THE SUFFERING SERVANT

Main focus of this chapter: Mark's unique portrait of Jesus as the one who demonstrates God's love through miracles and in suffering faithfully.

Introduction

As we have seen in previous chapters, each of the four gospels is a unique portrait of Jesus Christ. Each has its own angle of vision, its own perspective and its own way of telling the story.

The Gospel according to Mark is the shortest of the gospel accounts. It is regarded by most Bible scholars to have been written before Matthew and Luke. Mark's account is a very fast paced drama. One of Marks favorite words is *"euthus"*, which is translated as "immediately." Mark uses this word at least forty times in the gospel narrative. Jesus is always going "immediately" from one action-packed event to another.

In Matthew, the emphasis is on Jesus as the Messiah King in the line of David. In Mark there are no genealogies, no angels to predict his miraculous conception or to announce his royal birth, no mention of the adoring shepherds, a jealous king or visiting Wise Men, very few prophecies of the Old Testament quoted, very few parables recorded and no record of the Sermon on the Mount.

Mark is painting a very different portrait of Jesus. Mark is telling us about the "Suffering Servant" Messiah. Matthew portrays a King who teaches and judges and rules. Mark portrays a Servant who demonstrates God's love through actions. Marks gospel begins with a quote from the prophet Isaiah:

> "The beginning of the gospel of Jesus Christ, the Son of God. As it is written in Isaiah the prophet, 'Behold, I send my messenger before they face, who shall prepare thy way; the voice of one crying in the wilderness: Prepare the way of the Lord, make his paths straight'."

This passage is quoted from the portion of Isaiah known as "The Book of the Consolation of Israel" (chapters 40 to 55). These chapters contain the four "servant songs" which we discussed in chapter 8. By beginning the gospel in this way, Mark focuses our attention upon the promises of God regarding the "Suffering Servant."

> "Surely he has borne our griefs and carried our sorrows; yet we esteemed him stricken, smitten by God, and afflicted. But he was wounded for our transgressions, he was bruised for our iniquities; upon him was the chastisement that made us whole, by his stripes we are healed. All we like sheep have gone astray; we have turned every one from his own way; and the Lord has laid on him the iniquity of us all."
>
> Isaiah 53:4-6

As we noted in chapter 8, the original message of the servant songs applied to the people of Israel – or more precisely, to those who suffered in the exile to Babylon. God had allowed them to suffer the indignities of forced relocation and exile, but God had redeemed them through suffering. After allowing the exiles to suffer for the collective unfaithfulness of their people, God restored them to the Promised Land. Mark tells us about Jesus who is the complete and final fulfillment of the ministry of the Suffering Servant. God will once again honor and redeem the suffering of his servant. God will bring salvation through the patient and faithful suffering of his Son Jesus.

Most people (in ancient times and now) have a hard time understanding why God allows suffering in the world – especially when the sufferers are faithful to God or are innocent of any wrong. We ask ourselves questions like: Why does a good and just God allow bad things to happen to good people and good things to bad people? Why be good if it doesn't keep you from harm? What good is it to be a "friend of God" if God doesn't take care of his friends? And so on.

The message of Isaiah, and even more of the gospel of Mark, is that suffering is not necessarily a sign of God's displeasure. Sometimes,being faithful to God means suffering for God's sake. Following God faithfully often means being persecuted for the love of God. God can and does work through the faithful suffering of his servants. Furthermore, the self-giving love and suffering of Jesus Christ is the instrument of God's redemption of the whole human race.

Most people (in the ancient world and now) have a hard time believing in a Messiah who suffers and dies and who, in dying destroys death, and in destroying death brings life without end. Most people have a hard time following a Messiah who demands self-giving love as a mark of true faith and the doorway to salvation. As we will see, even Jesus' family and closest followers had trouble understanding and believing Jesus' message and mission. But like it or not, this is the message of Mark's gospel. He invites everyone to believe in, follow and imitate the Suffering Servant Messiah.

Marks gospel is a "two act play." The first act (chapters 1-8) tells us who Jesus is – the Servant of God. The second act (chapters 9-16) recounts his ultimate act of suffering servanthood.

I. First Act:
The Servant of God Reveals His Identity Through Miracles

The first eight chapters of Mark tell us who Jesus is. His identity is fleshed out in what he does. Mark does not devote much space to Jesus teaching. (Matthew gives us fourteen parables; Mark gives us four). Instead, Mark focuses on miracles. Jesus performs miracles to demonstrate that God is at work in and through him. All the miracles performed by Jesus are directed to healing what is sick, restoring what is broken, bringing to life what is dead. God is at work in Jesus, restoring to perfection a world broken by sin. Jesus is the Servant of God brings God's love to bear on a sin sick world.

1) Demons Cast Out

(read Mark 1:21-34 and 5:1-19)

> *"And immediately, there was in the synagogue a man with an unclean spirit; and he cried out, 'What have you to do with us, Jesus of Nazareth? Have you come to destroy us? I know who you are, the holy one of God.' But Jesus rebuked him, saying, 'Come out of him!' And the unclean spirit, convulsing him and crying with a loud voice, came out of him. And they were all amazed, so that they questioned among themselves, saying, ' What is this, a new teaching? With authority he commands even the unclean spirits and they obey him'."*   1:23-27

> *"And the unclean spirits came out and entered the swine; and the herd, numbering about two thousand, rushed down the steep bank into the sea and were drowned in the sea."*   5:13

In these passages, Jesus demonstrates God's power over evil spirits (spiritual powers which influence human life and which are at war with God). Notice that the demons know who Jesus is even though the people do not yet understand. Jesus has God's power and authority over these powerful negative forces.

2) **Lepers Made Clean**
   (read Mark 1:40-45)

   "And a leper came to him beseeching him, and kneeling said to him, 'If you will, you can make me clean'. Moved with pity, he (Jesus) stretched out his hand, touched him and said, 'I will; be clean.' And immediately the leprosy left him, and he was clean."

Leprosy is almost unknown in the modern world. But as Jesus' time, it was widespread and dreaded disease. Not only were lepers physically impaired by the illness, but they were also outcasts from society, forced to live on the outskirts of town and beg for food. To heal such a person was to restore them to both physical health and social reintegration.

3) **Diseases Healed**
   (read Mark 2:1-12; 3:1-12; 5:21-34; 6:53-56; 7:31-37 and 8:22-26)

   "And when they got out of the boat, immediately the people recognized him, and ran about the whole neighborhood and began to bring sick people on their pallets to any place where they heard he was. And wherever he came, in villages, cities, or country, they laid the sick in the market places, and besought him that they might touch even the fringe of his garment; and as many as touched it were made well." (6:54-56)

These and many other passages demonstrate that God was working through Jesus to make whole that which was broken through illness. In all cases, these healings are a demonstration of God's power to heal and an invitation into a deeper level of spiritual health. People are healed in body in order to show them a deeper dimension of reality in God's kingdom.

4) **Calming of the Sea; Walking on Water; Feeding Thousands**
   (read Mark 4:35-41 and 6:32-51)

   "And he awoke and rebuked the wind, and said to the sea, 'Peace! Be still!' And the wind ceased, and there was a great calm. And he said to them, 'Why are you so afraid? Have you no faith?' And they were filled with awe, and said to one another, 'Who then is this, that even wind and sea obey him?'" (4:39-41)

These passages demonstrate God's power (at work in Jesus) over the forces of nature. To trust in Jesus is to trust in a power greater than any force which threatens our well-being. In Jesus, nothing can separate us from God's presence and peace and love. To trust in Jesus is to trust in God's willingness to provide for our daily bread and necessities of life.

5) Raising The Dead
(Read Mark 5:35-43)

> *"Taking the girl by the hand, he said to her, 'Talitha Cumi'; which means, 'Little girl, I say to you arise'. And immediately, the girl got up and walked."* (5:41-42)

This demonstrates God's power (at work in Jesus) over the final enemy – death. The raising of the dead girl is (like the raising of Lazarus in the gospel of John) a preview of what God will do in raising Jesus from death. In Jesus, God is demonstrating God's power and willingness to overcome sin and death. It should be noted that this miracle (like that of the raising of Lazarus) is a "restoration" not a "resurrection." The girl is restored to a normal biological life which will eventually end in death. She is not raised to eternal life without end. This miracle – great as it is- is a preview of the even greater miracle of Jesus' resurrection.

The miracles of Jesus, as remarkable as they are, are not the ultimate sign of his servanthood. They are done to demonstrate who Jesus is – the unique servant of God. The miracles are done demonstrate the power of God at work in Jesus and to invite those who experienced them into a relationship with Jesus. As we read along in the gospel, it slowly begins to dawn on Jesus' followers that he is somebody special, but they still do not completely understand his identity. Therefore, the culmination of Act 1 is Peter's recognition of Jesus' true identity.

II. The Turning Point of Mark's Gospel: Peter's Confession/ Peter's Confusion
(Read Mark 8:27-33)

> *"Peter answered him, 'You are the Christ'. ...And Peter took him and began to rebuke him. But turning, he rebuked Peter, and said, 'Get behind me Satan! For you are not on the side of God but of men.' "*

Up to this point, Peter and the other disciples had been following Jesus for a long time, perhaps a couple of years. They have observed his many miracles and signs of God's kingdom; they have heard his many teachings about the kingdom of God. Now Jesus is about to give his followers a "mid-term exam." He asks them what other people are saying about him, and they give him various answers. But he presses them for a more personal response: "Don't tell me what everybody else thinks. What do you think. Who do you say I am."

Peter answers on behalf of the other disciples" "You are the Christ." ("Christ" means "the anointed One" or "the Messiah"). We call this "Peter's Confession." Peter was inspired by God to understand Jesus' true identity. And yet, ironically, Peter did not understand at all. Jesus begins to explain that he must suffer and die as part of his mission as the Messiah. Peter "rebuked" Jesus for talking this way. Peter thought it was great to follow a miracle working Messiah, but he did not want to hear about his hero and leader suffering and dying. Peter's confusion was shared by all of the disciples. They could not comprehend a suffering Messiah.

This passage recounting "Peter's Confession" and "Peter's Confusion" is the dramatic turning-point in Mark's gospel. Up to this point, the emphasis has been on Jesus' miracles and mighty acts. From this point forward, the emphasis will be on Jesus' suffering and death. As time goes on, the disciples begin (slowly) to realize the full extent of Jesus' mission. Only after his death and resurrection do they realize that He was the fulfillment of the "Suffering Servant" prophecy of Isaiah. In Jesus, God acts decisively to save his people through the suffering of His only Son.

III. Second Act: The Servant Saves Through Suffering

1) Jesus Prepares His Disciples For His Death
(Read 9:30-32 and 10:32-45)

"But they did not understand the teaching and were afraid to ask." (9:32)

"For the Son of man came not to be served, but to serve, and to give his life as a ransom for many." (10:45)

In these two passages, Jesus continues teaching his disciples the meaning of his true mission and of what it means to follow the Suffering Servant Messiah. It is clear from these passages that Peter and the other disciples were finding it very hard to accept what Jesus was telling them and "afraid to ask" for too many details. Jesus knew that they would have a hard time accepting his mission, and an even harder time following him during his time of suffering and death. He knew that they would abandon him and yet he didn't give up on them. He loved them despite their flaws.

2) The Agony In the Garden
(Read 14:26-50)

After the Last Supper, Jesus went to prepare for his final and complete act of love. As this passage makes clear, Jesus had a very human fear of suffering and death. He would have preferred to bring salvation through some other means than his own death. He prayed to be spared the agony if possible.

> *"Jesus said to them 'My soul is very sorrowful, even to death; remain here, and watch.' And going a little further, he fell on the ground and prayed that if possible, the hour might pass from him. And he said, 'Abba, Father, all things are possible to thee; remove this cup from me; yet not what I will, but what thou wilt."* (14:33-36)

This passage also makes clear that Jesus freely and faithfully chose to fulfill his mission of a sacrificial death to atone for the sins of all humanity. He was not dragged to the cross against his will. He made a conscious choice to be obedient to God rather than to give in to his own human fears and run away. The Son of God loved each one of us enough to freely die on our behalf.

3) Death of the Messiah
(Read 15:1-39)

> *"And at the ninth hour, Jesus cried out with a loud voice... 'My God, my God, why has thou forsaken me?' ...And Jesus uttered a loud cry, and breathed his last. And the curtain of the temple was torn in two, from top to bottom. And when the centurion, who stood facing him, saw that he thus breathed his last, he said, 'Truly, this was the Son of God.'"* (15:34 and 37-39)

The moment of truth has arrived. Jesus fulfills his mission and demonstrates that he is faithful and obedient to the Father even to the end. At the moment of death, the Roman soldier utters the words of revelation "Truly this is the son of God." This passage is highly ironic. The disciples have all fled the scene in fear of their own lives. The pagan soldier alone testifies to Jesus' identity and mission.

4) The Resurrection of the Suffering Servant
(Read 16:1-20)

> *"Do not be amazed; you seek Jesus of Nazareth, who was crucified. He is risen, he is not here; see the place where they*

Mark: Triumph of the Sufering Servant

laid him. But go, tell his disciples and Peter that he is going before you to Galilee; there you will see him as he told you."
(16:6-7)

The account of the resurrection in Mark's gospel is very short. There are several theories about why this is so. Some scholars believe that Mark wanted to place more emphasis on Jesus' suffering and death and less emphasis on his triumph over death. Other scholars think that the last page of the original version of the gospel was lost, thus leaving out many of the resurrection episodes. Still others think that the brief resurrection account fits in with Mark's terse writing style. Whatever the case may be, it is clear that Jesus did in fact triumph over death in the resurrection. In his act of suffering, the power of sin and death were overturned. The resurrection is a sign that God honored the suffering of his faithful servant and Son. Jesus' death was an atoning sacrifice for the sins of all humanity. All of the sacrifices of the Old Testament are prefigurations of this perfect, once and for all sacrifice.

Once again, Jesus' disciples were slow to understand and believe what had happened. When the angel told them that Jesus had been raised from the dead, *"they went out and fled from the tomb; for trembling and astonishment had come upon them; and they said nothing to anyone for they were afraid."* (16:8)

Later, after the disciples had a chance to tell one another what had happened, Jesus appeared to them and, *"he upbraided them for their unbelief and hardness of heart because they had not believed those who saw him after he had risen."* (16:14)

Mark's version of the gospel shows the disciples to be quite reluctant saints – slow to understand, slow to believe in the resurrection and "hard of heart." To some Christians, this is an embarrassment. But it should not be so. The disciples were normal human beings who had normal doubts and fears. The disciples came to understand who Jesus was only very slowly because this was something new in the history of the world – the Messiah had never come before and they didn't know exactly what to expect. They came to believe in the resurrection only when they experienced the risen Lord Jesus in their midst; only when they could no longer deny what they saw. They found it difficult to believe in the resurrection because it is an unbelievable event!!!

The disciples' reluctance of faith ought to stand as a comfort to us when we are going through times of doubt and fear; times when God doesn't seem to make sense; times when we have a hard time understanding, or believing in, the resurrection of Jesus. Christian faith is not always easy to believe. Christian life is not always easy to live faithfully. In the disciples we have living examples of people who experienced the same obstacles that we face and who persevered in faith. They should serve as an inspiration to us.

QUESTIONS FOR DISCUSSION AND REFLECTION

1) God worked through Jesus to perform miracles, and these miracles drew people's attention to the fact that God was working in the world through Jesus. Do miracles still happen? What are some miraculous things that you have seen or heard about, which have opened your eyes to God's work in the world? When we read the gospel of Mark, we see Jesus performing miracles very frequently and very obviously. This seems to be a big contrast with the way God works miracles in our lives today. Why do you think this is so? (Was Mark exaggerating the miraculous deeds of Jesus? Did God work "overtime" to show that Jesus was the Messiah and has since slipped back to "part-time" miracle working? Are we less inclined to seek and notice miracles today than people were then? Does modern technology, science and medicine divert our attention and expectations to other ways of solving problems?)

2) Read Mark 9:14-29. Many of the accounts of "demon" possession in the Bible, sound like symptoms of what we have learned through modern science to identify as epilepsy and various mental illnesses. In Mark's gospel, Jesus "cast out" the demons and healed these people. How should we understand these passages in light of what we have learned through modern science? Are all references to "demons" to be understood as a primitive way of describing illnesses that we now understand differently? Or are there malevolent spiritual forces at work in human life? Did you know that the practice of exorcism is on the rise in many parts of the world today, including parts of "secularized" Europe? What would explain this?

3) God allowed Jesus to suffer on behalf of the whole human race. What are some ways that God's people are required to suffer with, or on behalf of, others? Discuss ways that God continues to bring good things out of hurtful situations.

PRAYER REFLECTION

Read Mark 8:27-38. Can you relate Peter's Confession / Peter's Confusion to your own life? Are there times when following Jesus seems exciting and inspirational and other times when it seems frightening and confusing? Do you ever wonder how far we can go with "taking up our own Cross and following Jesus"?

Take a few minutes to think about the times when you have found it fearful or embarrassing to admit to following Jesus. Ask yourself honestly, what is the source of your fear? Disapproval by other people? Diminished personal autonomy?

Now take a few minutes to think about the times when following Jesus seemed clear and right and true. Ask yourself, what was it about these times that gave you courage, hope and clarity of vision?

Now take some time in prayer to ask God for the strength and faith to be steadfast in your resolve to follow Jesus in the face of opposition.

BIBLE MEMORY VERSE

Jesus said: "If anyone would come after me, let him take up his cross and follow me. For whoever would save his life will lose it; and whoever would loses his life for my sake and the gospel's will save it. For what does it profit a man to gain the whole world and forfeit his life?"

Mark 8:34-36

CHAPTER 13

LUKE:
THE MAN OF COMPASSION

Main focus of this chapter:
Luke's unique portrait of the human nature of Jesus

Introduction

As we have seen in previous chapters, each Gospel writer paints a different portrait of Jesus, a new perspective, a different point of view. Matthew portrayed Jesus as the Messiah – King. Mark portrayed him as the Suffering Servant. Luke paints a portrait of the human side of Jesus. All of the Gospel authors believe that Jesus is God's "only begotten Son" and is therefore both human and divine. But Luke lays the strongest emphasis on Jesus' human nature. Also, he places great emphasis on Jesus' compassion for his fellow human beings. Luke constantly tells of Jesus' identification with the people who are hurting.

According to early Church tradition, Luke was a physician (not quite a "medical doctor" in the modern sense of the word, but one who cared for the sick with very primitive knowledge and technology). As such, he would have been very familiar with the horrible effects of many diseases which people suffered and the constant fears under which they lived. Perhaps because of his first hand experience with pain and suffering, Luke chose to emphasize Jesus' response to hurting people.

In Luke's gospel, we see a compassionate and very human Jesus. In portraying Jesus in this way, Luke drives home a very important truth. God cares for the people we are most likely to forget. God accepts those whom we humans are likely to reject. God's love goes out in extra measure to those who are lost and hurting. Through Jesus, God identifies with human pain and suffering. Through Jesus, God reaches out to save those who are not able to save themselves (that's all of us, whether we realize it or not).

Luke: The Man of Compassion

I. Humble Beginnings

The celebration of Christmas, as we know it, would not have been the same without the gospel according to Luke. If you didn't know the details reported only in the gospel of Luke, you would have to eliminate 99% of all Christmas carols. Luke tells us about the Annunciation (Luke 1:26-38) and about Mary's Song (Luke 1:46-55). Luke alone tells us why Jesus came to be born in Bethlehem under the reign of Caesar Augustus, that there was no room at the inn, that he was born in a Manger, that he was first visited by shepherds and angels singing "Glory to God in the highest." (Luke 2:1-20)

From the beginning of Luke we see God's intention to reach out to all humanity in Jesus. Jesus was not born into a wealthy or powerful family in an important center of world commerce and political influence, Instead, he was born to a poor family in an obscure corner of the Roman empire. His birth was first witnessed by those in the lowest level of society – shepherds. Yet amidst these humble circumstances, God was doing something new and important. So angels announced his birth.

1) The Song of Mary (read Luke 1:39-55)

This song of Mary (widely known as "The Magnificat" from the first word of the Latin translation) was Mary's birth announcement to her kinswoman Elizabeth. In it, we see the purposes of God choosing Mary to give birth to the savior of the world.

> "He has shown the strength of his arm, he has scattered the proud in the imagination of their hearts, he has put down the mighty from their thrones, and exalted those of low degree; he has filled the hungry with good things, and the rich he has sent away empty. He has helped his servant Israel, in remembrance of his mercy, as he spoke to our fathers, to Abraham and his children forever." Luke 1:51-55

God is not impressed with human power, material prosperity, social prestige or military might. From the beginning of Israel's history, God has called the "nobodies" of the earth to follow Him. God rescued slaves from Egypt, restored a demoralized people from exile in Babylon, preserved a faithful nation in the midst of centuries of war and violence against them. Now God is completing that work by sending a Savior for all people – not just the powerful, rich, famous, and beautiful. As we will see emphasized in the rest of the gospel of Luke, God wants to turn the world as we know it upside down with love for all humanity. Jesus invites all of his followers to join him in exalting "those of low degree and filling the hungry with good things."

2) The Genealogy of Jesus
(read 3:23-38)

This is not the most exciting reading in the world, but it makes a very important point, especially when compared with the genealogy cited in Matthew 1:1-16. Matthew calls Jesus "the son of David, the son of Abraham" and then traces his lineage to each of these ancestors. His point is that Jesus is an heir to the royal throne of David ("an everlasting kingdom") and also an heir to the promise given to Abraham ("by you shall all nations of the earth be blessed").

Luke is making a very different point in his genealogy. He cites David and Abraham, but he traces it back even further. He goes all the way back to Adam (3:38). In tracing Jesus back to Adam, he is making the point that Jesus is related to all humanity – not just the people of Israel. He has come to welcome every tribe, race, people and nation. He is the Savior and brother of all humanity. Jesus came to redeem the whole human race –all of the descendants of Adam.

II. Public Ministry: "To Set At Liberty Those Who Are Oppressed"

When American politicians announce that they are running for President, they usually go back to their home town and surround themselves with old friends and relatives. In so doing they are making a symbolic statement about their roots and identification with everyday people. When Jesus began his public ministry, he did something similar. He went to his home town (Nazareth) and entered the synagogue on the Sabbath. He was among people who had known him all his life; people with whom he had worked, learned and played; people with whom he worshipped and served God. On this day, he deliberately made a statement about his own future and what he felt God was calling him to do with his public ministry.

> "And he came to Nazareth where he had been brought up; and he went to the synagogue, as his custom was, on the Sabbath day. And he stood up to read; and there was given to him the book of the prophet Isaiah. He opened the book ad found the place where it is written, 'The Spirit of the Lord God is upon me, because he has anointed me to preach good news to the poor. He has sent me to proclaim release to the captives and recovering of sight to the blind, to set at liberty those who are oppressed, to proclaim the acceptable year of the Lord.'"
>
> Luke 4:16-19

Jesus chose this passage to illustrate his mission. He then closed the book and announced: *"Today this scripture has been fulfilled in your hearing."* He meant that his life would be a living demonstration of this prophecy. In the narrative that follows, we see Jesus bringing liberation to those who are oppressed with various diseases and misfortunes. In Luke's account the main emphasis of Jesus' miracle ministry is on healing.

(Read the following passages)

Healing Simon's Mother and Others	(4:38-41)
Healing Lepers and a Paralytic	(5:12-26)
Healing the Centurion's Slave	(7:1-10)
Restoring Life to the Widow's Son	(7:11-17)
Healing the Demon-Possessed Man	(8:22-32)
Healing the Hemorrhaging Woman	(8:40-42 and 49-56)
Restoring Life to Jairus' Daughter	(8:40-42 and 49-56)

In all of these passages, Jesus show his compassion for those who are suffering. He demonstrates the willingness of God to heal, restore and forgive. These miracles of healing are one aspect of the salvation that is ours in the kingdom of God. Physical healing is an outward sign of the spiritual healing that is the result of the believer's faith in the savior of the world. Jesus saves us from the destructive powers of sin, sickness and death.

III. Teachings on Compassion

Jesus divided his time between performing miracles and teaching about the kingdom of God. His miracles demonstrated the kingdom while his teaching helped everyone understand how to discover and live into the kingdom which "is in the midst of you." His teaching constantly reinforces a common theme: God is compassionate and merciful. Therefore, we also must be compassionate and merciful to our fellow human beings. God cares for those whom the world rejects. Therefore, we also must care for the outcasts.

His teachings on the kingdom follow a threefold pattern:

**1) God is Compassionate and Merciful:
The Lost Sheep, The Lost Coin, The Lost Son**
(Read Luke 15:1-32)

The message of these three consecutive teachings is that God actively seeks out those who are lost. The shepherd cares for the ninety-nine sheep who don't get lost, but he devotes extra effort to find the one who got lost. The woman devotes extra effort to find the lost coin. The father appreciates the "good" son who stayed home and helps. But he rejoices when the wayward son comes to his sense and returns home. That's the way God is. That's why God sent his only Son into the world – to seek and save the lost; to reconcile sinners to God.

2) God Accepts Those Whom the World Rejects: Banquet for the Outcasts
(Read Luke 14:7-24)

The message of these parables is that God is not impressed with human pride and self-righteousness. All who accept the invitation are welcomed into the Kingdom of God. Those who, because of their religious heritage, think that they have an honored place in the kingdom may be surprised in the end.

3) Therefore, We Must be Compassionate and Merciful:

> The Good Samaritan (read Luke 10:25-37)
> The Rich Man and Lazarus (read 16:19-31)
> The Repentance of Zacchaeus (read Luke 19:1-10)

The point of these three episodes is that we who believe in a loving, merciful, compassionate God are to imitate (as far as we are able) the character of God. Faith needs to be translated into acts of compassion for those who are hungry, those who are beaten down and left for dead. Repentance means imitating the generosity of God.

IV. Death and Resurrection

As we have seen, each gospel writer tells the story of Jesus differently. This is especially true in describing his suffering, death and resurrection. Each gospel writer provides different details which paint a different portrait of Jesus in his final hours on earth and in his final triumph over sin and death.

Luke provides three details which speak volumes about Jesus' character: 1) his prayer for Peter, 2) his prayer for forgiveness for his persecutors, 3) his words to the repentant thief on the cross.

1) Jesus prays for Peter

All of the gospel accounts record Peter's denial of Jesus, In each case, they report that Jesus predicted Peter' denial. In Luke, we have another detail:

> *"Simon, Simon, behold, Satan demanded to have you, that he might sift you like wheat, but I have prayed for you that your faith may not fail; and when you have turned again, strengthen your brethren." And he (Peter) said to him, "Lord I am ready to go with you to prison and to death." He said, "I tell you Peter, the cock will not crow this day until you three times deny that you know me."*
>
> Luke 22:31-34

Not only did Jesus know that Peter would deny him. He also had compassion on Peter's weakness of character and faith. He prayed that Peter would recover from his failure and would become a source of strength to others who were struggling with their faith.

2) Jesus Prays For His Persecutors

> *"And when they came to the place which is called 'The Skull', they crucified him, and the criminals, one on the right and one on the left. And Jesus said, 'Father forgive them; for they know not what they do.'"*
>
> Luke 23:33-34

Not only did Jesus have compassion on his wayward friends, he asked for forgiveness for his enemies also. This kind of forgiveness is hard enough to muster up for everyday hurts and slights. It is nearly beyond imagination to be able to forgive someone who is actively killing you. This super-human capacity to forgive is one sign of Jesus' divine nature.

3) Jesus' Promise to the Thief

> *"One of the criminals who were hanged railed at him (Jesus), saying 'Are you not the Christ? Save yourself and us!" But the other rebuked him, saying, 'Do you not fear God, since you are under the same sentence of condemnation? And we indeed justly; for we are receiving the due reward of our deeds; but this man has done no wrong. And he said, 'Jesus remember me when you come into your kingdom.' And he said to him 'Truly, I say to you, today you will be with me in paradise.'"*
>
> Luke 23:39-43

Soldiers often speak of "fox-hole conversions." In other words, people (who have never before shown much interest in religion) often turn to God when they are confronted with their own imminent death. This appears to be such a moment. The thief is about to die and he repents and asks to be included in the kingdom of God. Under the circumstances, we might expect Jesus to question his motives: "Why didn't you seek God before now?" Instead, Jesus accepts his repentance as true and promises him an inheritance in "paradise." Jesus came "to seek and save the lost" and this prodigal son is welcomed home even at the hour of his death. Jesus' compassion, forgiveness and mercy extends even to last minute conversions. It is never too late to repent and turn to Christ. It is never too late to ask for God's forgiveness. It is never too late to be included in the kingdom. No one has messed up his or her life so badly that Christ can't make it whole.

4) The Stranger on the Road to Emmaus
(read Luke 24:1-35)

Each of the gospel writers presents the resurrection of Jesus in a different way. This passage is the longest and most detailed resurrection account in the entire New Testament. The most interesting feature of this account is the disciples' gradual and growing recognition of the risen Lord.

Most people have had the experience of meeting an acquaintance whom we have not seen for a long time. For a whole variety of reasons, we do not immediately recognize the person. The person may have gained (or lost) a lot of weight; may have changed hairstyles or clothing; may have grown (or shaved off) a beard; may be in an entirely different role than you are expecting (your high school math teacher in a bikini at the beach!) and so on. In such cases, there is a nagging feeling in the back of your mind: "I know I know that person from somewhere. Her face is so familiar. Where have I seen her before?" And finally, after searching the inner chambers of your memory, a light suddenly goes on: "Oh yeah, that's who it is!!! I knew she looked familiar."

Something like that was going on in this account of the resurrection. Two disciples were heading home to Emmaus, a small village seven miles from Jerusalem. They were demoralized and dejected. Their hero was dead. Some women had told them of angels who reported that Jesus had risen from the dead. But apparently they didn't fully understand or believe the women. They were confused. As they were walking, a stranger began to walk with them and struck up a conversation. They did not know that it was Jesus: "their eyes were kept from recognizing him." As they began to tell the stranger what happened to Jesus, the stranger began to explain the scriptures concerning the Messiah. At this point, the disciples began to sense something familiar about this stranger ("did not out hearts burn within us as he talked to us on the road?") but they still didn't recognize him.

As they drew near to their destination, it was getting dark. In an act of simple hospitality, they invited the stranger to stay with them for a meal and lodging for the night. When they sat down to a simple meal, the stranger "took the bread, and blessed it, and broke it and gave it to them." This is the exact same thing that Jesus did at the Last Supper; he took, blessed, broke, and gave the bread saying "Do this in remembrance of me." In that instant, a light went on in the disciples mind. The disciples recognized him. It all became clear. The Jesus who took, blessed, broke and gave the bread at the Last Supper was the same Jesus who was present at this holy meal. At that mystical moment, he vanished out of their sight. And they ran back to tell the others "how he was known to them in the breaking of the bread."

This passage tells us two important things:

1) We meet the risen Lord in the Scriptures ("did not our hearts burn within us as he explained the Scriptures"). He is the real teacher when we read Scripture.

2) We welcome and receive the risen Lord in "the breaking of the bread" at Holy Communion. He is the real priest at the holy meal which he commanded us to share in his memory.

QUESTIONS FOR DISCUSSION AND REFLECTION

1) As we have seen, the central message of the gospel according to Luke is that God accepts those whom human society rejects, if we believe this is true, and if we wish to follow Jesus faithfully, what are some things that we ought to change in our perception of, and behaviors towards, other people?

For example, how do you think Jesus would relate to (and want us to relate to) the following: people with AIDS, "welfare mothers", alcoholics and drug addicts, people who panhandle and don't take a bath very often, convicted murderers, child molesters? Does accepting people mean we need to hang around with them, be friends, invite them to our house for dinner? Where do we "draw the line" between acceptance and compromising our own physical safety?

2) Read Luke 15:11-32. This is most often called "the parable of the prodigal son", but neither Jesus nor the gospel writer gave it that title. It could also be called "the parable of the forgiving father" or "the parable of the resentful older brother." Try to enter into each of these characters and experience what they must have felt at each turn in the story. How does it feel to be the father who watches his son waist everything the father has worked for? How does it feel to be the son who realizes what a mess he has made of his life? How does it feel to be the older brother who does everything right and gets no recognition or appreciation? Which one do you think Jesus intended to be the "main character" in this parable? To whom is the message directed: those who have messed up their lives and need to "come home", those who need to forgive, resentful "older brothers" or "all of the above"? How does this parable speak to you personally? Have you ever been in one (or all) of these roles?

3) Read Jesus' prayer for Peter (Luke 22:31-34). Jesus knew Peter's weakness of character, but he prayed that this weakness would be turned to strength and would be used to strengthen others. Have you ever prayed that God would use the weaknesses and sins in your life to be a source of strength for others who are struggling with similar issues?

4) The disciples met Jesus on the road to Emmaus (Luke 24:1-35), but didn't recognize him. Have there been times in your life when Jesus was reaching out to you, but you didn't recognize his presence until later?

5) The disciples knew Jesus in the breaking of the bread. Describe ways that you draw closer to Jesus in the Holy Communion.

6) Jesus promised the thief that he would be with Jesus in paradise (Luke 23: 39-43). Do you think this passage would encourage people to wait until the last minute to "get right with God"? How is this passage like the parable of Luke 15:11-32?

PRAYER

The following is a devotional prayer which may be used after receiving communion or at any other time of prayer. Spend some quiet time reflecting on the areas of your spiritual life, your thoughts, attitudes and behavior which need to be transformed by Jesus' living presence. Use this prayer as a method of asking Christ into those parts of your life that need his healing touch.

"Heart of Jesus, think of me.
Eyes of Jesus, look on me.
Face of Jesus, comfort me.
Hands of Jesus, bless me.
Arms of Jesus, hold me.
Body of Jesus, feed me.
Blood of Jesus, wash me.
Jesus, make me thus thine own,
Here and in the world to come."
(*St. Augustine's Prayer Book* p. 108)

BIBLE MEMORY VERSE

"And he came to Nazareth where he had been brought up; and he went to the synagogue, as his custom was, on the Sabbath day. And he stood up to read; and there was given to him the book of the prophet Isaiah. He opened the book ad found the place where it is written, 'The Spirit of the Lord God is upon me, because he has anointed me to preach good news to the poor. He has sent me to proclaim release to the captives and recovering of sight to the blind, to set at liberty those who are oppressed, to proclaim the acceptable year of the Lord.'"

Luke 4:16-19

Chapter 14

JOHN:
THE ETERNAL WORD OF GOD

Focus Of This Chapter:
John's unique portrait of the divine nature of Jesus

Introduction

We have now come to the fourth and final gospel:"according to John." As we have seen, each of the gospels paints a different portrait of Jesus. But John's is the most different of all. Many of the early "Church Fathers" called John "the spiritual gospel" and we will soon discover why.

Most of us have been passengers on an airplane. After takeoff, as the plane ascends higher into the sky, people, cars and buildings look much different than they do when we are "on the ground." In just a few minutes, we develop a much different perspective. It's the same world, but it looks a lot different from 3,000 feet. That experience of a changed perspective is a good analogy for understanding the gospel according to John in comparison to Matthew, Mark and Luke - the "synoptic" gospels. These earlier three gospels are based on a common collection ("synopsis") of memories about Jesus life and teaching. Each shares the same basic outline of Jesus' life, but chooses to emphasize a different aspect of it. John is unique in that it does not follow the basic biography that we find in the others. In John, we have no lists of ancestors (called "genealogies"), none of the heart-warming stories from which Christmas pageants are made, no King Herod, no flight to Egypt, no accounts of his youth, no temptation in the wilderness, no Sermon on the Mount, no parables, no Transfiguration and so on. John seems to have no interest at all in the earthly biography of Jesus. Instead, John tells a very different story – a "heavenly biography." As Matthew, Mark and Luke begin with a "ground level" perspective, John begins at 100,000 feet. For Matthew and Luke, the story of Jesus begins in Bethlehem. For John, the story begins at the heart of the universe.

John: The Eternal Word of God

> *"In the beginning was the Word, and the Word was with God and the Word was God. He was in the beginning with God; all things were made through him, and without him was not anything made that was made. In him was life, and this life was the light of men. The light shines in the darkness and the darkness has not overcome it. The true light that enlightens every man was coming into the world. He was in the world, and the world was made through him, yet the world knew him not. He came to his own home and his own people received him not. But to all who received him, who believed in his name, he gave power to become children of God; who were born, not of blood nor of the will of man, but of God. And the Word became flesh and dwelt among us, full of grace and truth; we have beheld his glory, glory as of the only Son from the Father. ...No one has ever seen God; the only Son, who is in the bosom of the Father, he has made God known."*
>
> John 1:1-14 and 18

This opening passage gives us the basic pattern for John's gospel as a whole, and for each individual passage. Every episode in the gospel is an illustration of the basic pattern of 1) The Word descending from heaven, 2) the Word made flesh (Jesus) showing forth the love and purpose of God on earth and 3) the Word returning to heaven and calling us to follow him there. Every episode and every conversation in the gospel of John has a double meaning. Every earthly event points us (and invites us) to experience a heavenly reality. The earthly Jesus is really the heavenly Word who uses every opportunity to lead us to "my Father's House" where "I have gone to prepare a place for you."

The gospel of John can be divided into three parts which demonstrate the threefold pattern of descent, manifestation and return.

Part I: **The Word / Son "Comes Down" From Heaven To Earth**
(John 1:1-18)

Part II: **The Word / Son Reveals His Identity To The World**
(John 1:19 to 12:50)

Part III: **The Word / Son Returns To Heaven And Invites Us To Follow**
(John, chapters 13 through 21)

We will now consider each of these parts in turn.

The Living Word of the Living God

I. The Word / Son "Comes Down" From Heaven To Earth
(read Genesis 1:1-31 and Proverbs 8:22-36 before continuing)

These Old Testament passages are a preparation for John's introduction. They illustrate the creative power of God. In the Genesis 1 passage, God speaks and creation happens. God's Word is the instrument of creation. In the Proverbs 8 passage, God's Wisdom is a partner in the creative energy. These passages (to be understood as theological truth set to poetry - not astrophysics) are the basis for John's opening verses:

> *"In the beginning was the Word, and the Word was with God and the Word was God. He was in the beginning with God; all things were made through him, and without him was not anything made that was made. In him was life, and this life was the light of men. The light shines in the darkness and the darkness has not overcome it."*

The eternal creative Word and Wisdom of God are what we humans can know about the essential nature of God. Now, God has chosen to translate his essential nature even more clearly in the language of a human life: *"And the Word became flesh and dwelt among us, full of grace and truth; we have beheld his glory, glory as of the only Son from the Father. ...No one has ever seen God; the only Son, who is in the bosom of the Father, he has made God known."*

More than any other gospel writer, John wants to emphasize the "divine nature" of Jesus. He is not just a prophet; not just a miracle worker; not just a great moral teacher – although (John would say) he certainly is all of those. But he is more than that. He is God "in the flesh." He alone came from heaven. He alone gives us the power to go back to heaven, to the heart of God: *"The true light that enlightens every man was coming into the world. He was in the world, and the world was made through him, yet the world knew him not. He came to his own home and his own people received him not. But to all who received him, who believed in his name, he gave power to become children of God; who were born, not of blood nor of the will of man, but of God."*

Later Christian reflection interpreted this and other similar passages to formulate "the doctrine of the Incarnation" (based on the Latin word for "in the flesh.") Jesus was God "in the flesh." When we look to the life, death, and resurrection of Jesus, we see clearly the true person, purpose and power of God.

II. The Word / Son Reveals His Identity To The World

In the second part of John's gospel (from 1:19 through chapter 12), Jesus reveals himself to the world. Each of these chapters is a nearly self-contained unit which focuses on a particular title or symbolic statement about Jesus' identity and mission. In each case, the narrative, dialogue and miracles are intended to point the reader to "heavenly things." Here is a brief summary of the themes of each chapter.

Chapter	Theme
2	Jesus, The New Wine, New Temple
3	Jesus, The Giver of Eternal Life
4	Jesus, The Giver of Living Water
5	Jesus, The Healer
6	Jesus, The Bread of Life
7	Jesus, The Teacher "Greater Than Moses"
8	Jesus, The Liberator From Sin
9	Jesus, The Healer of Blindness
10	Jesus, The Good Shepherd
11	Jesus, The One Who Raises The Dead
12	Jesus, The Light of The World

We will consider a few of these themes in more detail.

1) The Giver of Eternal Life
(read Chapter 3)

"Truly, truly I say to you, unless one is born of water and the Spirit, he cannot enter the Kingdom of God. ...No one has ascended to heaven except he who descended from heaven, the Son of man. And as Moses lifted up the serpent in the wilderness, so must the Son of man be lifted up, that whoever believes in him may have eternal life. For God so loved the world that he gave his only Son, that whoever believes in him may not perish, but have eternal life. For God did not send his Son into the world to condemn the world, but that the world might be saved through him."

John 3:5 and 13-17

This passage is very important. It tells us how we are to receive the salvation only Jesus can deliver, because "no one has ascended to heaven except he who descended from heaven." But important as it is, it's also confusing. Nicodemus wants to know what does Jesus mean by being "born again"? In the first instance, Jesus says, being "born again" is not a physical birth but a spiritual reception of God's saving purpose. One needs to believe in God's saving mission as summarized in the final words: ***For God so loved the world that he gave his only Son, that whoever believes in him may not perish, but have eternal life. For God did not send his Son into the world to condemn the world, but that the world might be saved through him.*** " So believing and receiving God's saving work, made available through Christ is important. But there is also the important qualifying phrase "by water and the Spirit." This has been interpreted to refer to the sacrament of Baptism, also commanded by Jesus in the Great Commission (in Matthew 28) and explained by Paul (in Romans 6:3-14).

The meaning of these combined passages have been vigorously debated by different Christian groups throughout history. Some Christian groups say that being "born again by water and the Spirit" means "being baptized." Other Christian groups say that, to be "born again" a person must make a deep, personal and conscious decision to accept Jesus Christ as their Savior and Lord. When, and only when, a person has made this deep and personal commitment of faith can he or she be truly "born again."

Which one of these views is correct? Both!

First of all, a person must be baptized to enter into the life, death and resurrection of Jesus. This is God's chosen instrument for connecting us to the saving work God has done through Christ. This is the sacrament commanded by Jesus to connect us to his saving work. No one can be "born again" without being baptized. (See Matthew 28:19; Mark 16:16; Romans 6:3-14 and I Peter 3: 21)

Secondly, every baptized person must make a deep, personal and conscious decision to accept Jesus Christ as Savior and follow him as Lord. To be baptized and fail to do this is like being legally "married" but refusing to live with your spouse. It is a functional denial of the status conferred by the sacrament. Baptism is not a magic act which operates against our will. Rather, it is God's invitation to cooperate with God's purpose for our life. When a person is baptized "by water and the spirit," God connects that person to the saving power of Christ, wipes away the penalty of sin and give us an inheritance in heaven. But each person must consciously receive and apply the blessings that God makes available. In the sacrament of baptism, God offers the greatest gift of all. But without a living faith, the offered gift remains unopened. To use a different analogy, God plants the seed of authentic

Christian faith and life in our soul at Baptism. In so doing, God has initiated something that we cannot do for ourselves. But it is our responsibility to water and nurture the seed into a full plant and to remove obstacles to its continual growth and health. (See Romans 6:1-23 for an extended exhortation on living up to the implications of being baptized into the death and resurrection of Christ.)

2) **I Am the Bread of Life**
   (read Chapter 6)

   "I am the living bread which came down from heaven; if anyone eats of this bread, he will live forever; and the bread which I shall give for the life of the world is my flesh....Truly, truly, I say to you, unless you eat the flesh of the Son of man, and drink of his blood, you shall not have life within you; he who eats my flesh and drinks my blood has eternal life and I will raise him up on the last day. For my flesh is food indeed and my blood is drink indeed. He who eats my flesh and drinks my blood abides in me and I in him."

   John 6:51 and 53-56

Unlike Matthew, Mark and Luke, John makes no specific mention of the in institution of Holy Communion ("Take. Eat. This is my Body. Do this in remembrance of me.") And yet, ironically, John seems more focused on the Holy Communion reality than all of the others. The whole sixth chapter is an extended meditation on the phrase "I Am the Bread of Life." The chapter begins with the miraculous multiplication of bread and the feeding of the multitudes, which is reported by all of the other gospels. However, John shows a deeper meaning. It's not about multiplied bread. It is a sign of who Jesus is- the Bread of Life. Just as God provided manna to the ancient Israelites, so he now, through Jesus, provides food for the journey to the ultimate promised land of eternal life.

These passages about Holy Communion (in John chapter 6 and elsewhere) have provoked much disagreement between different Christian groups throughout history. Exactly what did Jesus mean when he told his followers "This is my body. This is my blood."? What did he mean when he invited his followers to "eat my flesh and drink my blood"? Is he claiming a "Real Presence" of his person in the physical elements of bread and wine? Or is he saying that those who receive these physical elements of bread and wine in faith will experience a spiritual closeness to him? As with our previous discussion of Baptism, we need to avoid "either/or" thinking on these questions. Jesus gave us a physical action with physical elements and promised to be uniquely present in the physicality of the sacrament: "This is my body" (Not "this symbolizes my body.") He promised to be uniquely and personally present under the physical signs of bread and wine when we remember him in this physical act of worship. Holy Communion is rightly understood, and rightly received, only by the person who approaches the physical elements of communion with a deep trust that Jesus in mysteriously present and that we can grow closer to him by calling to our conscious memory what he has done for us and our salvation. To receive the physical elements of Holy Communion without the active faith and sincere prayer of the person receiving it offers no spiritual benefit. (see I Corinthians 11:23-29)

3) The Healer of Blindness
(read Chapter 9)

"Whether he is a sinner, I do not know; one thing I know, that though I was blind, I now see. ...Never since the world began has it ever been heard that anyone opened the eyes of a man born blind. If this man were not from God, he could do nothing."

The irony of this passage is that Jesus heals the physical blindness of a man, but the real malady is the willful spiritual blindness of the Pharisees. The healed man is able to see – both physically and spiritually. But the Pharisees persist in their refusal to see. Theirs is the true blindness. Jesus came to heal the spiritual blindness of the world by demonstrating God's redeeming love and healing power in tangible ways. Through Jesus, God is using dramatic miracles to get our attention, but some refuse to recognize God's hand at work. This was true then and continues to be so. Many people are given eyes to "see" the reality of God through Jesus. Many people either are not able, or stubbornly refuse, to see. Those of us who have been given eyes of faith to see the love of God through Jesus have a mission like that of the healed blind man: to share what we have seen with those who do not yet see. The healed blind man did not have all the answers, but he told others of his own experience: **"one thing I know, that though I was blind, I now see."** We are also called to share with others our experience of the healing power of God in Christ.

4) The Good Shepherd
(read chapter 10)

"I am the good shepherd; I know my own and my own know me... My sheep hear my voice and I know them, and they follow me."

In Jesus' time and place, sheep and shepherds were a normal part of everyone's daily life just as cars, T.V., computers and cell phones are part of our experience. For that reason, the Bible is full of references to shepherding. In the Old Testament, God is often called the "Shepherd of Israel." Corrupt kings and religious leaders are often referred to as "false shepherds." In this passage, Jesus is identified with God as the trustworthy shepherd of God's people. Herding sheep is a very demanding and all-consuming occupation. Sheep are not independent thinkers. They instinctively and uncritically follow other sheep. Consequently, one of the challenges of shepherding is keeping one's own sheep from wandering off with another herd. To prevent this, each shepherd must develop his own special call and train his herd to respond to the sound of his own voice – and not respond to another shepherd's voice. If sheep are not so trained, they are soon lost to other herds. Jesus is the Good Shepherd in the spiritual sense. His followers must be trained to hear his voice among all of the competing voices of the world. In a world of many voices which compete for our attention and which lead us in bad directions, we need to develop the capacity to hear his voice and follow. We develop the capacity to hear Jesus' voice through prayer, worship, study of the Bible, biblical commentaries, the spiritual writings and biblical reflections of other Christians and of the teachings of the Church and in serving others in Jesus' name.

5) The Resurrection and The Life
(read chapter 11)

"I am the resurrection and the life; he who believes in me, even though he die, yet shall he live, and whoever lives and believes in me shall never die. Do you believe this? She said to him, 'Yes Lord; I believe that you are the Christ, the Son of God, he who is coming into the world.' "

The raising of Lazarus is a prefiguration of Jesus' own resurrection and a demonstration of God's power over sin and death. Death is the ultimate enemy of all human aspiration and hope. Resurrection is God's ultimate victory over our ultimate enemy. In Jesus, God demonstrates God's willingness to save, redeem and reconcile fallen humanity. Resurrection is God's final "yes" to God's creation. In raising Lazarus, Jesus demonstrates God's willingness to extend the resurrection reality to all who trust in him for salvation. This is the last and complete revelation of who Jesus is. Now the stage is set for the third and final section of John's gospel.

III. The Word / Son Returns To Heaven

In the first section (1:1-18) the Word / Son of God "came down" from heaven. In the second section (chapters 2 through 12), the Word /Son has revealed his identity, mission and purpose. Now, in the final section (chapters 13 through 21) the Word / Son of God is going back to heaven. But he is not going back alone. *"In my Father's house, there are many rooms...I go to prepare a place for you, that where I am you may be also."* In this last section, we have an extended invitation to follow where Jesus has leads: *"I Am the Way, the Truth and the Life; no one comes to the Father except through me."*

1) A New Commandment (read chapter 13)

Jesus is just about to return to his "Father's house" and he knew it. He prepared his friends for his departure by telling them how to relate to each other after he is gone. During the course of the Last Supper, he teaches by example: washing his disciples' feet. In Jesus' time, it was expected of a good host to provide this service at a social gathering and was a task reserved for the lowest servant or slave in the household. It was a disagreeable but necessary job because the energy source for all forms of transport was animal power. Therefore, the streets were paved with manure and foot washing was a matter of basic hygiene as well as hospitality. Jesus takes this humble and humbling task upon himself to make a point.

> *"If I then, your Lord and Teacher, have washed your feet, you also ought to wash one another's feet. For I have given you an example, that you also should do as I have done for you."* (v. 14)

Later in the supper, he explains the significance of the foot washing:

> *"A new Commandment I give to you, that you love one another; even as I have loved you, that you also love one another. By this all men will know that you are my disciples, if you have love for one another."* (vs. 34 -35)

This "love command", along with the foot-washing and the act of Holy Communion, points to the ultimate act of love, as Jesus prepares to give his life for his friends on the Cross. The "new" commandment is not simply to "love one another", which was already well taught and understood, but "as I have loved you." Jesus calls his friends, and his followers in every generation, to love each other with life-giving, and self-emptying love.

2) That They All May Be One
(read Chapter 17)

> *"And now I am no more in the world, but they are in the world, and I am coming to thee. Holy Father, keep them in thy name,*

> *which thou hast given me, that they may be one, even as we are one. ...I in them and thou in me, that they may become perfectly one, so that the world may know that thou hast sent me and hast loved them even as thou hast loved me."*
>
> (vs. 11 & 23)

Chapter 17 is what is known as Jesus' "High Priestly Prayer" in which he prays for his disciples and for all Jesus' people throughout history: *"I do not pray for these only but for all who believe in me through their word."* (v. 20) His prayer and intention for all of his followers through time is that we all be united in truth and in loyalty to Jesus and in charity to one another. This prayer is a constant vision and challenge for all Christians in every time and place. It is not an exaggeration to say that we have failed to live into the vision and challenge more than we have succeeded. Christian unity in truth, loyalty and love is not just a nice ideal. It is the express intention of our Lord for which we are duty-bound to hope, pray and work.

3) It Is Finished
(read Chapter 19)

> *"After this Jesus, knowing that all was finished, said (to fulfill the scripture), 'I thirst'. A bowl of vinegar stood there; so they put a sponge full of vinegar on hyssop and held it to his mouth. When Jesus had received the vinegar, he said, 'It is finished'; and he bowed his head and gave up his spirit."* (vs. 28-30)

Moving from the Last Supper to the Cross is, at first glance, a study in contrasts. The scene shifts from acts of servanthood, words of wisdom and prayers of consecration to unspeakable acts of cruelty and hatred: "Crucify him." And yet, despite the apparent contrast, these are two movements in one great act of love. God so loved the world that he sent his one and only Son to live and die for us. The Cross is the climax of his mission of love and salvation. He ends his life with one simple word "tetelestai" (translated into English as three words: "it is finished"). We might paraphrase it: "mission accomplished."

John gives us a detail not available in the other gospel accounts. Jesus death occurred on "the day of Preparation for the Passover" (vs. 14 & 31). This was the hour when the lambs were being ritually slaughtered by the priests for the Passover meal (as commanded in Exodus 12). In giving us this detail, John is making a very important theological point. Jesus is the final and complete Passover Lamb, who delivers the world from slavery and sin, and who opens the way to the Promised Land. The first Passover is a prefiguration of this final and complete Passover. In the first Passover, the people of Israel were liberated from slavery in Egypt. In this second Passover of Jesus Christ, the whole of humanity is liberated from slavery to sin and death.

4) Resurrection Appearances

Each of the resurrection appearances in John has a special message and purpose. Each extends the invitation to follow Jesus back to the Father's house where he is going to prepare a place for us.

Mary Magdalene: A Grief Healed   (read 20:1-18)

> " 'Woman, why are you weeping? Whom do you seek?' Supposing him to be the gardener, she said to him, 'Sir, if you have taken away my Lord, and I will take him away'. Jesus said to her 'Mary'. She turned to him and said 'Rabonni' (which means 'Teacher')." (vs. 15-16)

Mary Magdalene was deeply indebted to Jesus. Through her contact with Jesus, a dramatic change had occurred in her life. We don't know exactly how Jesus helped Mary. An ancient Church tradition (not found in the Bible) holds that Mary was a prostitute and that Jesus rescued her from that sordid life. The Bible simply says that "seven demons" had been cast out of Mary, which is a biblical way of saying that she really had a lot of problems. Perhaps she was mentally ill. Maybe she drank a lot to anesthetize her illness. Maybe she sold her body to buy her drink. Maybe all of the above? Whatever happened, Mary was deeply indebted and deeply attached to Jesus. And she was overwhelmed with grief at his death. In this poignant encounter, she mistakes him for the gardener and requests his body for a proper burial. It is only when he speaks her name that she recognizes him. Suddenly all of the memories come back. Suddenly, she experiences again the healing power of his voice. In that one instant, her grief is transformed into hope; her brokenness is healed.

In our lives, we face grief and loss, either through death or through profound loss of what we hold most dear. Jesus is risen from death, and he calls each one of us, as he called Mary, by name. Because he lives; because he calls us; because he invites us to his Fathers' house, we need not be overwhelmed by our grief and loss.

The Power To Forgive   (read 20:19-23)

> "Jesus said to them again 'Peace be with you. As the Father has sent me, so I send you.' And when he had said this, he breathed on them and said, 'Receive the Holy Spirit. If you forgive the sins of any they are forgiven. If you retain the sins of any, they are retained.' " (vs. 21-23)

Different Christian communions have varied understandings of this authority to forgive and how it should be exercised. Roman Catholics, Eastern Orthodox and "high church" Anglicans exercise it within the "Sacrament of Reconciliation" (or "Penance" or "Confession") administered by an ordained priest who is invested with apostolic authority. Protestant groups exercise it within the context of congregational prayers of confession and appeals to God for forgiveness or with private prayer in which a person (ordained or not) prays on behalf of another, asking for forgiveness. In all cases, these sacramental acts and prayers are seen as an extension of the ministry that Jesus commended to his followers. It is never seen as one human being forgiving another on his own personal authority, which would be an arrogant usurpation of God's sole prerogative to forgive. In all of the various Christian communities, the goal is to faithfully fulfill Jesus' command.

"Doubting Thomas" Becomes Believing Thomas   (read 20: 24 -29)

"My Lord and my God."

Thomas, like many of us needs evidence for his faith. In the early verses of this passage, he is "Doubting Thomas" (a name he has been unfairly stuck with for two thousand years). After some evidence, he begins to have doubts about his doubts. In the end, he confesses complete faith in the risen Lord. Like Thomas, many of us desire tangible proof of faith. And sometimes, we receive evidence to help us in our belief. But there are other times when evidence is not forthcoming. In those barren times, we need to remember Jesus' final words to Thomas in this passage: "Blessed are those who have not seen, and yet believe." The writer closes this episode with a summary of why he wrote the gospel:

> *"Now Jesus did many other signs in the presence of his disciples which are not written in this book; but these are written that you may believe that Jesus is the Christ, the Son of God, and that believing you may have life in his name."*
> John 20:30-31

The Bible is the living word of the living God. Through it, Jesus continues to speak to us and to draw us to himself. He continues to call us to the Father's house where he has gone to prepare a place for us.

QUESTIONS FOR DISCUSSION AND REFLECTION

1) Read again John 1:1-18. Then read Genesis 1:1-27 and Proverbs 8:22-36.

How are these passages similar and different? Do the passages from Genesis and Proverbs give us a better understanding of what John was trying to say about Jesus? Why do you think John began his gospel account this way instead of with a genealogy as in Matthew and Luke? Now read Hebrews 1:1-3. How is this the same as, or different from, John 1?

2) Compare the compassionate and very human portrait of Jesus in Luke's gospel to the very spiritual and heavenly portrait of Jesus in John's gospel. Which one of these portraits is most appealing to you? How would our understanding of Jesus be different if one of these were left out of the Bible?

3) Read the story of Jesus healing the blind man in John chapter 9. The central irony of this passage is that one person (the blind man) is healed of his blindness and "sees" who Jesus really is, while many others (the Pharisees) persists in their spiritual blindness and refuse to see Jesus' true identity, even though there is ample evidence that God is working through him. Think about your own life. Have there been times when you have been spiritually blind? Times when your eyes were opened to see yourself, God, or the world in a new light? What happened to change your perspective?

4) Read John 3. What was Jesus trying to teach Nicodemus? How is this account like the healing of the blind man in Chapter 9? How is it like Jesus appearing to Thomas in chapter 20? What does it mean to be "born again" (chapter 3), to "see" (chapter 9) and to "believe without seeing" (chapter 20)? How does your own personal experience of faith in Jesus compare with the symbolism of these passages? Have you had a moment in which you were "born again" or began to "see" Jesus, or were able to have a deep level of faith without being able to "see"? Why do you think John used so many different symbols to invite us into a deeper relationship with Jesus?

5) In John 17, Jesus prays that his followers "may be perfectly one." Why do you think so many of Jesus followers are not united with each other in the basic teachings of faith?

What are the main points that you think all Christians should be able to agree on? What are the areas of legitimate difference of opinion? Are differences of culture or worship style evidence of disunity – or just different ways that God relates to different types of people? What can we do to reconcile disagreeing groups of Christians?

PRAYER EXERCISE

Go to a quiet place. Take some time to still your thoughts and your spirit. Picture in your mind the image of Jesus as the Good Shepherd. Think about the times in your life when you have been lost. (For example, lost in the woods, lost on the highway, lost in indecision about the direction of you life, lost in knowing what God expects of you.) Picture Jesus speaking to you, lifting you up on his shoulders and carrying you to a safe place. Now ask Jesus to keep returning to you in your times of being lost. Now say slowly, the "Jesus Prayer" : **"Lord Jesus Christ, Son of the living God, have mercy on me, a sinner."** Repeat this prayer slowly ten times.

BIBLE MEMORY VERSE

"In the beginning was the Word, and the Word was with God and the Word was God. He was in the beginning with God; all things were made through him, and without him was not anything made that was made. In him was life, and this life was the light of men. The light shines in the darkness and the darkness has not overcome it. The true light that enlightens every man was coming into the world. He was in the world, and the world was made through him, yet the world knew him not. He came to his own home and his own people received him not. But to all who received him, who believed in his name, he gave power to become children of God; who were born, not of blood nor of the will of man, but of God. And the Word became flesh and dwelt among us, full of grace and truth; we have beheld his glory, glory as of the only Son from the Father. …No one has ever seen God; the only Son, who is in the bosom of the Father, he has made God known."

John 1:1-14 and 18

Chapter 15

ACTS: GOSPEL OF THE HOLY SPIRIT

Main focus of this chapter:
How Jesus continues to work on earth through the Holy Spirit

Introduction

Most of us are familiar with "sequels" in the movie business. Someone produces a big hit (like "Batman") which attracts millions of people and millions more dollars. Then two years later, the producer cranks out a sequel in hopes of capitalizing on the previous success (Batman II, III and so on). This is not a new idea. The Bible has sequels too. "Acts of The Apostles" is the sequel to "The Gospel According to Luke."

The Sequel   Luke begins the book of Acts with these words:

"In the first book, O Theophilus, I have dealt with all that Jesus began to do and teach until the day that he was taken up, after he had given commandment through the Holy Spirit to the disciples whom he had chosen. To them he presented himself alive after his passion by many proofs, appearing to them forty days and speaking of the kingdom of God."

Acts 1:1-3

The "first book" was "the gospel according to Luke." In it, Luke recorded all that Jesus began to do and teach. In this sequel, we will discover what Jesus continues to do and teach through the "acts" of the apostles, who are empowered, inspired and directed by the Holy Spirit. The title "Acts" was widely used in the ancient world to describe the great accomplishments of famous people. In meant, in other words, "The Great Deeds of…" the hero of a particular story. Many Bible scholars have observed that the "Acts of the Apostles" could also be called "the Gospel of the Holy Spirit." The human actors are the apostles, but the real "mover and shaker" is the Holy Spirit.

ACTS: GOSPEL OF THE HOLY SPIRIT

The Leading Role Luke continues his introduction of main character.

"And while staying with them he (the risen Jesus) charged them not to depart from Jerusalem, but to wait for the promise of the Father, which he said 'you heard from me, for John baptized with water, but before many days, you shall be baptized with the Holy Spirit."

Acts 1:4-5

In Luke's version of the Great Commission, Jesus tells his disciples to "go." But before they "go", they need to "wait" for the "promise of my Father." They need to wait for the leader to show up. (Luke 24:44-49)

The Scope of the Mission

Luke then tells where the Holy Spirit will lead them.

"But you shall receive power when the Holy Spirit has come upon you; and you shall be my witnesses in Jerusalem and in all Judea and Samaria and to the end of the earth."

Acts 1:8

In this brief introduction, Luke gives us the three main themes of the book of Acts: 1) Jesus will continue what he has already begun - no longer here "in the flesh", but through the Holy Spirit, 2) the Holy Spirit will be the motive force in the Church, 3) the mission of the Church is to all humanity – "the end of the earth."

I. The Promise of The Father: "Power From On High"

In the closing verses of Luke's gospel, Jesus says *"Behold, I send the promise of my Father upon you; but stay in the city until you have received power from on high."* (Luke 24:49) To get a fuller picture of what he meant by that, we need to look at the gospel according to John, in which Jesus gives an extended teaching on the Holy Spirit. This teaching takes place during the Last Supper on the night before Jesus died. He tells his disciples that he is about to die, and that things will never be the same again. But, even though he is leaving, he promises that he will never abandon them. In the following passages, Jesus assures them that the Holy Spirit will continue the ministry that Jesus began and that he (Jesus) will be personally present with them through the Holy Spirit.

"I will not leave you desolate; I will come to you. Yet a little while and the world will see me no more, but you will see me;

because I live, you will live also. In that day, you will know that I am in my Father, and you in me, and I in you. ... the Counselor, the Holy Spirit, whom the Father will send in my name, he will teach you all things, and will bring to your remembrance all that I have said to you."

John 14:18-20,25-26

"when the Counselor comes, whom I shall send from my Father, even the Spirit of truth, who proceeds from the Father, he will bear witness to me."

John 15:26

"It is to your advantage that I go away, for if I did not go, the Counselor would not come to you; but if I go, I will send him to you. ...I have yet many things to say to you but you cannot bear them now. When the Spirit of truth comes, he will guide you into all truth. ...He will take what is mine and declare it to you."

John 16:7,12-14

After rising from death and ascending into heaven, Jesus "sits at the right hand" of God. But God continues to live and work in the lives of believing people on earth, through the personal presence of the Holy Spirit. These promises of Jesus came to fruition on the fiftieth day after his Resurrection.

The "Doctrine of The Trinity" is a key element of the Church's normative interpretation of the Bible and is of critical importance in rightly interpreting and understanding the meaning of Pentecost. The One God is fully present in each "person" of the Trinity. When the Father created the universe, the Son and Holy Spirit were fully present in the act of Creation. When the Son died on the Cross, the Father and the Holy Spirit were fully present in the Atoning Sacrifice. On Pentecost, the Father and the Son were fully present as the Holy Spirit descended on the disciples in the upper room.

II. Pentecost: The Promise Fulfilled

The day of Pentecost has special symbolic significance. In the Old Testament, it was originally a feast of "first fruits" for the wheat harvest – a time to thank God for providing abundant food. In later Jewish tradition held that the Law was given to Moses on the fiftieth day after the Passover. ***"Shavout"*** (the fiftieth day after Passover) is the day for Jews to give thanks for the giving of the law. This is another example of God working through Old Testament traditions to infuse them with a new meaning. On the fiftieth day (that's what "Pentecost" means) after Jesus' Passover from death to resurrection life, God was about to act decisively again.

> *"When the day of Pentecost had come they (the disciples) were all together in one place. And suddenly a sound came from heaven like the rush of a mighty wind, and it filled all the house where they were sitting. And there appeared on them tongues as of fire, distributed and resting on each one of them. And they were all filled with the Holy Spirit and began to speak in other tongues as the Spirit gave them utterance."*
>
> Acts 2:1-4

From this moment on, the Holy Spirit began to work through the disciples in spectacular ways. The apostles received the "go power" to preach the gospel effectively and convincingly. Jesus was present, leading his disciples as he had promised them. The Church began to fulfill the Great Commission. This pentecostal moment was not just a one-time event. The Holy Spirit was given to the Church and to each individual Christian for all time. And while it is true that the Church, and individual Christians, go through times of greater and lesser awareness of the Holy Spirit, still the power and presence are always with us. Why? Because Jesus promised us that he would never abandon his followers on earth. The Holy Spirit is always present even if we don't always acknowledge him.

In the next two sections, we will look at two individuals through whom the Holy Spirit worked to reach people "in Jerusalem, Judea, Samaria and the end of the earth."

III. Peter, The First Preacher
(Read Acts chapter 2 before proceeding)

As we see in this chapter, the very first work of the Holy Spirit was to attract many people to the message of the gospel. After Peter boldly proclaimed what God had done through the life, death and resurrection of Jesus, many in his audience were "cut to the heart." In other words, they found his message convincing, wanted to respond positively and asked, "What shall we do?" Peter replied:

> *"Repent, and be baptized every one of you in the name of Jesus Christ for the forgiveness of your sins; and you shall receive the gift of the Holy Spirit. For the promise is to you and your children and to all that are far off, every one whom the Lord our God calls to him...So those who received his word were baptized, and there were added that day about three thousand souls. And they devoted themselves to the apostles teaching and fellowship, the breaking of bread and the prayers."*
>
> Acts 2:37-42

On this amazing day, three thousand people responded positively to Peter's message, a fact which must have amazed him and every one of the other disciples. In one morning, they had been transformed from a small group of slightly bewildered people, not quite sure what to do next, to bold leaders of a new movement to reach the whole world. The remainder of the book of Acts tells the rest of that story.

But before Peter could reach the world, he needed to be convinced that that was a good thing to do. Like many followers of Jesus, then and since, Peter did not get the full picture all at once. The Holy Spirit had to work on him to help him see the need to reach non-Jews (the Gentiles). Like most Jews, Peter regarded Gentiles as "unclean." Peter, like all of the first believers in Jesus, were Jews. As such, they assumed that one needed to be converted to Judaism before becoming a follower of Christ. Remember, at this point, the word "Christian" had not yet been invented. Jews who believed in Jesus were simply "believers." They all continued to practice their Jewish faith. Peter, like every other Jew, would have assumed that anyone who believed in Jesus would need to first become a Jew. We will now see how the Holy Spirit changed Peter's mind.

Two Visions, One Message
(Read Acts chapter 10 before continuing.)

It happened at Caesarea, a predominantly Roman city on the Mediterranean sea and a long way from Jerusalem. A Roman soldier named Cornelius, "a devout man who feared God with all his household, gave alms liberally to the people, and prayed constantly to God", had a vision. During a time of prayer, an angel told him to seek out Peter, whom he had never met before and who was visiting Joppa, a city nearby.

One day later, Peter had a vision of his own. While preparing a meal, he saw a vision of a many animals, reptiles and birds, all considered "unclean" in Jewish law, being lowered in a sheet. A voice came to him "Rise Peter, kill and eat." He replied "No Lord, for I have never eaten anything unclean or common." The voice replied, "What God has cleansed, you must not call common." The message was repeated three times. But Peter was still unsure of its meaning. As he sought to figure it out, messengers came from Cornelius asking Peter to visit. At the same time, the Spirit prompted him to go.

When Cornelius explained his vision to Peter, the meaning of Peter's own vision became clear to him, *"Truly I perceive that God shows no partiality, but in every nation anyone who fears him and does what is right is acceptable to him."* Peter then went on to share the gospel of Jesus with Cornelius and his household. While he was still speaking, the Holy Spirit "fell on all who heard the word" and they began to speak in tongues as the disciples did on Pentecost. Peter saw this as evidence that God had indeed chosen these "unclean" Gentiles to be part of the Jesus movement. *"Then Peter declared, 'Can anyone forbid water for baptizing these people who have received the Holy Spirit just as we have?' And he commanded them to be baptized in the name of Jesus Christ."*

In this event, the Holy Spirit paved the way for Peter and the other disciples to understand that faith in Jesus is intended for all humanity. God is doing a new thing to extend salvation to "the end of the earth", but it took Peter and the other disciples a long time to fully understand what God was doing. This was the fulfillment of God's promise to Abraham, that through his descendants, "shall all nations of the earth bless themselves." (Gen. 22: 18)

Even though the vision was given to Peter, his main concern was reaching his fellow Jews. Paul was God's "chosen instrument" to bring the name of Jesus Christ to the Gentiles. And to him we now turn.

IV. Paul, The First Itinerant Missionary

We will discuss the conversion and theology of Paul at greater length in the next chapter. In this chapter, we will focus on his missionary journeys.

After his conversion to Christ (recorded in Acts, chapter 9), Paul went on to become one of the great itinerant missionaries of all time and to set a standard for all later evangelism and church-planting endeavors. The first half of the book of Acts focuses on many different early disciples. The latter half of the book focuses almost entirely on the trials, triumphs and tribulations of Paul. Paul established a pattern of "planting" Christian communities which has been used by many mission organizations since. He established a local community of believers, trained local people to lead it, and then moved on to start new communities elsewhere. He kept in touch with these communities by letters and personal messengers. Many of these letters have survived and are now part of the New Testament.

One of Paul's early mission trips was to Antioch (in modern day Turkey) where he taught the locals for a year before moving on. It was here that a new name was invented: *"And in Antioch the disciples were for the first time called Christians."* (Acts 11:26)

Paul focused on coastal cities (Philippi, Thessalonica, Corinth, Ephesus) as well as inland cities (Antioch, Derbe, Lystra). Paul was not a soft-spoken , personal one-on-one evangelist. His style was abrasive and confrontational. His strategy was to find a public forum for discussing religious ideas, take the pulse of the crowd and then craft his message to his particular audience. Sometimes this strategy worked well (as in Derbe – see Acts 14:19-28 and

Corinth – see Acts 18:1-11)). Often, it got him in big trouble (as in Antioch of Pisidia – see Acts 13). Sometimes, he had great success and great calamity in the same place (as in Ephesus – see Acts 19).

At other times, he got mixed results. His missionary effort in Athens, even though not overwhelmingly successful, offer a model for bringing the Christian message to others in a multi-cultural world. As he enters the city, we are told "his spirit was provoked within him when he saw that it was full of idols." And yet, when it came time to speak to the polytheists of Athens, he reigned in his provoked spirit and presented the gospel in terms and symbols that they could accommodate in their own world-view. The following is a summary of Acts 17:16-34.

> *"Men of Athens, I perceive that in every way you are very religious. For as I passed along, and observed objects of your worship, I found also an altar with an inscription 'To an unknown god'. What you therefore worship as unknown, I now proclaim to you."*

He then goes on to tell the story of the Creator God, even quoting a Greek poet:

> *"As one of your poets has said "in him (the Creator God) we live and move and have our being."*

He then concludes his presentation by bringing them the explicit message of the gospel:

> *"the times of ignorance God has overlooked, but now he commands all men everywhere to repent, because he has fixed a day on which he will judge the world in righteousness by a man whom he has appointed, and of this he has given assurance to all man by raising him from the dead."*

In the end, some mocked him, but others responded positively. The point is that he contextualized his presentation of the gospel. He took the time to understand the world-view of another culture and attempted to "meet people where they live." This offers a good model for missionaries in every time and culture.

Paul's efforts to bring the gospel to the Gentiles (without first converting them to Judaism) eventually get him in big trouble with the Jewish followers of Jesus in Jerusalem. The story of his trials and tribulations is covered in Acts, chapters 21 through 26. At the end of his ordeal in the Jewish legal system, he is sent to Rome for his case to be heard by Caesar. Chapters 27 and 28 tell us of his long and arduous trip to Rome. The book closes on a triumphant note. Paul's legal troubles have gotten him a chance to preach the gospel in the heart of the polytheistic empire, whose Caesar is supposed to be a god. *"And he lived there for two years at his own expense, welcomed all who came to him, preaching the Kingdom of God and teaching about the Lord Jesus Christ quite openly and unhindered."*

The book of Acts ends with an optimistic eye to the future. The Great Commission is well on its way to being fulfilled. Through the efforts of Peter, Paul and others, the gospel has been carried "from Jerusalem, to Judea, to Samaria and to the end of the earth."

V. The Ongoing Work of The Holy Spirit in The Church

The Holy Spirit is the spirit of the Risen Lord Jesus Christ. Jesus is always with us through the work and power of the Holy Spirit. The Holy Spirit is given to every believing Christian just as really and truly as to the first Christians. So the book of Acts is not to be read only as an ancient history lesson.

The ongoing work of the Holy Spirit in the life of the Church as a whole, and in the life of each individual Christian, may be summarized as follows.

1) The Holy Spirit connects us to the Father and the Son and is a conduit for Jesus' abiding presence in our lives. (see John chapters 14, 15 and 16)

2) The Holy Spirit builds up the Body of Christ on earth and equips each member of the Body of Christ for the work of ministry. (See Ephesians 4: 4-16 and Romans 12:6-8)

3) The Holy Spirit is the living presence of Christ in the sacraments, in preaching, teaching, faith sharing, healing, miracles and other ministries of the Church. (See 1 Corinthians 12:7-12)

4) The Holy Spirit leads the Church into all truth, interpreting the unchanging truth of the gospel in the context of an ever-changing world. (See John 16:7-14 and Acts 10 and Acts 15)

5) The Holy Spirit confirms and strengthens faith, hope and love in the lives of those who seek to follow Jesus and seek God's will. Draws unbelievers to faith in Christ (See Romans 8:9-27)

QUESTIONS FOR DISCUSSION AND REFLECTION

1) Review each of the five categories outlined in the previous section on the ongoing work of the Holy Spirit. Read each of the Bible passages. Try to identify the times in your own life when you experienced the leading of the Holy Spirit in the ways described in these passages.

2) Look at the fruits of the Holy Spirit listed in Galatians 5:22-23 and the gifts of the Holy Spirit listed in Romans 12:6-8. What are some of the gifts and fruits that God has given you? What are some that you see at work in others, but do not see in yourself? What are some of the gifts that you think could be cultivated in your life?

PRAYER EXERCISE

Several theologians have said, "The Holy Spirit is the forgotten person of the Trinity." What they mean by that is that most people have some idea about "Our Father - The Creator." And many are able to relate to the man Jesus. But they don't spend much time thinking about the Holy Spirit.

Many people who have a beginning awareness of God, and even some who have a stronger faith in God, often seem unaware of the presence of the Holy Spirit in their own life. Are you in that category? Have you ever consciously asked for the empowering of the Holy Spirit? Have you ever asked for a specific gift of the Holy Spirit? Have you ever been conscious of using one of the gifts or fruits of the Holy Spirit?

Wherever you are in your spiritual journey, take some time now to pray for God to show you what you need to be shown about the Holy Spirit at work in your life. Ask for the continued grace to grow in the power and anointing of the Holy Spirit.

BIBLE MEMORY VERSE

"When the day of Pentecost had come they (the disciples) were all together in one place. And suddenly a sound came from heaven like the rush of a mighty wind, and it filled all the house where they were sitting. And there appeared on them tongues as of fire, distributed and resting on each one of them. And they were all filled with the Holy Spirit and began to speak in other tongues as the Spirit gave them utterance."

Acts 2:1-4

Chapter 16
PAUL'S GREAT EPISTLES: "I AM NOT ASHAMED OF THE GOSPEL"

Main focus of this chapter: The life and teaching of the most influential author of the New Testament

Introduction

In this chapter, we will summarize the epistles (letters) of Paul - the largest body of writing attributed to one author in the entire New Testament. Paul's writings have been very influential in the subsequent development of Christian theology over the centuries. At the time of deep controversy during the Protestant Reformation of the 16th century, Paul's authority and influence reached new heights as each side claimed to be the correct interpreters of Paul. It is no exaggeration to say that, second only to Jesus, Paul has been the most influential person in Christian theology and practice throughout history.

The letters traditionally attributed to Paul are: Romans, I and II Corinthians, I and II Thessalonians, Galatians, Philippians, Philemon, Colossians, Ephesians, I and II Timothy, and Titus. For a variety of reasons, many scholars think that the latter five books on this list are "deutero-Pauline" (written by Paul's disciples after his death and attributed to him). The reasons for this assessment are complex and beyond the scope of this brief summary. Whether or not these scholars are correct, the fact remains that these books are part of the canonical scriptures and (even if written by Paul's disciples) reflect his thought. Therefore, we will include them all in our general summary of Paul's writings. We will begin with a brief summary of Paul's life, followed by a section on Paul's "Big Picture" theology (What is God Doing?) and a section on his "Pastoral" theology (How do we humans respond to what God is doing?).

I. A Brief Biography of Paul
1) A Changed Life

Have you ever met someone who has changed your life? Someone who helped you see the world (and your place in the world) in a very different way?

The Living Word of the Living God

A school teacher or college professor, a coach, a mentor in your job, a husband or wife? Or maybe it was an experience that changed your life. A chance meeting which led to a lifelong friendship, a disaster that cause you to question and change your priorities, a visit to a foreign country very different from your own, falling in love, falling out of love, the death of a loved one, the birth of a loved one? Saul (later called Paul) met a person and had an experience on the road to Damascus. This person changed everything he ever thought about the world and his place in it. This experience caused him to reexamine the purpose and priorities in his life.

When we first hear of Saul, he is a vehement and violent persecutor of those who believe in Jesus. He approved of, assisted others in, the murder of Stephen.: *"Then they cast (Stephen) out of the city and stoned him; and the witnesses laid their garments at the feet of a young man named Saul."* (Acts 7:58) Following this, he actively persecuted and threatened to murder anyone who believed in Jesus. But in the midst of one of his persecutions, something happened to change his life forever. He met someone, was knocked to the ground and struck blind, and his life was never the same again.

> *"Saul, still breathing threats and murder against the disciples of the Lord, went to the High Priest and asked him for letters to the synagogues in Damascus, so that if he found any belonging to the Way, men or women, he might bring them bound to Jerusalem. Now as he journeyed he approached Damascus, and suddenly a light from heaven flashed about him. And he fell to the ground and heard a voice saying to him, 'Saul, Saul, why do you persecute me?' And he said, 'Who are you Lord?' And he said "I am Jesus, whom you are persecuting; but rise, enter the city, and you will be told what you are to do'."*
>
> Acts 9:1-6

At that moment, Saul began to have a profound change in his life. As was the case with the other people who met the risen Lord Jesus, it took Saul a while to come to grips with what he experienced. In the immediate aftermath of this incident, he was blinded by the light emanating from the risen Christ. The blind Saul was led into the city and met follower of Jesus named Ananias, who prayed with him and later taught him and prepared him to be baptized. During Ananias' prayer, "something like scales fell from his eyes" and he could see again. Shortly later, he was baptized and began a new life of service to Jesus and his followers. From that time on, Saul worked tirelessly to tell everyone in the whole world about this person he met on the road to Damascus.

Shortly after his encounter with the risen Jesus, Saul changed his name to "Paul" (which means "little one"). Although his motives for doing so are never explained, many scholars think the name change is a sign of an emerging humility. This humility is reflected in many different places in his writings, as in the following.

> "He (the risen Lord Jesus) appeared to all of the apostles. Last of all, as to one untimely born, he appeared also to me. For I am the least of the apostles, unfit to be called an apostle, because I persecuted the church of God. But by God's grace, I am what I am, and his grace toward me is not in vain. On the contrary, I have worked harder than any of them."
>
> I Corinthians 15:7-10

His humility is based on the conviction that God radically intervened in his life. And even though unworthy because of his previous behavior, God chose him for a mission to reach "the gentiles" (non-Jews).

> "For you have heard of my former life in Judaism, how I persecuted the church of God violently and tried to destroy it. ... But... he who set me apart before I was born, and had called me through his grace, was pleased to reveal his son to me, in order that I might preach him among the gentiles."

2) A Missionary to Gentiles (Non-Jews)

From this point on, Paul became a major figure in the spread of the Jesus message to the non-Jewish world (which is to say to the vast majority of people in the world). He worked tirelessly and relentlessly for the rest of his life to tell anyone who would listen about the person who changed his life. He helped to establish churches in many of the major cities of the Roman empire and wrote letters to many of the churches he helped to start. We have thirteen of those letters which comprise a major part of the New Testament and give us a very good window into the faith and life of the first followers of Jesus.

This mission to the gentiles was radical and controversial among Jews who believed in Jesus. Why? Because they thought that faithful followers of Jesus should be (or become) Torah-observant Jews. They should keep the dietary laws, the Sabbath laws, offer the Temple sacrifices and the men should be circumcised. They made the very reasonable argument that Jesus was a devout and observant Jew who never stopped being so. All of the first disciples of Jesus were Jewish and Jesus never told them to abandon the traditional practice of their Jewish faith.. Therefore, any new disciple of Jesus should follow the example of Jesus and his first followers by becoming observant Jews in full compliance with the revealed will of God in the Old Testament. This was a matter of faithfulness to God. God had ordained the law of the Old Testament and God had sent his Son to complete and fulfill the saving work that God had begun in the Old Testament. Therefore, every believer in Jesus should joyfully embrace the Torah-observant Jewish life. Gentile converts to Jesus should be circumcised (and observe all other Jewish norms) before being baptized. (This line of reasoning continues today in "Jews For Jesus" and other "messianic Jewish" movements, as well as some non- Jewish Christian groups, such as Seventh Day Adventists.)

Paul countered this argument with a very different line of reasoning. Paul insisted that God had acted to do something radically new in the life, death and resurrection of Jesus. In Jesus, God had begun a "New Covenant" which brings the Old to completion, and for which the Old had been a preparation.. In this New Covenant, God was offering salvation (previously available only to observant Jews) to all people. The "Chosen People" had now become all humanity. The "Promised Land" had now become the whole world. Through the life, death and resurrection of Jesus, God was fulfilling God's own promises to Abraham in the Old Covenant: that his descendants would be a blessing to all peoples of the earth.

> *"Thus Abraham 'believed God and it was reckoned to him as righteousness'. So you see that it is the people of faith who are sons of Abraham; and the scriptures, foreseeing that God would justify the Gentiles by faith, preached the gospel beforehand to Abraham saying, 'In you shall all nations be blessed'. ... (Therefore) in Christ Jesus the blessing of Abraham might come upon the Gentiles, that we all might receive the promise of the Spirit through faith."*
>
> Galatians 3:6-9 and 14

In Paul's view, the Old Testament had been given by God to Moses as a temporary measure. It was given to train the Jewish people to understand the purpose and character of God, and to shape Israel as God's own people in preparation for the salvation in Christ.

> *"Now before faith (in Christ) came, we were confined under the law, kept under restraint until faith should be revealed. So that the law was our custodian until Christ came, that we might be justified by faith. But now that faith has come, we are no longer under a custodian; for in Christ Jesus we are all sons of God through faith."*
>
> Galatians 3:23-27

In light of what God was doing, Paul reasoned, it was imperative that the Gentiles be brought directly to faith in Christ without taking the intermediate (and unnecessary as he saw it) step of conforming to the Old Testament law. In Paul's view, God had completely fulfilled the promises of the Old Testament in Christ, and therefore, it was working at cross purposes with God to insist on gentiles becoming Jews.

> *"For as many as you as were baptized into Christ have put on Christ. There is neither Jew nor Greek, there is neither slave nor free, there is neither male nor female; for you are all one in Christ Jesus. If you are Christ's, then you are Abraham's offspring, heirs according to the promise."*
>
> Galatians 3:28-29

Through Christ, God had broken down all dividing walls of religious distinction and social status (exemplified in, but not limited to, the distinctions between Jews and gentiles, male and female, slave and free). God is reaching out to redeem every human being, making old distinctions irrelevant. Through faith in Christ, everyone is equal before God. Paul dedicated his life to putting this conviction into practice. He traveled extensively, and at great personal cost and discomfort, to bring the message to the gentiles. In his letters, we can see his zeal and passion to be an effective instrument of God in this great work.

In his first letter to one of his earliest group of gentile converts in Thessalonica (in northeast Greece on the Mediterranean coast), we can detect his joy (and perhaps astonishment) that the gentiles are responding to his efforts.

> *"We give thanks to God always for you all, constantly mentioning you in our prayers...For we know brethren beloved by God, that he has chosen you...and how you turned to God from idols to serve a living and true God, and to wait from his Son from heaven, whom he raised from the dead, Jesus who delivers us from the wrath to come."*
>
> I Thessalonians 1:2,4,9-10

Paul saw these conversions of gentiles as evidence of God's approval and confirmation of his mission strategy of not requiring gentiles to become Jews. Paul's opponents (called "the circumcision party" in Acts11:2) continued to press their own view against him. They are steadfast in their view that faithfulness to God requires both circumcision and baptism. (In this New Testament argument, the word "circumcision" is shorthand for all the Old

Testament ritual requirements. This difference of opinion is discussed at great length in Galatians and in more generally in Romans. The "Jerusalem Conference," recorded in Acts 15, is convened to settle the matter and resolves it in Paul's favor. After much discussing and arguing and praying, a decision is made.

> *"For it has seemed good to the Holy Sprit and to us to lay no greater burden upon you (gentile converts to Christ) than these necessary things: that you abstain from what is sacrificed to idols and from blood and from what is strangled, and from sexual immorality. If you keep yourselves from these things you will do well."*
>
> Acts 15:28-29

After this decision, many of the apostles focused on bringing Jewish people to faith in Christ. These Jewish converts to Christ continued to practice all of the rituals of Judaism. For many years, the main body of believers in Jesus were observant Jews and continued to worship alongside other Jews in the Temple in Jerusalem. But Paul's mission was legitimized by this Jerusalem decision and he continued to bring Christ to the gentiles. Eventually Paul's view became the "mainstream" of Christianity for two reasons: first, because gentile converts far outnumbered Jewish converts and secondly, because the Jesus followers were later expelled from the Jewish community by the rabbis. Christianity has been very successful in adapting to many different racial, cultural and ethnic groups throughout the world. This success is largely owing to the flexible missionary strategy and to the universalizing missionary theology that are Paul's gifts to the Church. We now turn to the theology that supported the mission.

II. Paul's "Big Picture" Theology: What Is God Doing?

Paul's longest and most influential letter is "Romans" (so named because it was written to the fledgling Christian community in Rome). In this letter, Paul writes what some scholars have called his "Missionary Manifesto." In this letter, he presents a universalizing missionary theology. (We use the word "universalizing" here to indicate that salvation is needed by, and available to, all people. Paul certainly would not endorse the modern notion that all people will be saved, with or without their agreement and active participation.) Paul's missionary theology may be summarized under four headings: 1) Universal Human Need, 2) God's Universal Offer of Salvation, 3) The Necessary Human Response and 4) The Universal Mission Imperative.

1) **The Universal Condition:
   Everyone needs salvation – no exceptions.**

All human beings are spiritual sons and daughters of Adam and Eve. We are alienated from God through sin. The evidence of this alienation is sin and death. This is true for non-Jews as well as faithful Jews.

For non-Jews, who have never had the benefit of knowing the explicit will of God revealed in the Old Testament, there is a "natural revelation" that is available to any rational person observing the world:

> *"For the wrath of God is revealed from heaven against all ungodliness and wickedness of men who by their wickedness suppress the truth. For what can be known about God is plain to them, because God has shown it to them. For ever since the creation of the world his invisible nature, namely his eternal power and deity, has been clearly perceived in the things that have been made. So they are without excuse; for although they knew God, they did not honor him as God...."*
>
> Romans 1:18 -21

This implicit knowledge of God's moral law is imprinted on the human conscience and therefore, ignorance is no excuse. They are accountable to God.

> *"When the Gentiles who have not the (Old Testament) law do by nature what the law requires...They show that what the law requires is written on their hearts, while their conscience also bears witness and their conflicting thoughts accuse or perhaps excuse them on that day when... God judges the secrets of men."*
>
> Romans 2:14-18

For Jews, there is the advantage of a better explicit knowledge of the will of God, *"for the Jews are entrusted with the oracles of God."* To be part of God's chosen people was indeed a privilege, but the purpose was to prepare the world for God's saving work in Christ, not to secure a special "elite" status for Jews. The Jewish special knowledge of God does not change the fundamental and universal problem because *"all men, both Jews and Greeks are under the power of sin, as it is written: 'None is righteous, no not one; no one understands, no one seeks for God. All have turned aside, together they have gone wrong; no one does good, not even one.'"* (Romans 3:2,9-12)

2) God's Universal Offer of Salvation through Jesus Christ

In the life, death and resurrection of Jesus Christ, God has done something for all humanity that we can never do for ourselves. By the self-offering of Jesus on the Cross, God has made an atoning sacrifice for our sins. God has reached down to save us, not because we deserved it, but because we needed it.

> *"While we were still weak, at the right time Christ died for the ungodly.... God shows his love for us in that while we were yet sinners Christ died for us. Since, therefore, we are now justified by his blood, much more shall we be saved by him from the wrath of God. For while we were enemies, we were reconciled to God by the death of his Son, much more now that we are reconciled shall we be saved by his life."*
> Romans 5:6,8-10

3) The Necessary Human Response to God's Offer of Salvation

The only appropriate human response to God's offer of salvation is to accept it in faith. By "faith" Paul means much more than intellectual agreement (as in "I believe that two plus two equals four"). He means a deep knowledge of, and trust in, God's saving purpose (as in "When I was a child and sick as a dog with chicken pox, I knew in the depth of my heart that my mother loved me by the way she took care of me."). When a person, through living faith, believes, accepts and receives the message of what God has done for us in Christ, then that person receives the benefits of God's work. It is God's pure gift that "justifies" (brings to a right relationship with God) those who have a living faith and trust in God.

> *"...since all have sinned and fall short of the glory of God, they are justified by his grace as a gift, through the redemption which is in Christ Jesus, whom God put forward as an expiation by his blood to be received in faith....It will be reckoned to us who believe in him that raised from the dead Jesus our Lord, who was put to death for our trespasses and raised for our justification."*
> Romans 3:22-25 and 4:24-25

4) The Universal Mission Imperative

Because there is a universal human need for salvation, and because God has extended his offer of salvation to all people, and because people everywhere need to know how to respond to God before they can respond, it is therefore imperative that we tell everyone in the whole world about our need and about God's great offer of salvation.

> *"The word is near you, on your lips and in your heart...if you confess with your lips that Jesus is Lord and believe in your heart that God raised him from the dead, you will be saved. For man believes with his heart and so is justified, and he confesses with his lips and so is saved. For the scripture says 'everyone who calls upon the name of the Lord will be saved.' ... But how are men to call upon him in whom they have not believed? And how are they to believe in him of whom they have never heard? And how are they to hear without a preacher? And how is one to preach unless he is sent?"*
>
> Romans 10:8-11,14-15

The obvious answer to this series of rhetorical questions is that people cannot believe what they have never heard. Therefore, it is the responsibility of everyone who has received the gift of salvation to extend that gift to those who have not heard. For this reason, Christianity is necessarily a missionary faith. There is a God-given mandate to extend God's universal offer to everyone. To do any less than that would be unfaithful to the God who saved us. The mandate to tell every human being about God's saving work in Christ is not an "optional" activity for a few. It is the core mission of the Church. Paul begins the letter to Romans with a summary of this mission imperative:

> *"Paul, a servant of Jesus Christ, called to be an apostle, set apart for the gospel of God, which he promised beforehand through the prophets in the holy scriptures, the gospel concerning his Son, who was descended from David according to the flesh and designated Son of God in power according to the Spirit of holiness by his resurrection from the dead, Jesus Christ our lord, through whom we have received grace and apostleship to bring about the obedience of faith for the sake of his name among all the nations, including yourselves, who are called to belong to Jesus Christ"*
>
> Romans 1:1-6

He spent his life fulfilling this God-given mission "to bring about the obedience of faith for the sake of his name to all nations." He invites and challenges every Christian in every time and place to do the same. His motivation is to extend to every human being the liberating forgiveness of God which he himself had experienced.

> *"For I am not ashamed of the gospel: it is the power of God for salvation to everyone who has faith...For in it, the righteousness*

of God is revealed through faith for faith, as it is written, 'He who through faith is righteous shall live'."
Romans 1:16-17

III. Paul's "Pastoral" Theology: How Should We Respond To God?

The gospel is "the power of God for salvation to everyone who believes" In the life, death and resurrection of Jesus, God has rescued us "while we were yet sinners." So how should we humans receive and respond to this work of God? How does a person's life look different after having been "saved?" What is the evidence of a vital and living faith in Christ? To these questions, Paul had a hundred very good answers. The following is a brief summary.

1) A New Creation "In Christ"

When a person receives and believes the gospel message "in faith", that person is connected to the saving work of God through Jesus Christ. When a person comes to a living faith in Jesus, a spiritual transformation occurs - a transformation of being in which a believer's life is connected to the life of Jesus. Paul's term for this spiritual transformation was that the new believer was "in Christ."

> *"From now on therefore, we regard no one from a human point of view; even though we once regarded Christ thus, we regard him so no longer. Therefore, if anyone is in Christ, he (or she) is a new creation; the old has passed away, behold the new has come."*
> 2 Corinthians 5:16-17

This new status is symbolized and initiated in the sacrament of baptism and actualized in faithful living. Baptism connects us to the death-destroying and eternal-life-giving power of God. What God did with Jesus in his death and resurrection, God now does with us through our spiritual connection to Jesus through baptism and living faith.

> *"Do you not know that all of you who have been baptized into Christ Jesus were baptized into his death? We were buried with him therefore by baptism into death, so that as Christ was raised from the dead by the glory of the Father, we too might walk in the newness of life. For if we have been united to him in a death like his, we shall certainly be united to him in a resurrection like his.*

> *... But if we died with him, we shall also live with him. For we know that Christ being raised from the dead will never die again; death no longer has dominion over him. The death that he died he died to sin once for all, but the life that he lives, he now lives to God. So you also must consider yourselves dead to sin and alive to God in Christ Jesus, our Lord..*
>
> Romans 6:3-5 and 8-11

This sacramental and spiritual connection to the dying and rising Christ means that the person and personality of Jesus ought to be manifest in our life. This does not mean that our own personality is obliterated, but that we take on the character and love of Christ.

> *"I have been crucified with Christ. It is no longer I who live but Christ who lives in me; and the life that I now live, I live by faith in the Son of God, who loved me and gave himself for me."*
>
> Galatians 2:20

2) A Living Sacrifice

Recognizing, and being grateful for, this new life of Christ in us, we are called, challenged and inspired to offer our lives to God in humble service.

> *"I appeal to you therefore, brethren, by the mercies of God, to present your bodies as a living sacrifice, holy and acceptable to God which is your spiritual worship. Do not be conformed to this world, but be transformed by the renewal of your minds that you may prove what is the will of God, what is good and acceptable and perfect."*
>
> Romans 12:1-2

God no longer needs the dead sacrifice of bulls and goats. God desires a living sacrifice of a human life offered to the saving work of God. Good works should be done, not in hope of gaining God's favor, but as an expression of gratitude for all that God has done for us.

> *"For by grace you have been saved through faith; and this is not your own doing, it is the gift of God – not because of works lest any man should boast. For we are his workmanship, created in Christ Jesus for good works which God has prepared beforehand that we should walk in them."*
>
> Ephesians 2:8-10

A life given to the works of mercy and love is the evidence of the life-changing presence of Jesus Christ at work in the believing person. Therefore, we should take serious inventory of our lives to see where we have fallen short of the glory of God and strive to embody the love of Christ that God has given to us so generously,

> *"Work out your own salvation with fear and trembling, for God is at work in you both to will and to work for his good pleasure."*
> Philippians 2:12-13

And we should always recognize that a life surrendered to God's will is itself a gift. When we open our lives to the indwelling purpose of God, he give us both the will and the inner strength to do more than we ever thought possible.

> *"Now to him who by the power at work within us is able to do far more abundantly than all we ask or think, to him be glory in the church and in Christ Jesus forever and ever. Amen"*
> Ephesians 3:20-21

3) "Already But Not Yet": A Life-Long Process of Transformation

The transformation of a person's life "in Christ" is an "Already, But Not Yet" experience. Already we are a "new creation, the old has passed away, behold the new has come." Already, we can recognize the character of Jesus infusing our personality with his presence, so that "it is no longer I who live but Christ who lives in me." But not yet is the process of transformation complete. Paul speaks of his own life as a ""loss" of all the trappings of self-righteousness in order to "gain" the true goodness given to him through Christ.

Already, he has begun a journey to ever deeper identity with Christ:

> *"For his sake I have suffered the loss of all things, and count them as refuse, in order to gain Christ and be found in him, not having a righteousness of my own, based on law, but that which is through faith in Christ, the righteousness from God that depends on faith; that I may know him and the power of his resurrection, and may share in his sufferings, that it possible I may attain the resurrection of the dead. "*
> Philippians 3:8-11

But not yet is the journey complete:

> *"Not that I have already obtained this or am already perfect; but I press on to make it my own because Christ Jesus has made me his own. Brethren, I do not consider that I have made it my own; but one thing I do: forgetting what lies behind and straining forward to what lies ahead, I press on to the goal for the prize of the upward call of God in Christ Jesus."*
>
> Philippians 3:12-14

Paul is well acquainted with human frailty, including his own. He knows that the journey to be conformed to the will an purpose of God is difficult and filled with many obstacles and temptations. His focus is not on his own strength or weaknesses. His confidence is entirely based on the saving purpose of God in Christ: *"I press on to make it my own, because Christ Jesus has made me his own."*

Paul recognizes that human beings (including himself) can often obscure the presence and life of Christ in themselves. It is therefore necessary to remind ourselves that "it's not about us" but about Christ working through us. Christ transforms us "from the inside out" and we need to acknowledge the source, not focus on the outward appearances.

> *"For what we preach is not ourselves, but Jesus Christ as Lord, with ourselves as your servants for Jesus sake. For it is the God who said 'Let light shine out of darkness', who has shone in our hearts to give the knowledge of the glory of God in the face of Christ. But we have this treasure in earthen vessels, to show that the transcendent power belongs to Christ and not to us."*
>
> 2 Corinthians 4:5-7

4) "You Are the Body of Christ"

The identity of Christ within the individual believer is not the end of the matter. The church of Jesus Christ, in every time and place in history is collectively "The Body of Christ" on earth. Jesus walked the earth for a brief period of time, but he continues to walk the whole earth through his living Body – the Church.

> *"For just as the (human) body is one and has many members, and all of the members of the body, though many, are one body, so it is with Christ. For by one Spirit we are all baptized into one Body – Jews and Greeks, slaves or free-all were made to drink of one Spirit."*
>
> 1 Corinthians 12:12-13

Therefore, Paul says, we cannot think of the Church as a collection of autonomous individuals, each pursuing their own agenda with no regard for the others. We need to recognize in each other the presence of Christ. Because of Christ's presence, we need to honor each other – even when we don't agree. In honor of his presence, we need to love each other even when it is not always possible to like each other. Drawing on an extensive comparison to the interdependence of the various parts of the human body, Paul reminds us that no one is indispensable and everyone is needed.

> *"And if the ear should say 'Because I am not an eye, I do not belong to the body', that would not make it any less apart of the body. ...If the whole body were an eye, where would be the hearing? If the whole body were an ear, where would be the sense of smell? But as it is, God has arranged the organs in the body, each of them as he chose. ... As it is, there are many parts but one body. The eye cannot say to the hand, 'I have no need of you', nor again the head to the feet,' I have no need of you'.*

He then compares the human body to the living Body of Christ:

> *"If one member suffers, all suffer together; if one member is honored, all rejoice together. Now you are the body of Christ, and individually members of it.*
>
> 1 Corinthians 12:16-21, 26-27

This spiritual truth has far-reaching implications, many of which are spelled out in the rest of this letter to the Corinthians, and which have continuing relevance for every Christian community in every time and place in history. The Church is God's own invention - the body of Christ. Other members of the Body of Christ are our brothers and sisters in one Body, even when we don't like or agree with them; even when our cultures and priorities and political affiliations are at odds with each other; even when our government is at war with their government. Believers in Jesus can (and do) disagree and argue about important things. But we can never in good faith and in good conscience denigrate, despise or disrespect other members of the Body. To do so is to deny and despise the person at the heart of our life together: Jesus Christ.

Summary

Paul's life was changed dramatically by his encounter with the risen Lord Jesus. He changed from being a persecutor of the followers of Jesus to a zealous and unrelenting messenger: "I am not ashamed of the gospel. It is the power of God for salvation to all who believe." He endured many hardships, angry mobs and imprisonment to tell anyone who would listen about the Christ who changed his life. And he eventually died a martyr's death in Rome.

This changed man in turn changed the face of history. He was God's "chosen instrument" to bring God's salvation to the gentiles. He gave us a "missionary manifesto" that is still relevant and still inspires missionaries today. Through Paul's words and example, millions of people have come to know the liberating power of Christ throughout the world.

QUESTIONS FOR DISCUSSION AND REFLECTION

1) The central event of Paul's life was his encounter with the risen Lord Jesus. Because of this encounter with Jesus, he changed his direction.. He dedicated the rest of his life to telling others about the saving power of God in Jesus.

There are at least three types of faith in God that we can have.

The first is "formal" faith. This focuses on official teachings (I believe that the Bible is the word of God) and practices (I pray "the Lord's Prayer" before I go to bed).

The second is "shared" faith. This focuses on sharing beliefs and practices with other people (I learned about Jesus in Sunday School and pray with my family at meal time).

The third is "personal" faith. This is when you make a personal decision to relate to God, to pray in earnest and to commit your life to serving God.

Read Philippians 3:1-16. How would you describe Paul's level of faith as he describes it in this passage? How would describe your own level of faith? Have you ever made a conscious and personal commitment to Jesus Christ as your Lord and Savior?

2) Almost everyone has an experience in life of which they are ashamed. Many people are aware of ongoing moral struggles in their life that they seem to have no power to control. Read Romans 7:13 through 8:2. How would you describe Paul's moral crisis? What is his source of hope about his status before God? What does this have to tell us about our own moral struggles and our relationship to God?

3) Paul worked tirelessly to tell everyone he could about the wonderful thing that happened to him when he met the Risen Lord. What are some of the really important people , events or things in your life that you are excited to tell others about? What is the key to your excitement about these people, events and things (Do they make you happy, sad, proud, hopeful?) Is faith in Jesus one of the people or events on your list?

PRAYER EXERCISE

Read Philippians 4:4-9. Did you realize that Paul wrote these words when was in prison waiting to die? Are there people or events in your life that make you sad, angry, frustrated or depressed? Is it possible to apply Paul's message to your own life? Ask God to show you how to refocus the source of your unhappiness in light of these words.

BIBLE MEMORY VERSE

"Do you not know that all of you who have been baptized into Christ Jesus were baptized into his death? We were buried with him therefore by baptism into death, so that as Christ was raised from the dead by the glory of the Father, we too might walk in the newness of life. For if we have been united to him in a death like his, we shall certainly be united to him in a resurrection like his. ... But if we died with him, we shall also live with him. For we know that Christ being raised from the dead will never die again; death no longer has dominion over him. The death that he died he died to sin once for all, but the life that he lives, he now lives to God. So you also must consider yourselves dead to sin and alive to God in Christ Jesus, our Lord.."

Romans 6:3-5 and 8-11

Chapter 17

THE LATER EPISTLES: "NOW YOU ARE GOD'S PEOPLE"

Main focus of this chapter:
Practical advice on Christian life, hope and leadership

In the last chapter, we summarized the main themes of Paul's writings, primarily Romans, 1 and 2 Corinthians, Philippians and Ephesians. In these letters, we have considered the "ground floor" theology of the early Christian movement. In this chapter we will summarize several themes found in the later epistles. These include the "Pastoral Epistles" (I and II Timothy, and Titus), the "Catholic" or "General" epistles (I and II Peter, James, Jude, and I, II and III John) and Hebrews. Their primary focus is on the practical day-to-day realities of Christian life and the issues of leadership, discipline, direction and encouragement of the Church. Many Bible scholars believe that these letters were written in the "second generation" of the Christian movement because they are concerned with organizational matters which reflect a more mature institutional life of the Church. In this brief summary, we will include the later letters of Paul which seem to fall in this later category.

As we mentioned in chapter 9, when we read the epistles, we are reading "someone else's mail." These letters were not abstract theological essays. They are practical letters written to address real life problems and challenges in the early Christian communities. They are more like advice from "Dear Abby" than a doctoral dissertation on "What Is God Like?" However, the advice given is thoroughly informed by the writers' beliefs about God's nature and purpose, and about an adequate and faithful human response to God. That is why we continue to find meaning in these letters even though the original context is very different from our own.

We will summarize these "pastoral" letters under three main pastoral themes: Christian Life, Christian Hope and Christian Leadership.

I. Christian Life

As we have noted in the last chapter, much of the New Testament is concerned with how we live our lives in response to what God has done for us in Christ. Paul casts a great vision of presenting ourselves as "a living sacrifice" to God. But, what does that mean in practical terms? Here are a few examples from the epistles. There are many more to be found on every page and the reader is encouraged to explore beyond this brief summary introduction.

1) Development of Christ-like Character

Shaping the character of a child is a primary job of every conscientious parent. And shaping the character of Christians is one of the primary concerns of the New Testament writers. This process is shaped by the indwelling presence of Christ. When we respond to Christ with a living faith and engaged prayer life, he allows us to share in his nature.

> *"His (God's) divine power has granted us all things that pertain to life and goodness, through the knowledge of him (Jesus) who called us to his own glory and excellence, by which he has granted to us his precious and very great promises, that through these you may escape from the corruption that is in the world because of passion and become partakers of the divine nature."*
> 2 Peter 1:3-4

However, this is not a passive process in which we wait for Christ to "do something to" us. Rather, it requires our active and intentional cooperation. Following Jesus means being shaped by his example and growing into his likeness. This does not mean that we become physical clones of the historical Jesus of Nazareth. It means that we develop a Jesus-centered character - the virtues, values, moral vision, mission priorities and relational style that we see in Jesus. It means that we embody the love, humility and God-centered orientation that flows from the words and actions of Jesus. And when grow into the spiritual, moral and character likeness of Jesus, it helps us to understand him more thoroughly.

> *"For this reason make every effort to supplement your faith with virtue, and virtue with knowledge, and knowledge with self-control, and self-control with steadfastness, and steadfastness with godliness, and godliness with brotherly affection, and brotherly affection with love. For if these things are yours, and abound, they keep you from being ineffective or unfruitful in the knowledge of our Lord Jesus Christ."*
> 2 Peter 1:5-8

2) Showing Mercy and Offering Practical Help to Poor People

In the parable of the Good Samaritan, Jesus concludes by saying "you go and do likewise." In Matthew 25, Jesus tells us that when we feed a hungry person in his name, we are in fact feeding him. Jesus said he came to "bring good news to the poor" and he sends his followers to do the same. These teachings of Jesus are reflected in the epistles.

> *"Be doers of the word and not hearers only, deceiving yourselves. ...What does it profit, my brethren, if a man says he has faith but has not works? Can his faith save him? If a brother or sister is ill-clad and in lack of daily food, and one of you says, 'Go in peace, be warmed and filled', without giving him them the things needed for the body, what does it profit? So faith by itself, if it has no works, is dead."*
>
> James 1:22 and 2:14-17

> *"By this we know love, that he (Jesus) laid down his life for us; and we ought to lay down our lives for the brethren. But if anyone has this world's goods and sees his brother in need, yet closes his heart against him, how does God's love abide in him? Little children, let us not love in word or speech but in deed and truth"*
>
> I John 3:16-18

3) Love, Mutual Concern and Respect For Other Christians

Jesus taught that all ethical questions and commitments can be boiled down to two simple commands: love God with your whole being and love your neighbor as yourself. Several of the epistles offer a different emphasis. See how much God has loved us, therefore, we ought to be inspired to imitate the love of God. This love is evidence (both to those who do, and those who do not yet, believe) of God at work in our community of faith.

> *"Beloved, let us love one another because love is of God, and he who loves is born of God and knows God. He who does not love does not know God; for God is love. In this the love of God was made manifest among us, that God sent his only Son into the world, so that we might live through him. In this is love, not that we loved God, but that he loved us and sent his Son to be the expiation for our sins. Beloved, if God so loved us, then we ought to love one another. No man has ever seen God; if we love one another, God abides in us and his love is perfected in us."*
>
> `I John 4:7-12

In another passage, love, mutual respect and forgiveness are put in the context of assuming the character of Christ and growing into his life among the Christian community "in the one body."

> *"Put on then, as God's chosen ones, holy and beloved, compassion, kindness, lowliness, meekness and patience, forbearing one another and, if one has a complaint against another, forgiving each other; as the Lord has forgiven you, so you also must forgive. And above all these put on love, which binds everything together in perfect harmony. And let the peace of Christ rule in your hearts, to which you indeed were called in the one Body. And be thankful....And whatever you do in word or deed, do everything in the name of the Lord Jesus, giving thanks to God the Father through him."*
>
> Colossians 3:12-17

As anyone who has any level of participation in a Christian community will know, the advice given in the two passages above has two contradictory aspects. First, it has continuing relevance. Secondly, it is often ignored in the heat of disagreements and controversy. It is sad (and worse than sad) when followers of Christ do not even try to love and forgive one another as Christ loved and forgave us.

4) Love and Mutual Respect in Marriage, Family Life and Slavery

In the Roman cultural/legal context in which the New Testament is written, husbands were the absolute rulers of a household. Wives could be dismissed at the whim of a husband without any legal recourse. Infanticide was widely practiced as a method of family planning: new born infants would be allowed to live, or left to die, based on the decree of the father. Slavery was widely practiced because slaves were "war booty" from Roman military conquests. Slaves had no rights and were often severely mistreated by their masters. Jewish customs and law at the time were only slightly more favorable to women than in the Roman context. It is important to consider this context when reading New Testament passages on marriage and family life. Modern readers find these passages to be highly approving of male dominance and female subservience - and when compared to modern American attitudes and practices, this impression is accurate. But in the context of the ancient Roman and Jewish culture, they are remarkable because of their emphasis on mutual respect and fair treatment. The first four sentences of the following passage would have been compatible with the prevailing cultural norms; but the latter four sentences were radically at odds with them.

The Later Epistles: "Now You are God's People"

> *"Be subject to one another out of reverence for Christ. Wives, be subject to your husbands, as to the Lord. For the husband is head of the wife as Christ is the head of the church, which is his body, and is himself its savior. As the church is subject to Christ, so let wives be subject in everything to their husbands. Husbands love your wives, as Christ loved the church and gave himself up for her, that he might sanctify her, having cleansed her by the washing of water with the word, that he might present the church to himself in splendor, without any spot or wrinkle, or any such thing, that she might be holy and without blemish. Even so, husbands should love wives as their own bodies. He who loves his wife loves himself. For no man ever hates his own flesh, but nourishes it and cherishes it, as Christ does the church, because we are members of his body."*
> Ephesians 5:21-30

The foundational conviction in the passage above is that husbands and wives are members of the body of Christ. Mutual respect and love is based on the conviction that Christ is alive in each partner and that we should respect each other out of reverence for his presence there. Other passages hold up the same truth with respect to relations with other members of the household.

> *"Children, obey your parents in everything, for this pleases the Lord. Fathers, do not provoke your children, lest they become discouraged. Slaves, obey in everything your earthly masters, not with eye service, as men pleasers, but in singleness of heart, fearing the Lord. ...Masters, treat your slaves justly and fairly, knowing that you also have a Master in heaven."*
> Colossians 3:20-22 and 4:1

Many modern readers are understandably perplexed that the New Testament writers did not denounce the practice of slavery. One can only respond that this was a very common Roman (and not Jewish) practice at the time, that the New Testament writers were part of a very small Jewish movement who had no political or social influence with the Romans and that therefore, challenging an entrenched Roman institution would have been ineffective at best and suicidal at worst. To ask why the New Testament writers didn't oppose slavery is like asking why they didn't seek a medical cure for leprosy. It was a real problem that caused widespread human misery, but finding a "solution" was probably not on their "radar screen" as a possibility.

However, we do see evidence that, on a personal level, they tried to ameliorate the human suffering of slavery, as the passage above indicates. Also, we have one example (which may well be indicative of similar efforts by others) to persuade Christian slave holders to regard their slaves as brothers and sisters in Christ. In the following passage, Paul is writing to his friend Philemon (who was converted to Christ by Paul) to show mercy on his runaway slave (who was also converted to Christ by Paul). Philemon has the right to severely punish his slave for running away. But Paul urges mercy. The slave's name is Onesimus (which means "useful" in Greek) and is the basis for a pun in Paul's plea. Uncharacteristically for Paul, the tone of this appeal is subtle. He appeals to his friend to see his runaway slave as "a brother in the Lord" and to treat him as such.

> *"I appeal to you for my child Onesimus whose father I have become in my imprisonment. Formerly he was useless to you, but now he is indeed useful to me and to you. I am sending him back to you, sending my very heart. I would have been glad to keep him with me, in order that he might serve me on your behalf during my imprisonment for the gospel; but I preferred to do nothing without your consent in order that your goodness might not be by compulsion but by your own free will. Perhaps that is why he was parted from you for a while, that you might have him back forever, no longer as a slave but more than a slave, as a beloved brother, especially to me but how much more to you, both in the flesh and in the Lord. So if you consider me your partner, receive him as you would receive me."*
>
> Philemon 10-17

In sum, the Roman cultural context of marriage and family and slaveholding was radically different from our own. The New Testament writers did not seek to reform these cultural norms. Instead, they sought to bring the love of Christ to bear on various relationships, focusing on personal commitment to Christ and enjoining Christ-like behavior from his followers. The advice given in these letters can help us apply the love of Christ to our own cultural norms for marriage, family life and employer/employee relationships.

II. Christian Hope

In the very early Christian communities, there was a widespread expectation that Jesus would return very soon and that the world as we know it would be transformed into the Christ's Kingdom in which God would be "all in all." As time went on, however, it became obvious that the second coming of Christ would not happen as soon as some had expected. This then created a pastoral problem. Many became confused and began to lose hope.

The Later Epistles: "Now You are God's People"

Several of the epistles address this matter by reminding everyone that God is not on the same timetable as we are. They repeat a message we often hear from Jesus in the gospels: "Don't worry about God's timing, which is beyond human knowing. Focus on being faithful in thought, word and deed, which is within our power."

> *"But do not ignore this one fact, beloved, that with the Lord one day is as a thousand years, and a thousand years as one day. The Lord is not slow about his promise as some count slowness, but is forbearing toward you, not wishing that any should perish, but that all should reach repentance. ...But according to his promise, we wait for new heavens and a new earth in which righteousness dwells. Therefore, beloved since you wait for these, be zealous to be found in him, without spot or blemish, and at peace. And count the forbearance of the Lord as salvation."*
> 2 Peter 3:8-9 and 13-15

Other passages remind us of the patience and hope-filled expectation of our ancestors in faith and exhort us to learn from their example. The longest, and most eloquent of these passages is found in Hebrews chapter 11 and 12. It begins with a short and memorable statement of firm conviction.

> *"Now faith is the assurance of things hoped for, the conviction of things not seen. For by it, the men of old received divine approval. By faith, we understand that the world was created by the word of God, so that what is seen was made out of things that do not appear."*
> Hebrews 11:1-3

The author then goes on to list several heroes of the faith from the Old Testament (Abel, Noah, Abraham, Moses and many others). About half way through the chapter, he reminds us that these heroes of faith trusted God, even when there was little or no immediate encouragement to do so, and even died before seeing the fulfillment of their hopes.

> *"These all died in faith, not having received what was promised, but having seen it and greeted it from afar, and having acknowledged that they were strangers and exiles on the earth. For people who speak thus make it clear that they are seeking a homeland. If they had been thinking of that from which they had gone out, they would have had an opportunity to return. But as it is they desire a better country, that is, a heavenly one. Therefore*

> *God is not ashamed to be called their God, for he has prepared for them a city."*
>
> Hebrews 11:13-16

He then concludes the eleventh chapter by connecting the expectant hope of the Old Testament to the fulfilled hope of the New Testament.

> *"And all these, though well attested by their faith, did not receive what was promised, since God had foreseen something better for us, that apart from us they should not be made perfect."*
>
> Hebrews 11:39-40

He then brings this extended reflection to its grand conclusion, calling everyone to be inspired by the Old Testament heroes and preeminently, by Jesus, to be expectant in hope and to trust God to finish what God has begun.

> *"Therefore, since we are surrounded by so great a cloud of witnesses, let us also lay aside very weight and sin which clings so closely, and let us run with perseverance the race that is set before us, looking to Jesus, the pioneer and perfecter of our faith, who for the joy that was set before him endured the cross, despising the shame, and is seated at the right hand of the throne of God."*
>
> Hebrews 12:1-2

The message of these and many other biblical passages is that human timing and God's timing are often very different. The short term adversities of life can cause us to lose our perspective and lose our hope in God's saving purposes. In such circumstances, we need to encourage each other to renew our faith, trust and hope in God. And we can teach each other by example, to live the truth of Hebrews 11:1 "Faith is the assurance of things hoped for, the evidence of things not seen."

III. Christian Leadership

In his final "Great Commission", Jesus gave his followers a very big job to do: "Go and make disciples of all nations." He trained twelve "apostles" (which means "sent ones") to lead his followers. He told them what to teach and how to pray. He promised to send the Holy Spirit to lead and guide them. He told them what to do, but he said very little about how to do it. So, the earliest Christians had to "make it up" as they went along – under the promised guidance of the Holy Spirit. Consequently, we see in the New Testament, the development of leadership roles for sound teaching, positive direction and discipline. In later Church history, these leadership roles changed as new challenges called for new solutions. It is a source of endless discussion (and sometimes intense disagreement) about how to most faithfully apply these biblical patterns of leadership and discipline as new situations and new challenges arise in an ever changing world. It is left to each generation, guided by the Holy Spirit, to employ and adapt these New Testament models in fulfilling the mission given to us by Jesus.

1) Gifts For Ministry

Jesus promised that he would send the Holy Sprit to empower, teach and guide the Church "into all truth." Therefore, leadership in ministry is itself a gift of the Holy Spirit. Leadership in the Christian movement should never be thought of as a "job" in the secular sense, nor as an "office" in the bureaucratic sense. It is a gift and calling from the Holy Spirit – a sacred trust to be respected and used as God intends.

> *"There is one body and one Spirit, just as you were called to the one hope that belongs to your call, one Lord, one faith, one baptism, one God and Father of us all, who is above all and in all and through all. But grace was given to each one of us according to the measure of Christ's gift. ... And his gifts were that some should be apostles, some prophets, some evangelists, some pastors and teachers..."*
>
> Ephesians 4:4-7 and 11

2) To Equip the Saints for Building Up the Body

Leadership gifts are not given so that some people can "do ministry" while other people watch them do it. The purpose of leadership in the Church is for leaders to help others to grow into mature Christian disciples who will discover their own ministry and, in turn, help others to grow in ministry maturity.

> *"...to equip the saints for the work of ministry, for building up the body of Christ, until we all attain to the unity of the faith and the knowledge of the Son of God, to mature manhood, to the measure of the stature of the fullness of Christ."*
>
> Ephesians 4:12-13

3) To Grow Up In Every Way Into Christ, The Head

The purpose of every leader, and of every member, of the Church is to help each other grow into the moral likeness of Christ. When it is being what God wants it to be, the Church is the living Body of Christ on earth. The Church makes visible on earth the invisible realities of God's kingdom.

> *"...so that we may no longer be children, tossed to and fro and carried about by every wind of doctrine, by the cunning of men, by their craftiness and deceitful wiles. Rather, speaking the truth in love, we are to grow up in every way into him who is the head, into Christ, from whom the whole body, joined and knit together by every joint with which it is supplied, when each part is working properly, makes bodily growth and upbuilds itself in love."*
>
> Ephesians 4:14-16

The end result of faithful leadership is a spiritually mature community of disciples who in turn make disciples of others. As the above passage attests, good leadership means saying "no" to many trends in the surrounding culture which distort the Christian gospel and distract followers of Christ. In any and every cultural context, there will be forces which confuse us. Good leaders keep us focused during the storms of life. A healthy Christian community is engaged in the storms, but is not shipwrecked by them.

4) Preach the Word, In Season and Out of Season

The chief duty of a pastor is to preach the gospel and teach disciples. This truth is often obscured in modern Church life. Pastors are expected by others (and often themselves) to be counselors, administrators, fund-raisers, entertainers, community organizers, publishers, webmasters, recruiters for every conceivable activity and mediators of conflict (just to name a few). While these duties are not intrinsically evil, and many of them good and necessary, the accumulated weight of them can drown out any time or energy to focus on the main thing. The main thing is twofold: proclaiming the gospel so that people may receive Christ as their Lord and teaching people so that they may know what it is to become a mature disciple of Jesus.

> *"I charge you in the presence of God and of Christ Jesus who is judge of the living and the dead, and by the appearing of his kingdom: preach the word, be urgent in season and out of season, convince, rebuke and exhort, be unfailing in patience and teaching. For the time is coming when people will not endure*

sound teaching, but having itching ears they will accumulate for themselves teachers to fit their own likings and will turn away from listening to the truth and wander into myths. As for you, always be steady, do the work of an evangelist, fulfill your ministry."

2 Timothy 4:1-5

In every time and place, there will always be the opportunity for people to turn away from the truth. The work of a pastor is to tirelessly define the Christina faith over, and often against, the prevailing cultural winds. A faithful pastor can expect to encounter opposition from those with "itching ears" who have an investment in the prevailing cultural winds. This job is often thankless and always difficult. It requires intelligence, flexibility and persistence. It deserves the highest level of priority and attention in the life of a Christina leader and of the community he or she leads.

5) Bishops, Presbyters and Deacons

Jesus called and commissioned "apostles" ("sent ones") to lead his disciples. In the very early Christian movement, however, there was a need to better differentiate roles and ministries. In the book of Acts(chapter 6), we see the apostles selecting seven men for a special "servant" ministry in order to free the apostles to devote themselves to the teaching ministry. This servant ministry later became formalized into the role of "Deacon" (from the Greek word "diaconos" which means "servant"). Later still, we see the apostolic ministry separated into two separate roles of "Presbyters" (from the Greek word "presbuteros" which means "elder") and "Bishop" (from the Greek word "episcopos" which means "overseer"). In the following passages, we see a later development in the Church in which, it is assumed, these "offices" are well established and established roles.

Bishops

"If anyone aspires to the office of a bishop, he desires a noble task. Now a bishop must be above reproach, the husband of one wife, temperate, sensible, dignified, hospitable, an apt teacher, no drunkard, not violent but gentle, not quarrelsome and no lover of money. He must mange his own household well, keeping his children submissive and respectful in every way; for if a man does not know how to manage his own household, how can he care for God's church?"

1 Timothy 3:1-5

Presbyters

"So I exhort the elders (presbuterous) among you, as a fellow elder and a witness of the sufferings of Christ as well as a partaker of the glory that is to be revealed. Tend the flock that is in your care, not by constraint but willingly, not for shameful gain, but eagerly, not as domineering over those in your charge but being examples of the flock. And when the chief Shepherd is manifested, you will obtain the unfading crown of glory."

1 Peter 5:1-4

Deacons

"Deacons likewise must be serious, not double-tongued, not addicted to much wine, nor greedy for gain; they must hold to the mystery of the faith with a clear conscience. And let them be tested first; then if they prove themselves blameless, let them serve as deacons."

1 Timothy 3:8-10

At the time of Church history that these passages were written, these "offices" seem to be "semi-permanent" roles of leadership. Within a couple of generations (in letters written by Church leaders after the New Testament), we see them being solidified into "permanent" orders of ministry and with a discernible order of authority. Bishops were overseers, usually of a city with several congregations. Presbyters were in charge of local congregations as the bishop's delegated representative. And Deacons were servant ministers whose main job was to feed the poor, working under the supervision of the Bishop. In later generations, the title "presbuteros" has been translated into English as "priest" and this is the normal usage in the Roman Catholic Church, Eastern Orthodox Church and Anglican Communion.

Apostolic Succession

Still later in Church history, this "threefold order" of apostolic ministry became identified with "the apostolic succession" in which a bishop's authenticity was legitimated by having been ordained in a direct line of bishops leading to the original twelve apostles. In the emergent Christian movment, rival teachers and widely divergent interpretations arose in various Christian communities. This trend is already evident in the New Testament epistles. Paul and John especially devote much of their writing to distinguishing between authentic and false teachers of the Christian faith. After the death of the original apostles, a new question arose. Now that the original "eyewitnesses" were no longer alive, who was qualified to settle arguments between rival Christian teachers ? Who was qualified to decide in matters of biblical interpretation ? How would Christian communities decide which teachers and teachings were most trustworthy? How would Christian communities hold one another accountable to the "faith once delivered to the saints"? Who was qualified to decide which books would be included in the canon of the New Testament ? The consensus of the early Church was that bishops who could be identified with an unbroken line of authority from the apostles (called "apostolic succession") were more trustworthy teachers of the faith.

This doctrine is still believed and practiced by the Roman Catholic Church, the Eastern Orthodox Church and the Anglican Communion. In these Christian communities which hold to the doctrine of apostolic succession, the ministry of Bishop, Priest and Deacon is regarded as a permanent and life-long office. At the time of the Reformation in the 16th century, many Protestant groups rejected (or radically reformulated) the doctrine of "apostolic succession" and the various leadership roles.

In rejecting the authority of the Roman Catholic Church, they appealed to (what they regard to be) a more authentic "apostolic succession" founded on a true teaching of the Bible rather than on an institutional pedigree. Similarly, in modern Protestant denominations, there are a variety of leadership roles which they consider to be closer to the Biblical model. These often include a threefold pattern of 1) bishops, 2) some adaptation of pastor, elder, presbyter and 3) deacons, but they are generally understood as temporary elective offices and not life-long.

It would be a mistake to think that "apostolic succession" is an anachronistic and irrelevant doctrine. The situation of the world-wide Church in the 21st century is, at least in some respects, very similar to the early centuries of Christianity. There are many rival and divergent interpretations of authentic Christian faith. Many Christian communities are experiencing extreme institutional stress arising from these divergent teachings and practices. There is an ongoing and urgent need to maintain institutions and norms of mutual accountability in Christian teaching and practice for the sake of presenting a credible witness to those who have not yet heard or received the gospel.

Summary

The "pastoral" and "catholic" epistles address many practical issues of Christian life, Christian hope and leadership within the Christian movement. The overarching themes of all of these epistles is that Christianity is a communal faith – not an individualistic enterprise. In scholarly circles, it is said: "Jesus promised us a Kingdom but he left us a Church." The comment is intended to be ironic, or maybe even cynical, but it is true. Jesus promised us a Kingdom as the goal, and he left us a Church as the vehicle to help us get to the desired destination. We do not get to the Kingdom alone. We go there together or we do not go at all. In every generation and in every part of the world, there are unique temptations, distractions and distortions which lead us away from the Kingdom that Jesus promised. He calls us together in communities to help each other lead a faithful life, to sustain the hope that we have and to lead each other through a wilderness to the Promised Land.

> *"And his gifts were that some should be apostles, some prophets, some evangelists, some pastors and teachers to equip the saints for the work of ministry, for building up the body of Christ, until we all attain to the unity of the faith and the knowledge of the Son of God, to mature manhood, to the measure of the stature of the fullness of Christ, so that we may no longer be children, tossed to and fro and carried about by every wind of doctrine, by the cunning of men, by their craftiness and deceitful wiles. Rather, speaking the truth in love, we are to grow up in every way into him who is the head, into Christ, from whom the whole body, joined and knit together by every joint with which it is supplied, when each part is working properly, makes bodily growth and upbuilds itself in love."*

QUESTIONS FOR REFLECTION AND DISCUSSION

1) Medical professionals have long observed that some people do much better than others in recovering from serious illnesses. Several clinical studies and much anecdotal evidence suggest that the most important factor in recovery and health is hope. Those who have a strong will to live and confidence that things will get better tend to recover faster and more often than those without hope.

Are there situations in your life (or in the lives of people you know and love) that cause you to lose hope in a better future, in God's love in the Kingdom of God that Jesus promised?

When you are feeling hopeless, how do you respond? When someone you know is feeling hopeless, how do you respond to them? Do you think your response can make a difference?

Read the following passages:
Romans 8:18-25
2 Peter 3:8-10

How do these passages speak about hope, hopelessness and the way to address each?

2) One of the great crises in American society today is the breakdown of the nuclear family (that is: father and mother in intact marriage raising their children to adulthood together). The most obvious victims of family breakdown are children. Multiple studies have shown that these children are statistically more likely to: live in poverty, be uneducated, go to jail and have children out of wedlock (which perpetuates the cycle).

Read the following passages:
Ephesians 5:21-33
Colossians 3:18 through 4: 6
1 Timothy 5:1-24

The New Testament gives us several models for family life. Some people think these are hopelessly outmoded and not relevant to our modern world. Others say that they are directly applicable without any alteration. Others say that the general principles are applicable, but need to be adjusted to modern realties. Which do you think is the best way to apply these passages to our modern life?

How would you apply the messages of these passages to the problems we face in our society?

3) In the modern world, we see many problems in Christian communities: divisive arguments about sexual ethics, what to do about poverty, women's rights, human rights, discipline for misbehaving clergy, and so on. And there are many different models of leadership in Christian communities. Some are led by very strong, clear and centralized lines of human authority and accountability, for example the Roman Catholic Church. Some are led by more local authority structures centered on an individual congregation, for example many Baptist churches.

Read the following passages:
Titus chapters 1 and 2
1 Corinthians chapter 5

What kind of leadership is being recommended in these passages? What are the problems they are seeking to remedy? Do you see any similar problems arising in churches today? What do you think is the most effective and faithful leadership model (more centralized or more localized)? What is the "upside" and "downside" of centralized and localized leadership models?

PERSONAL REFECTION

Read slowly Colossians 3:12-17. This passage exhorts us to "put on" several attitudes and behaviors. The implication is that we are not adequately clothed and that we need to add another layer. Think about the relationships in your life, with your family, friends, church community, co-workers and so on. Do any examples come to mind in which you need to "put on" some of the attitudes and behaviors mentioned in this passage? What difference do you think it would make if you did?

The passage ends with the exhortation: "whatever you do in word or deed, do it in the name of the Lord Jesus." Take a moment to think about a specific relationships in your life, perhaps one with which you have some difficulty. Do your words and deeds meet the standard set in this passage? Take some prayer time to ask God for the grace to "put on" the attitudes and behaviors suggested in the passage.

THE LATER EPISTLES: "NOW YOU ARE GOD'S PEOPLE"

BIBLE MEMORY VERSE

"Put on then, as God's chosen ones, holy and beloved, compassion, kindness, lowliness, meekness and patience, forbearing one another and, if one has a complaint against another, forgiving each other; as the Lord has forgiven you, so you also must forgive. And above all these put on love, which binds everything together in perfect harmony. And let the peace of Christ rule in your hearts, to which you indeed were called in the one Body. And be thankful....And whatever you do in word or deed, do everything in the name of the Lord Jesus, giving thanks to God the Father through him."
Colossians 3:12-17

Chapter 18

THE BOOK OF REVELATION ("APOCALYPSE")

Main focus of this chapter:
How to understand one of the most perplexing books of the Bible

We now consider that last book of the Bible which is an appropriate bookend complimenting the first book. Genesis tells us of Creation "in the beginning"- at the dawn of time. Revelation tells us of the "new heaven and a new earth" at the end of time. Genesis recounts humanity's misuse of the tree of life and expulsion from the Garden. Revelation foretells our return to the tree of life "and the leaves of the tree were for the healing of the nations." Genesis speaks with sorrow of the curse of human sin and its growing web of destruction. Revelation speaks with joyful anticipation of a time when "there shall no more be anything accursed, but the throne of God and of the Lamb shall be in it, and his servants shall worship him; they shall see his face and his name will be written on their foreheads." Genesis portrays a Creator God who pronounces his work "very good." Revelation portrays a Redeemer God who brings his work to completion in a time beyond time in which "death will be no more, neither will there be mourning, nor crying, nor pain anymore, for the former things have passed away." Placing Genesis at the beginning and Revelation at the end frames the Bible as one coherent narrative of a loving God who never gives up on the people and universe he has created.

I. How Should Revelation Be Interpreted?

The title of this book is taken from the very first verse: "The Revelation of Jesus Christ which God gave him to show to his servants what must soon take place...." The English word "Revelation" is a translation of the original Greek word "apocalypsis" which means literally "the unveiling of what is hidden." This leads inevitably to several questions: "what exactly is being unveiled? What must soon take place? When will it happen?" For the past two thousand years, the various answers to this question have fallen into three general categories.

First, there are some who think that, because the book was written at the time of severe persecution of Christians by Roman emperors, all of its symbolic language refers to current events around 95 A.D. For that reason, it has no relevance whatsoever for later generations of readers except as an interesting historical commentary.

Second, many have sought to interpret the book as a coded message about the details and timing of the end of the world. In almost every generation, but especially in times of great social upheaval, many have applied the symbolic message of this book to their own time and situation. For example, many have identified the "antichrist" with a particular person (the Pope, Hitler, Stalin, Saddam Hussein, Ronald Reagan etc., etc.), identified the battle of Armageddon with current military events (the Black Plague, the Thirty Years War, the American Civil War, World Wars I and II, the atom bomb, the Gulf Wars) and predicted the exact date of "the end" (the year 1,000 A.D., the completion of the Reformation of the 16th century, the year 2,000 A.D.). In the twentieth century many books were written (and widely read)using this method of interpretation. So far, every attempt to predict the exact date of "the end" in this way has proven false.

Third, many people read Revelation as a message of absolute conviction that God will bring to completion the work that God has begun in and through the people of Israel, through the life, death and resurrection of Jesus and through the Church in history. In this method of interpretation, the highly symbolic language and imagery of the book is intended to convey the same Christ-centered message we find in the Gospels and Epistles but in a very different medium. Its purpose is to encourage Christians to "hang in there" during times of hardship and persecution. In this interpretation, the book of Revelation is relevant for every time and place because the spirit of "antichrist" is always present in world events when people work against the purposes of God, the Evil One is always active in persuading people to rebel against God, and Christ is always alive and triumphant before the throne of the Father interceding for his Church on earth. The exact timing of "the end" is God's business. The business of the Church on earth is to be faithful and steadfast in the face of temptation, persecution and opposition.

We will return to the subject of which of these three methods of interpretation is best in the discussion section at the end of the chapter.

Revelation is a very complex book with rich symbolism building on previous biblical texts. It has many levels of meaning and possible lines of interpretation which are beyond the scope of this brief overview. This introduction is offered to help the reader see the overall structure and the main themes of the book. There are many excellent commentaries which will help the interested reader dig deeper into this "mother lode" of biblical symbolism.

II. Basic Structure of the Book of Revelation

Bible scholars have many theories about the basic structure. We will use the following. (adapted from Raymond E. Brown *Introduction to the New Testament* Doubleday, New York 1997, p.774)

Prologue	1:1-3
Letters to the Seven Churches	1:4 – 3:22
Seven Revelations	4:1 – 22:5
1) Visions of the Heavenly Court	4:1 – 5:14
2) Seven Seals	6:1 – 8:1
3) Seven Trumpets	8:2 – 11:19
4) Visions of the Woman, Dragon, Beasts and the Lamb	12:1 – 14:20
5) Seven Plagues and Seven Bowls	15:1 – 16:21
6) Judgment of Babylon, The Great Harlot	17:1 – 19:10
7) Victory of Christ and the New Creation	19:11 – 22:5
Epilogue - Final Blessing	22:6-21

III. Summary of the Main Themes of Revelation

Prologue 1:1-3

> *"The revelation of Jesus Christ which God gave him to show to his servants what must soon take place; and he made it know by sending his angel to his servant John..."*

The introduction tells us that this is not a generic "spiritual vision." It is rooted in the ongoing life and ministry of Jesus Christ, who has died, is risen and is alive forevermore. The message of this book should never be set against, or above, or below, the other New Testament writings. It is a complementary part of the whole narrative of God's work in and through Jesus. It is given for a specific reason: to show his servants what God is up to and to encourage them to persevere in faith, hope and love.

Letters to the Seven Churches (1:4 – 3:22)

The reader will quickly notice that the number "seven" comes up frequently. This is a number symbolizing "completeness." This is frequently used throughout the Bible but never more often than in Revelation. It probably derives from Genesis, when God rested on the seventh day because Creation was completed. So even though there are letters to seven individual congregations, the message to "seven" is intended for the whole church – the complete Church. The various messages to these seven churches (Ephesus, Smyrna, Pergamum,Thyatira, Sardis, Philadelphia and Laodicea – all in modern day Turkey) are very similar to the messages we find in the various epistles. They encourage and commend good behavior and solid faith. They exhort everyone to greater levels of faith, devotion and service. And they rebuke lukewarm faith, bad behavior and false teaching

Seven Revelations (4:1 – 22:5)

In the main body of the book, we find seven revelatory visions. These visions do not move in an obviously straightforward narrative fashion from beginning to end. They are more like a symphony which repeats certain themes for added emphasis. However, the book does move to its grand conclusion, as we shall see.

1) Visions of the Heavenly Court (4:1 – 5:14)

This vision of God's throne in the heavenly court is very similar to the visions recorded in Ezekiel chapter 1, Isaiah chapter 6 and 1 Kings chapter 22. A throne, winged creatures flashes of lightening, peals of thunder and hymns of praise to the Almighty. This vision, however has one significant addition, introduced by a question: "Who is worthy to open the scroll and break its seals?" (The scroll represents the ultimate purposes of God.) *"and no one in heaven, on earth or under the earth was able to open the scroll or look into it."* Then the question is answered by one of the heavenly court: *"Weep not; lo the Lion of the tribe of Judah, the Root of David, has conquered, so that he can open the scroll with its seven seals….(then) I saw a Lamb standing as though it had been slain… and he went and took the scroll from the right hand of him who was seated upon the throne.*"

Then, the court of heaven sings a "new song" to the Lamb who was slain:

"Worthy art thou to take the scroll and to open its seals,
For thou wast slain and by thy blood didst ransom men for God
From every tribe, tongue and people and nation,
And hast made them a kingdom and priests to our God
And they shall reign on earth."

The message here is that Jesus is the one through whom, by his death and resurrection, God has made known his ultimate saving purpose for humanity. The remaining visions in the book flow from this foundational vision.

2) Seven Seals (6:1 – 8:1)

Now we move from heaven to earth. The seven seals are seven aspects of God's judgment upon a sinful world. The first four seals are the famous "Four Horsemen of the Apocalypse." The Old Testament background for this imagery is Zechariah 1:8-11 and 6:1-7. Each horse is a different color and represents a different man-made calamity: a white horse symbolizing conquest in war, a red horse symbolizing murder, a black horse symbolizing famine and a pale horse symbolizing Death and Hades. A fifth seal represents all of the believers in Jesus who have been killed for their faith by the Roman empire. A sixth seal describes cosmic disturbances which are God's punishment for the human atrocities symbolized in the first five seals. Then follows an interlude (chapter 7) in which the servants of God on earth (144,000) and "a great multitude which no one can number" in heaven are sealed upon their foreheads with the promise of protection from God.

We are now ready for the climax: the seventh seal is opened ! (8:1) But what is it? What does it signify? There is "silence in heaven for a half an hour" as everyone waits in suspense for the answer. But we can't know the answer because a new development has arisen. God has passed out seven trumpets to seven angels.

3) Seven Trumpets (8:2 – 11:19)

The seven trumpets symbolize more cosmic calamities which are God's judgment on human sin. These seven bear a close resemblance to the ten plagues in Egypt at the time of Moses: the first, fire and hail; the second, a mountain on fire flowing to the sea (volcanoes); a third, stars falling from heaven and rivers becoming bitter; a fourth, sun and moon darkened; a fifth, a plague of locusts; the sixth, an army of avenging angels to kill unrepentant humanity. And now, the climax: the seventh trumpet ! But not yet.

First, a word of encouragement to all of the followers of Jesus who are living in the midst of these calamities (chapter 10 and 11:1-13). The promise here is that, even though believers will have to pass through the same disasters as unbelievers, and even though many will scorn them, yet God will save them: *"after three days, the breath of life from God entered them, and they stood upon their feet, and great fear fell on those who saw them. Then they heard a loud voice from heaven saying to them, 'Come up hither!' And in the sight of their foes, they went up to heaven in a cloud."*

And now, the moment of climax: the seventh trumpet and the seventh seal reveal the same message – a message burned into the hearts and minds of millions of people all over the world by the "Alleluia Chorus" of "Handel's Messiah."

"The kingdom of the world has become the Kingdom of our God, and of his Christ. And he shall reign forever and ever."

A logical person might think that this would be a good place to end the book of Revelation. The seven churches have been encouraged, scolded and rebuked. The martyrs have been rewarded, The persecuted Christians have been given a reason to hope. The bad guys have been defeated. Our God and his Christ have won the ultimate victory. But a logical person would be wrong. There is much more to come. Having spent the last few chapters describing wars and other calamities on earth, we now go back to heaven.

4) Visions of the Woman, the Dragon, the Beasts and the Lamb (12:1 – 14:20)

The Dragon (Satan) began a war in heaven and was defeated by Michael and his angels. Therefore, the spiritual war begun in heaven now continues on earth. The Dragon has declared war on the Woman and her son. The Woman of chapter 12 has been identified with Eve, Mary and the Church. For the reference to Eve, recall God's words to the Serpent in Genesis 3:15 *"I will put enmity between your seed and her seed; he shall bruise your head and you shall bruise his heal."* For the reference to Mary, recall Mary fleeing into the wilderness to protect her son from Herod at the time of his birth. For the reference to the Church, see Rev.12:17: *"And the dragon was angry with the woman and went off to make war on the rest of her offspring, on those who keep the commandments of God and bear testimony to Jesus."*

The *"beast rising out of the sea"* (13:1) refers to the Roman empire (whose armies arrived by sea to conquer) which *"was allowed to make war on the saints and to conquer them."* The *"beast rose out of the earth"* (13:11) refers to the practice of Roman emperor worship (which was heavily practiced in Asia Minor where the seven churches are located).The Lamb of chapter 14 refers to Christ and his 144,000 true followers.(a symbolic number referring to the 12 tribes of Israel multiplied by the followers of the 12 apostles multiplied by 1,000). Again, the message is that even though the beast may give you a very hard time on this earth, in the end God wins the battle. *"Here is a call for endurance for the saints, those who keep the commandments of God and the faith of Jesus."*

5) Seven Plagues and Seven Bowls (15:1 – 16:21)

The Seven Plagues and Seven Bowls are very similar to the Seven Seals and Trumpets. Again, reference is made to the plagues visited upon the Egyptians and the deliverance of the people of Israel by God. At the climax, the seventh bowl is emptied and we hear the words "It is done" followed by an earthquake, both recalling the final climax of Jesus' crucifixion. The point here again is that (like the people of Israel suffering in Egypt before the Exodus and like Jesus suffering on the Cross before his resurrection) the calamities of the present time are "birth pangs" of God's act of liberation.

6) Judgment of Babylon, The Great Harlot (17:1 – 19:10)

In this section, we have an extended and detailed prediction of the destruction of "Babylon, the Great Harlot." Most bible scholars believe that this refers to the city of Rome, and more generally the Roman empire. There is a great lament: *"Fallen, fallen is Babylon the great !"* and a warning to all followers of Christ who may be tempted by her charms: *"Come out of her my people, lest you take part in her sins, lest you share in her plagues; for her sins are heaped high as heaven, and God has remembered her iniquities. Render to her as she herself has rendered…"*

The long lament of chapter 18 is a poignant and insightful summary of the human pride and greed that are the necessary drivers of any empire, ancient or modern. The warnings of this powerful chapter cut to the heart and speak to every generation. The enduring message is that we dare not place our ultimate hope in the acquisition of wealth because, as wonderful as it seems, it will fail us in the end.

So, if you can't place your ultimate trust in earthly kingdoms, then where can you place your ultimate hope? Read on.

7) Victory of Christ and the New Creation (19:11 – 22:5)

In chapter 20, we have the final judgment of the Devil (who is allowed a temporary reign on earth for "a thousand years") and is then thrown into the lake of fire "and " will be tormented day and night for ever and ever." Then the final judgment of every human being:

REVELATION: "A NEW HEAVEN AND A NEW EARTH"

> *"And I saw the dead, great and small, standing before the throne and books were opened. Also, another book, which is the book of life. And the dead were judged by what was written in the books and by what they had done. And the sea gave up her dead in it. And Death and Hades gave up the dead in them, and all were judged by what they had done. Then Death and Hades were thrown into the lake of fire. This is the second death, the lake of fire; and if anyone's name was not written in the book of life, he was thrown into the lake of fire."*
>
> Rev. 20:12-15

And now, the final climax:

> *"Then I saw a new heaven and a new earth; for the first heaven and the first earth had passed away, and the sea was no more. And I saw the Holy City, New Jerusalem coming down out of heaven from God, prepared as a bride adorned for her husband; and I heard a loud voice from Heaven saying 'Behold, the dwelling of God is with men. He will dwell with them and they shall be his people, and God himself will be with them; he wipe away every tear from their eyes, and death shall be no more, neither shall there be mourning nor crying nor pain any more, for the former things have passed away.' And he who sat upon the throne said, 'Behold, I make all things new'. And he said to me, 'Write this, for these words are trustworthy and true'. And he said to me, 'I am the Alpha and the Omega, the beginning and the end. To the thirsty, I will give from the fountain of life without payment. He who conquers will have this heritage. I will be his God and he will be my son."*
>
> Rev. 21:1-7

The summary message is repeated yet again: "No matter how rotten things are on this earth – and yes they sometimes really are rotten – God is in charge of his world. In his coming Kingdom, all evil will be punished and purged. All good will be validated and vindicated. God's love and goodness and mercy will conquer every enemy. The God who pronounced his creation "very good" in Genesis 1 is the same God who announces to his redeemed Creation "Behold, I make all things new. It is finished. I am the beginning and the end. It is as if the Creator God is saying: "My work is again 'very good' and will be so forever."

Epilogue – Final Blessing (22:6-21)

We now have a final promise from Jesus "I am coming soon" and a prayerful response "Amen. Come Lord Jesus."

QUESTIONS FOR DISCUSSION AND REFLECTION

1) At the beginning of this chapter, we outlined three possible ways of interpreting the book of Revelation. They are:

First, the symbolism of the book refers only to events and characters around the time of 95 AD when the book was written. Therefore, it has no relevance for us today.

Second, the symbols of the book are a secret code to tell us the exact details and timing for the end of the world. Therefore, we should "decode" them, find out the details, and plan accordingly.

Third, the symbols of the book are meant to express an absolute conviction that God is in charge of history, that the death and resurrection of Jesus give us the true meaning of God's purpose for history and that God will finish the job that God has begun.

Which of these three theories do you think is the best one? What are the strengths and weakness if each one? What difference does each one make in the way we live our lives today?

2) Compare Revelation , chapters 20 and 21 with I Corinthians 15:20-28. How are these passages the same? How are they different? If you see some differences, how would you resolve them?

3) Read Revelation, chapter 18. Do you see any parallels between ancient Rome and modern America?

PERSONAL REFLECTION

Think about this: If you knew for sure that Jesus was returning next Monday morning and that the final judgment was happening the following afternoon, how would you live your life differently in the mean time? Make a list and be specific. Now spend some time in prayer asking God for the grace and strength and will power to put your list into practice.

REVELATION: "A NEW HEAVEN AND A NEW EARTH"

BIBLE MEMORY VERSE

"Then I saw a new heaven and a new earth; for the first heaven and the first earth had passed away, and the sea was no more. And I saw the Holy City, New Jerusalem coming down out of heaven from God, prepared as a bride adorned for her husband; and I heard a loud voice from Heaven saying 'Behold, the dwelling of God is with men. He will dwell with them and they shall be his people, and God himself will be with them; he will wipe away every tear from their eyes, and death shall be no more, neither shall there be mourning nor crying nor pain any more, for the former things have passed away.' And he who sat upon the throne said, 'Behold, I make all things new'. And he said to me, 'Write this, for these words are trustworthy and true'. And he said to me, 'I am the Alpha and the Omega, the beginning and the end. To the thirsty, I will give from the fountain of life without payment. He who conquers will have this heritage. I will be his God and he will be my son."

Rev. 21:1-7

APPENDICES

1) Timeline of the Old Testament

2) Timeline of the New Testament

3) When the New Testament Books Were Written

4) Old Testament Prefiguration/ New Testament Recapitulation

5) Other Resources For Reading and Understanding the Bible

Appendix 1

Timeline of Old Testament People, Events and Books

The following timeline is intended to give the reader a general overview of the approximate timing of various events and persons as they relate to the written books of the Old Testament. A few of the following dates are well established because of multiple sources and agreed upon by most scholars. Many more of them are widely debated by various scholars for various reasons. Furthermore, the oral, written and editorial history of the Old Testament is a very complicated subject and is widely debated by scholars for reasons which are too complicated to explain here. This timeline should be interpreted as a "big picture" overview. Readers interested in a more detailed discussion are encouraged to consult relevant commentaries, some of which are listed in Appendix # 5.

APPENDICES

Date	Events and People	Old Testament Book
Prehistory	Creation, Adam/Eve, Cain/Able, Noah's Ark	Genesis 1-11
1,750 B.C.	Abraham, Isaac and Jacob	Genesis 12- 50
1,300 B.C.	Moses, Exodus, Wilderness, Promised Land	Exodus, Leviticus, Numbers, Deuteronomy
1,250 B.C.	Joshua, Conquest of Promised Land	Joshua
1,200 -1,000	Judges Lead Tribal Confederacy	Judges 1 Samuel
1,020 – 922	Kings Saul, David, Solomon	1 and 2 Samuel
	Tribes United in One Kingdom	1 Kings, 1 Chronicles
922 B.C.	Kingdom Divides: North (Israel), South (Judah)	1 and 2 Kings 2 Chronicles
922- 721	Two Parallel Kingdoms	Amos, Hosea Micah, Early Isaiah (chaps.1-39)

Date	Events and People	Old Testament Book
721 B.C.	Northern Kingdom destroyed by Assyrians	2 Kings, Early Isaiah
587 B.C.	Southern Kingdom destroyed by Babylonians	2 Kings, Early Isaiah
	Fall of Jerusalem, Temple Destroyed	Jeremiah, Habakkuk Ezekiel, Daniel
538 B.C.	Edict of Cyrus (Persian Empire)	Later Isaiah (chaps 40-66)
	Jews Begin to Return to Jerusalem	Ezekiel, Haggai, Zechariah
536-515 B.C.	City of Jerusalem and Temple Rebuilt	Ezra, Nehemiah
	Promised Land Resettled, Judaism Renewed	Joel
333 B.C.	Alexander (Greek Empire) Conquers Jerusalem	
167 B.C.	Maccabean Revolt (origin of Hanukkah)	1 and 2 Maccabees (in Apocrypha)
63 B.C.	Roman Empire Conquers Jerusalem	2 Chronicles
922-721	Two Parallel Kingdoms	Amos, Hosea Micah, Early Isaiah (chaps.1-39)

APPENDICES

Date	Events and People	Old Testament Book
721 B.C.	Northern Kingdom destroyed by Assyrians	2 Kings, Early Isaiah
587 B.C.	Southern Kingdom destroyed by Babylonians	2 Kings, Early Isaiah
	Fall of Jerusalem, Temple Destroyed	Jeremiah, Habakkuk Ezekiel, Daniel
538 B.C.	Edict of Cyrus (Persian Empire)	Later Isaiah (chaps 40-66)
	Jews Begin to Return to Jerusalem	Ezekiel, Haggai, Zechariah
536-515 B.C.	City of Jerusalem and Temple Rebuilt	Ezra, Nehemiah
	Promised Land Resettled, Judaism Renewed	Joel
333 B.C.	Alexander (Greek Empire) Conquers Jerusalem	
167 B.C.	Maccabean Revolt (origin of Hanukkah)	1 and 2 Maccabees (in Apocrypha)
63 B.C.	Roman Empire Conquers Jerusalem	

Appendix 2

Timeline of New Testament People, Events and Books

This timeline of the New Testament is much more precise than that of the Old Testament because the events happened in a much shorter period of time (100 years as compared to 2,000 years) and because there are more independent historical references available to verify and cross-reference the dates (for example the written correspondence of bureaucrats in the Roman empire). Please note that we give the date of 4 B.C. for the birth of Jesus. Why not 1 A.D. ? Most modern scholars think (for a variety of complicated reasons) that a miscalculation occurred when the "Christian calendar" became official in the third century and that therefore the real date is four years earlier than commonly thought. Thus, we calculate the beginning of Jesus' public ministry to begin 30 years later (26 A.D.) on the evidence of Luke 3:23. While the following timeline is more precise than that of the Old Testament, the same qualifications apply. This is intended to give a "big picture" overview and readers are encouraged to seek out further detail in the relevant commentaries, some of which are listed in Appendix # 5.

Appendices

Date	Events and People	New Testament Book
40 B.C.	Herod "the Great" is made King of Judah by the Roman Empire	Luke
30 B.C.	Caesar Augustus becomes Roman Emperor	Luke
20 B.C.	Temple Rebuilding Begun by Herod	
4 B.C.	Jesus is born. Herod Antipas (son of Herod "the Great") is tetrarch of Galilee. Herod Archelus (son of Herod "the Great") is ethnarch of Judea	Matthew and Luke
18 A.D.	Caiaphas becomes High Priest	
26 A.D.	Jesus begins his public ministry. Pontius Pilate become procurator of Judea	Matthew, Mark, Luke John
30 A.D.	Jesus' Crucifixion, Resurrection and Ascension Pentecost, Birth of the Church	Matthew, Mark, Luke, John, Acts

Date	Events and People	New Testament Book
31 – 40 A.D.	Conversion of Paul	Acts
40 – 56 A.D.	Paul's Missionary Journeys	Acts
56 A.D.	Paul Arrested in Jerusalem	Acts
56-64 A.D.	Paul in prison	Philippians, Ephesians, Philemon
64 A.D.	Paul martyred in Rome	
66-73 A.D.	Jewish Revolt against the Romans	
70.A.D.	Jerusalem and Temple Destroyed by Romans	

APPENDICES

Appendix 3

When the New Testament Books Were Written

Many people assume that Matthew, Mark, Luke and John were written before the epistles because they cover an earlier period of time. However, most biblical scholars believe that they came much later than many of the epistles. (See for example Luke 1: 1-4 for evidence that the gospels were later compilation of earlier writings about Jesus.) Here is a rough timeline of when some scholars believe the various New Testament books were written. There is much debate about the "later " letters of Paul (Ephesians, 1 and 2 Timothy and Titus). Many scholars think that they were written by Paul's disciples after his death. Others think that they were written in his lifetime. This timeline assumes the latter opinion is correct. As with the previous timelines in Appendices # 1 and #2, this is intended to give a "big picture" overview. Interested readers should consult relevant commentaries, some of which are listed in Appendix # 5, for more detailed analysis.

Date written	Books of New Testament
50-52 A.D.	1 and 2 Thessalonians
53 A.D.	Galatians
54-56 A.D.	1 and 2 Corinthians
57 A.D.	Romans
58 – 60 A.D.	Philippians, Colossians, Philemon
60-64 A.D.	Ephesians, 1 and 2 Timothy, Titus
70 A.D.	Mark
75 – 100 A.D.	Matthew, Luke, John, Acts 1 and 2 Peter, Hebrews, Revelation James, Epistles of John, Jude

Appendix 4

Old Testament Prefiguration / New Testament Recapitulation

"Prefiguration / Recapitulation" is a literary device used in the Bible to interpret "words from God" and "acts of God" in light of God's previous words and acts. People, events and promises of the Old Testament are seen to foreshadow people, events and promises fulfilled in the New Testament. In the internal logic of the Biblical narrative, God "repeats" words and actions for the purpose of establishing continuity and direction for God's people over time. This is a key element in understanding the relationship between the Old and New Testaments. It is especially evident in two New Testament books. First, letter to the Hebrews in which the sacrificial worship of the Old Testament is "a shadow of the good things to come" and Christ is "the true form of these realities". Secondly, Matthew's gospel, in which the phrase "this was to fulfill what the Lord had spoken by the prophet…" is used repeatedly. However, the logic of "prefiguration /recapitulation" (or "promise / fulfillment") is implicitly present in almost every New Testament book. The two main ideas behind all of these New Testament references is: 1) that the Bible is one coherent narrative of the One God's relationship with his people from Creation at the beginning of time to New Creation at the end of time and 2) that Jesus Christ is God's "last word" in the work of redemption. In Christ, God has summed up, and finished, all of the work begun in the Old Testament.

APPENDICES

Here is a list of some of the main themes of

Old Testament Prefiguration Biblical Texts	New Testament Recapitulation Biblical Texts
Adam ("man of dust" through whom sin entered the world) Gen 3	Jesus Christ (the "man of heaven" through whom sin is redeemed) I Corinthians 15
Abraham's trust in God. Gen. 12	Christian's trust in God's power to save. Romans 4
God gives Abraham sacrificial lamb instead of Isaac. Gen. 22	God gives his only Son as sacrifice. Rom. 5, 2 Cor. 5:21
Israel flight and return from Egypt Genesis, Exodus	Jesus flight and return from Egypt Matthew 2
Passover Lamb (blood on doors) Exodus 12	Jesus, Passover Lamb on Cross John 19, I Cor. 5:7

THE LIVING WORD OF THE LIVING GOD

"Prefiguration / Recapitulation" in the Bible.
Appendix 5

Helpful Books For Reading and Understanding the Bible

The following are books that I have found helpful in studying, reading and understanding the Bible. I have listed them in an ascending order of complexity. The reader is encouraged to begin with simpler books and move up as interest and time allow.

1) Simple and Easy –To- Read

Eugene H. Peterson *The Message.* Colorado Springs, Navpress, 2003.
This is a masterful paraphrase of the New Testament that is very helpful in understanding difficult passages.

The Serendipity Bible For Groups Grand Rapids, Zondervan, 1998.
This is a translation of the Bible with a user-friendly format for leading group study and discussion.

The Life Application Bible. Wheaton, Tyndale House Publishers,1996.
This Bible has a good running commentary on each page, offering insights, explanations and applications for many verses in the text.

"Life-Guide" Bible Studies Downer's Grove, InterVarsity Press.
A series of small booklets arranged for 8 to 12 session study and discussion groups with helpful hints for discussion leaders. The series offers a wide variety of topics, themes and specific books of the Bible.

2) A Little More Complicated But Good For Non-Scholars

John Motyer, John R.W. Stott eds. *"The Bible Speaks Today" Series* Leicester, UK InterVarsity Press.
This is a series of commentaries (verse by verse and chapter by chapter explanation) of various books of the Bible and of various biblical themes. Each is written by an individual author, usually an accomplished preacher and teacher, but written for a general audience. Each book is about 200 pages long.

3) For The More Academically Minded

Christian E. Hauer and William A. Young. *An Introduction to the Bible: A Journey into Three Worlds*. Upper Saddle River, NJ, Pearson/Prentice Hall, 2005.
This is a text used in college courses on the New Testament. It is filled with lots of useful introductions, insights and background on all sections of the Bible with good discussion questions for each chapter and a very good topical bibliography. It is 350 pages long.

Raymond Brown. *An Introduction to the New Testament*. New York, Doubleday, 1997.
Raymond Brown is a serious Bible scholar, but this book is written for a more general audience. It gives a good introduction to the New Testament and a good explanation of each individual book. It is over 800 pages long.

Paul Achtemeier, ed. *Harper's Bible Dictionary*. San Francisco, Harper & Row, 1985.
This is a very helpful guide to many names, events and themes in the Bible with contributions from many of the best scholars.

The Anchor Bible Commentary Series. New York, Doubleday.
Extensive and scholarly commentary on each individual book of the Bible. Each book is about 400 pages.

4) Books on Specific Themes in Biblical Study

Jaraslov Pelikan. *Whose Bible Is It ? A History of the Scriptures Through the Ages*. New York, Viking Press, 2005.
A very readable little book by a great scholar on how the Bible got to be the Bible and how different communities of Jews, Christians and Muslims read and regard it differently.

Gerhard von Rad *Old Testament Theology, volumes 1 and 2*. New York, Harper & Row, 1962
A very thorough and in-depth treatment of many Old Testament themes.

John Bright. *A History of Israel*. Philadelphia, Westminster, 1981. A thorough treatment of historical data as it relates to modern archeological evidence.

Abraham J. Heschel. *The Prophets* New York, Harper & Row, 1962. A great introduction to the world-view and passionate faith the Hebrew prophets.

Richard A. Burridge. *Four Gospels, One Jesus?* Grand Rapids, Eerdmans, 2005. An engaging explanation of the "symbolic" reading of the four gospel accounts, each contributing a unique portrait of Jesus.

Rowan Williams. *Resurrection: Interpreting the Easter Gospel.* Cleveland, Pilgrim Press, 2002.
A close look at several themes in the resurrection accounts in the gospels.

N.T. Wright. *The New Testament and the People of God* (Christian Origins and the Question of God, vol. 1). Minneapolis, Fortress Press, 1992.

N.T. Wright. *Jesus and the Victory of God* (Christian Origins and the Question of God, vol. 2). Minneapolis, Fortress Press, 1996.
A thorough treatment of the Jewish horizon of expectation regarding a Messiah and how Jesus fulfills this expectation.

N.T. Wright. *The Resurrection of the Son of God* (Christian Origins and the Question of God, vol. 3) Minneapolis, Fortress Press, 2003.
An exhaustive account of the Old Testament development of the belief in the Resurrection and of the New Testament witness to the Resurrection of Jesus.

ABOUT THE AUTHOR

Photo by Paul Corriveau

The Rev. Canon Tom Furrer has served in parish ministry in the Episcopal Diocese of Connecticut since 1986. He is currently the Rector of Trinity Church in Tariffville. He is also President of Kateri Medical Services, Inc., a non-profit corporation which funds and facilitates basic health care for residents of rural villages in Nigeria. In 2004, he was installed as a Canon of St. Michael's Cathedral in Kaduna in recognition of his efforts on behalf of the people of that diocese. He and his wife, Maryjane, have been married since 1976, have raised three adult daughters and are the proud grandparents of two grandchildren.

OTHER BOOKS OF INTEREST

C. S. Lewis

C. S. Lewis: Views From Wake Forest - Essays on C. S. Lewis
Michael Travers, editor

Contains sixteen scholarly presentations from the international C. S. Lewis convention in Wake Forest, NC. Walter Hooper shares his important essay "Editing C. S. Lewis," a chronicle of publishing decisions after Lewis' death in 1963.

"Scholars from a variety of disciplines address a wide range of issues. The happy result is a fresh and expansive view of an author who well deserves this kind of thoughtful attention."
Diana Pavlac Glyer, author of *The Company They Keep*

The Hidden Story of Narnia:
A Book-By-Book Guide to Lewis' Spiritual Themes
Will Vaus

A book of insightful commentary equally suited for teens or adults – Will Vaus points out connections between the *Narnia* books and spiritual/biblical themes, as well as between ideas in the *Narnia* books and C. S. Lewis' other books. Learn what Lewis himself said about the overarching and unifying thematic structure of the Narnia books. That is what this book explores; what C. S. Lewis called "the hidden story" of Narnia. Each chapter includes questions for individual use or small group discussion.

Why I Believe in Narnia:
33 Reviews and Essays on the Life and Work of C.S. Lewis
James Como

Chapters range from reviews of critical books , documentaries and movies to evaluations of Lewis' books to biographical analysis.
"A valuable, wide-ranging collection of essays by one of the best informed and most accute commentators on Lewis' work and ideas."
Peter Schakel, author of *Imagination & the Arts in C.S. Lewis*

C. S. Lewis Goes to Heaven: A Reader's Guide to The Great Divorce
David G. Clark

This is the first book devoted solely to this often neglected book and the first to reveal several important secrets Lewis concealed within the story. Lewis felt his imaginary trip to Hell and Heaven was far better than his book *The Screwtape Letters*, which has become a classic. Clark is an ordained minister who has taught courses on Lewis for more than 30 years and is a New Testament and Greek scholar with a Doctor of Philosophy degree in Biblical Studies from the University of Notre Dame. Readers will discover the many literary and biblical influences Lewis utilized in writing his brilliant novel.

C. S. Lewis & Philosophy as a Way of Life: His Philosophical Thoughts
Adam Barkman

C. S. Lewis is rarely thought of as a "philosopher" per se despite having both studied and taught philosophy for several years at Oxford. Lewis's long journey to Christianity was essentially philosophical – passing through seven different stages. This 624 page book is an invaluable reference for C. S. Lewis scholars and fans alike

C. S. Lewis: His Literary Achievement
Colin Manlove

"This is a positively brilliant book, written with splendor, elegance, profundity and evidencing an enormous amount of learning. This is probably not a book to give a first-time reader of Lewis. But for those who are more broadly read in the Lewis corpus this book is an absolute gold mine of information. The author gives us a magnificent overview of Lewis' many writings, tracing for us thoughts and ideas which recur throughout, and at the same time telling us how each book differs from the others. I think it is not extravagant to call C. S. Lewis: His Literary Achievement a tour de force."

Robert Merchant, *St. Austin Review*, Book Review Editor

Mythopoeic Narnia: Memory, Metaphore, and Metamorphoses in C. S. Lewis's The Chronicles of Narnia
Salwa Khoddam

Dr. Khoddam, the founder of the C. S. Lewis and Inklings Society (2004), has been teaching university courses using Lewis' books for over 25 years. Her book offers a fresh approach to the *Narnia* books based on an inquiry into Lewis' readings and use of classical and Christian symbols. She explores the literary and intellectual contexts of these stories, the traditional myths and motifs, and places them in the company of the greatest Christian mythopoeic works of Western Literature. In Lewis' imagination, memory and metaphor interact to advance his purpose – a Christian metamorphosis. *Mythopoeic Narnia* helps to open the door for readers into the magical world of the Western imagination.

Speaking of Jack: A C. S. Lewis Discussion Guide
Will Vaus

C. S. Lewis Societies have been forming around the world since the first one started in New York City in 1969. Will Vaus has started and led three groups himself. *Speaking of Jack* is the result of Vaus' experience in leading those Lewis Societies. Included here are introductions to most of Lewis' books as well as questions designed to stimulate discussion about Lewis' life and work. These materials have been "road-tested" with real groups made up of young and old, some very familiar with Lewis and some newcomers. *Speaking of Jack* may be used in an existing book discussion group, Sunday school class or small group, to start a C. S. Lewis Society, or as a guide to your own exploration of Lewis' books.

Pop Culture

To Love Another Person: A Spiritual Journey Through Les Miserables
John Morrison

The powerful story of Jean Valjean's redemption is beloved by readers and theater goers everywhere. In this companion and guide to Victor Hugo's masterpiece, author John Morrison unfolds the spiritual depth and breadth of this classic novel and broadway musical.

Through Common Things: Philosophical Reflections on Popular Culture
Adam Barkman

"Barkman presents us with an amazingly wide-ranging collection of philosophical reflections grounded in the everyday things of popular culture – past and present, eastern and western, factual and fictional. Throughout his encounters with often surprising subject-matter (the value of darkness?), he writes clearly and concisely, moving seamlessly between Aristotle and anime, Lord Buddha and Lord Voldemort.... This is an informative and entertaining book to read!"
    Doug Bloomberg, Professor of Philosophy, Institute for Christian Studies

Spotlight:
A Close-up Look at the Artistry and Meaning of Stephenie Meyer's Twilight Novels
John Granger

Stephenie Meyer's *Twilight* saga has taken the world by storm. But is there more to *Twilight* than a love story for teen girls crossed with a cheesy vampire-werewolf drama? *Spotlight* reveals the literary backdrop, themes, artistry, and meaning of the four Bella Swan adventures. *Spotlight* is is the perfect gift for serious *Twilight* readers.

Virtuous Worlds: The Video Gamer's Guide to Spiritual Truth
John Stanifer

Popular titles like *Halo 3* and *The Legend of Zelda: Twilight Princess* fly off shelves at a mind-blowing rate. John Stanifer, an avid gamer, shows readers specific parallels between Christian faith and the content of their favorite games. Written with wry humor (including a heckler who frequently pokes fun at the author) this book will appeal to gamers and non-gamers alike. Those unfamiliar with video games may be pleasantly surprised to find that many elements in those "virtual worlds" also qualify them as "virtuous worlds."

Memoir

Called to Serve: Life as a Firefighter-Deacon
Deacon Anthony R. Surozenski

Called to Serve is the story of one man's dream to be a firefighter. But dreams have a way of taking detours - so Tony Soruzenski became a teacher and eventually a volunteer firefighter. And when God enters the picture, Tony is faced with a choice. Will he give up firefighting to follow another call? Afer many years, Tony's two callings are finally united – in service as a fire chaplain at Ground Zero after the 9-11 attacks and in other ways he could not have imagined. Tony is Chief Chaplain's aid for the Massachusettes Corp of Fire Chaplains and Director for the Office of the Diaconate of the Diocese of Worchester, Massachusettes.

Poets and Poetry

Remembering Roy Campbell: The Memoirs of his Daughters, Anna and Tess
Introduction by Judith Lütge Coullie, Editor
Preface by Joseph Pearce

Anna and Teresa Campbell were the daughters of the handsome young South African poet and writer, Roy Campbell (1901-1957), and his beautiful English wife, Mary Garman. In their frank and moving memoirs, Anna and Tess recall the extraordinary, and often very difficult, lives they shared with their exceptional parents. Over 50 photos, 344 footnotes, timeline of Campbell's life, and complete index.

In the Eye of the Beholder: How to See the World Like a Romantic Poet
Louis Markos

Born out of the French Revolution and its radical faith that a nation could be shaped and altered by the dreams and visions of its people, British Romantic Poetry was founded on a belief that the objects and realities of our world, whether natural or human, are not fixed in stone but can be molded and transformed by the visionary eye of the poet. Unlike many of the books written on Romanticism, which devote many pages to the poets and few pages to their poetry, the focus here is firmly on the poems themselves. The author thereby draws the reader intimately into the life of these poems. A separate bibliographical essay is provided for readers listing accessible biographies of each poet and critical studies of their work.

The Cat on the Catamaran: A Christmas Tale
John Martin

Here is a modern-day parable of a modern-day cat with modern-day attitudes. Riverboat Dan is a "cool" cat on a perpetual vacation from responsibility. He's *The Cat on the Catamaran* – sailing down the river of life. Dan keeps his guilty conscience from interfering with his fun until he runs into trouble. But will he have the courage to believe that it's never too late to change course? (For ages 10 to adult)

"Cat lovers and poetry lovers alike will enjoy this whimsical story about Riverboat Dan, a philosophical cat in search of meaning."
Regina Doman, author of *Angel in the Water*

Fiction

The Iona Conspiracy (from The Remnant Chronicles book series)
Gary Gregg

Readers find themselves on a modern adventure through ancient Celtic myth and legend as thirteen year old Jacob uncovers his destiny within "the remnant" of the Sporrai Order. As the Iona Academy comes under the control of educational reformers and ideological scientists, Jacob finds himself on a dangerous mission to the sacred Scottish island of Iona and discovers how his life is wrapped up with the fate of the long lost cover of *The Book of Kells*. From its connections to Arthurian legend to references to real-life people, places, and historical mysteries, *Iona* is an adventure that speaks to eternal truths as well as the challenges of the modern world. A young adult novel, *Iona* can be enjoyed by the entire family.

www.ingramcontent.com/pod-product-compliance
Lightning Source LLC
Chambersburg PA
CBHW030312080526
44584CB00012B/540